BIGFOOT SIGHTINGS

TRUE TALES FROM ACROSS AMERICA

JIM WILLIS AND MICHAEL A. KOZLOWSKI

DETROIT

ABOUT THE AUTHORS

Michael A. Kozlowski lives in Detroit, Michigan, with his fiancée, Christen, and a whole gaggle of animals. He is an engineer, a singer/songwriter, an avid golfer, a huge sports fan (especially of his hometown Lions), and loves travelling and exploring. Mike (his mom is really the only one that calls him Michael) has written several short horror fiction stories for various magazines and online publications, many of which can be found in his collection, *Some Days Suck, Some Days Suck Worse*. Two horror/suspense thrillers in his "John Angel" series, *Angel of Death* and *Fallen Angel*, are currently available, with two more books currently in development. His first venture in to the "unexplained" genre was Visible Ink's *American Ghost Stories: True Tales from All 50 States*. Mike continues to write in the paranormal and horror fiction genres. You can keep up with his goings-on at his website, www.mikekozlowski.com.

Jim Willis earned his master's degree in theology from Andover Newton Theological School; he was also an ordained minister for over 40 years. He taught college courses in comparative religion and cross-cultural studies. In addition, Willis was a professional musician, high school orchestra and band teacher, arts council director, and even a drive-time radio show host. His background in theology and education led to his writings on religion, the apocalypse, cross-cultural spirituality, and the mysteries of the unknown, including Visible Ink Press' *Lost Civilizations: The Secret Histories and Suppressed Technologies of the Ancients* and *Hidden History: Ancient Aliens and the Suppressed Origins of Civilization*. Willis passed away in 2024.

BIGFOOT SIGHTINGS

TRUE TALES FROM ACROSS AMERICA

JIM WILLIS AND MICHAEL A. KOZLOWSKI

DETROIT

Copyright © 2026 by Visible Ink Press®

This publication is a creative work fully protected by all applicable copyright laws, as well as by misappropriation, trade secret, unfair competition, and other applicable laws.

No part of this book may be reproduced in any form without permission in writing from the publisher, except by a reviewer who wishes to quote brief passages in connection with a review written for inclusion in a magazine, newspaper, or website.

All rights to this publication will be vigorously defended.

Visible Ink Press®
43311 Joy Rd., #414
Canton, MI 48187-2075

Visible Ink Press is a registered trademark of Visible Ink Press LLC.

Most Visible Ink Press books are available at special quantity discounts when purchased in bulk by corporations, organizations, or groups. Customized printings, special imprints, messages, and excerpts can be produced to meet your needs. For more information, contact Special Markets Director, Visible Ink Press, 734-667-3211 or www.visibleinkpress.com.

Managing Editor: Kevin S. Hile
Cover Design: John Gouin, Graphikitchen, LLC
Proofreaders: Larry Baker and Christa Gainor
Indexer: Larry Baker

Cover image: Shutterstock.

ISBNs:
Paperback: 978-1-57859-869-4
Hardcover: 978-1-57859-881-6
eBook: 978-1-57859-882-3

Cataloging-in-Publication data is on file at the Library of Congress.

Printed in the United States of America.

10 9 8 7 6 5 4 3 2 1

TABLE OF CONTENTS

Preface: How This Book Came to Be
  by Michael A. Kozlowski xi
Preface: A Personal Experience
  by Jim Willis xvii
Introduction xxv

What's in a Name? 1
The Elephant in the Dark 7
Once There Were Giants 21
Let's Get Physical! 33
To Walk a Mile in Their Footsteps 47
Smile! You're on Candid Camera! 59
Victims of Circumstance 69
Howl at the Moon! 77
Don't Stop Believin' 83
Back to the Beginning 91
How Did We End Up Here? 101
Our First Teacher Is Our Own Heart 117
The Four Horsemen of Sasquatchery 141
O, Canada 157
The United States of Bigfoot 211
It's a Mad, Mad, Mad, Mad World 235
I'm Just Sayin' 255

Afterword 275
Photo Sources 283
Further Reading 285
Index 289

ALSO FROM VISIBLE INK PRESS

The Afterlife Book: Heaven, Hell, and Life after Death
by Marie D. Jones and Larry Flaxman
ISBN: 978-1-57859-761-1

The Alien Book: A Guide to Extraterrestrial Beings on Earth
by Nick Redfern
ISBN: 978-1-57859-687-4

Alien Mysteries, Conspiracies, and Cover-Ups
by Kevin D. Randle
ISBN: 978-1-57859-418-4

American Ghost Stories: True Stories from All 50 Books
by Michael A. Kozlowski
ISBN: 978-1-57859-799-4

Ancient Gods: Lost Histories, Hidden Truths, and the Conspiracy of Silence
by Jim Willis
ISBN: 978-1-57859-614-0

Angels A to Z, 2nd edition
by Evelyn Dorothy Oliver, Ph.D.; and James R. Lewis, Ph.D.
ISBN: 978-1-57859-212-8

Area 51: The Revealing Truth of UFOs, Secret Aircraft, Cover-Ups & Conspiracies
by Nick Redfern
ISBN: 978-1-57859-672-0

Armageddon Now: The End of the World A to Z
by Jim Willis and Barbara Willis
ISBN: 978-1-57859-168-8

The Astrology Book: The Encyclopedia of Heavenly Influences, 2nd edition
by James R. Lewis
ISBN: 978-1-57859-144-2

The Astrology Guide: Understanding Your Signs, Your Gifts, and Yourself
by Claudia Trivelas
ISBN: 978-1-57859-738-3

The Bigfoot Book: The Encyclopedia of Sasquatch, Yeti, and Cryptid Primates
by Nick Redfern
ISBN: 978-1-57859-561-7

Celebrity Ghosts and Notorious Hauntings
by Marie D. Jones
ISBN: 978-1-57859-689-8

Censoring God: The History of the Lost Books (and Other Excluded Scriptures)
by Jim Willis
ISBN: 978-1-57859-732-1

Conspiracies and Secret Societies: The Complete Dossier, 2nd ed.
by Brad and Sherry Hansen Steiger
ISBN: 978-1-57859-368-2

Control: MK Ultra, Chemtrails, and the Conspiracy to Suppress the Masses
by Nick Redfern
ISBN: 978-1-57859-638-6

Cover-Ups and Secrets: The Complete Guide to Government Conspiracies, Manipulations & Deceptions
by Nick Redfern
ISBN: 978-1-57859-679-9

Demons, the Devil, and Fallen Angels
by Marie D. Jones and Larry Flaxman
ISBN: 978-1-57859-613-3

Bigfoot Sightings

The Dream Encyclopedia, 2nd edition
by James R. Lewis, Ph.D.; and Evelyn Dorothy Oliver, Ph.D.
ISBN: 978-1-57859-216-6

The Dream Interpretation Dictionary: Symbols, Signs, and Meanings
by J. M. DeBord
ISBN: 978-1-57859-637-9

Earth Magic: Your Complete Guide to Natural Spells, Potions, Plants, Herbs, Witchcraft, and More
by Marie D. Jones
ISBN: 978-1-57859-697-3

The Encyclopedia of Religious Phenomena
by J. Gordon Melton
ISBN: 978-1-57859-209-8

The Fortune-Telling Book: The Encyclopedia of Divination and Soothsaying
by Raymond Buckland
ISBN: 978-1-57859-147-3

The Government UFO Files: The Conspiracy of Cover-Up
by Kevin D. Randle
ISBN: 978-1-57859-477-1

Haunted: Malevolent Ghosts, Night Terrors, and Threatening Phantoms
by Brad Steiger
ISBN: 978-1-57859-620-1

Hidden History: Ancient Aliens and the Suppressed Origins of Civilization
by Jim Willis
ISBN: 978-1-57859-710-9

Hidden Realms, Lost Civilizations, and Beings from Other Worlds
by Jerome Clark
ISBN: 978-1-57859-175-6

The Horror Show Guide: The Ultimate Frightfest of Movies
by Mike Mayo
ISBN: 978-1-57859-420-7

The Illuminati: The Secret Society That Hijacked the World
by Jim Marrs
ISBN: 978-1-57859-619-5

Lost Civilizations: The Secret Histories and Suppressed Technologies of the Ancients
by Jim Willis
ISBN: 978-1-57859-706-2

The Monster Book: Creatures, Beasts, and Fiends of Nature
by Nick Redfern
ISBN: 978-1-57859-575-4

Monsters of the Deep
by Nick Redfern
ISBN: 978-1-57859-705-5

Near Death Experiences: Afterlife Journeys and Revelations
by Jim Willis
ISBN: 978-1-57859-846-5

The New Witch Your Guide to Modern Witchcraft, Wicca, Spells, Potions, Magic, and More
by Marie D. Jones
ISBN: 978-1-57859-716-1

The New World Order Book
by Nick Redfern
ISBN: 978-1-57859-615-7

Nightmares: Your Guide to Interpreting Your Darkest Dreams
by J. M. DeBord
ISBN: 978-1-57859-758-1

Real Aliens, Space Beings, and Creatures from Other Worlds,
by Brad and Sherry Hansen Steiger
ISBN: 978-1-57859-333-0

True Tales from Across America

Also from Visible Ink Press

Real Encounters, Different Dimensions, and Otherworldly Beings
by Brad and Sherry Hansen Steiger
ISBN: 978-1-57859-455-9

Real Ghosts, Restless Spirits, and Haunted Places, 2nd edition
by Brad Steiger
ISBN: 978-1-57859-401-6

Real Miracles, Divine Intervention, and Feats of Incredible Survival
by Brad and Sherry Hansen Steiger
ISBN: 978-1-57859-214-2

Real Monsters, Gruesome Critters, and Beasts from the Darkside
by Brad and Sherry Hansen Steiger
ISBN: 978-1-57859-220-3

Real Vampires, Night Stalkers, and Creatures from the Darkside
by Brad Steiger
ISBN: 978-1-57859-255-5

Real Visitors, Voices from Beyond, and Parallel Dimensions
by Brad and Sherry Hansen Steiger
ISBN: 978-1-57859-541-9

Real Zombies, the Living Dead, and Creatures of the Apocalypse,
by Brad Steiger
ISBN: 978-1-57859-296-8

The Religion Book Places, Prophets, Saints, and Seers
by Jim Willis
ISBN: 978-1-57859-151-0

Runaway Science: True Stories of Raging Robots and High-Tech Horrors
by Nick Redfern
ISBN: 978-1-57859-801-4

The Sci-Fi Movie Guide: The Universe of Film from Alien to Zardoz
by Chris Barsanti
ISBN: 978-1-57859-503-7

Secret History: Conspiracies from Ancient Aliens to the New World Order
by Nick Redfern
ISBN: 978-1-57859-479-5

Secret Societies: The Complete Guide to Histories, Rites, and Rituals
by Nick Redfern
ISBN: 978-1-57859-483-2

The Spirit Book: The Encyclopedia of Clairvoyance, Channeling, and Spirit Communication
by Raymond Buckland
ISBN 978-1-57859-790-1

Supernatural Gods: Spiritual Mysteries, Psychic Experiences, and Scientific Truths
by Jim Willis
ISBN: 978-1-57859-660-7

Time Travel: The Science and Science Fiction
by Nick Redfern
ISBN: 978-1-57859-723-9

The UFO Dossier: 100 Years of Government Secrets, Conspiracies, and Cover-Ups
by Kevin D. Randle
ISBN: 978-1-57859-564-8

Unexplained! Strange Sightings, Incredible Occurrences, and Puzzling Physical Phenomena, 3rd edition
by Jerome Clark
ISBN: 978-1-57859-344-6

The Vampire Almanac: The Complete History
by J. Gordon Melton, Ph.D.
ISBN: 978-1-57859-719-2

Bigfoot Sightings

Also from Visible Ink Press

The Vampire Book: The Encyclopedia of the Undead, 3rd edition
by J. Gordon Melton, Ph.D.
ISBN: 978-1-57859-281-4

The Werewolf Book: The Encyclopedia of Shape-Shifting Beings, 2nd edition
by Brad Steiger
ISBN: 978-1-57859-367-5

Werewolf Stories: Shape-Shifters, Lycanthropes, and Man-Beasts
by Nick Redfern and Brad Steiger
ISBN: 978-1-57859-766-6

The Witch Book: The Encyclopedia of Witchcraft, Wicca, and Neo-Paganism
by Raymond Buckland
ISBN: 978-1-57859-791-8

The Witches Almanac Sorcerers, Witches and Magic from Ancient Rome to the Digital Age
by Charles Christian
ISBN: 978-1-57859-760-4

The Zombie Book: The Encyclopedia of the Living Dead
by Nick Redfern and Brad Steiger
ISBN: 978-1-57859-504-4

"Real Nightmares" E-Books by Brad Steiger

Book 1: *True and Truly Scary Unexplained Phenomenon*
Book 2: *The Unexplained Phenomena and Tales of the Unknown*
Book 3: *Things That Go Bump in the Night*
Book 4: *Things That Prowl and Growl in the Night*
Book 5: *Fiends That Want Your Blood*
Book 6: *Unexpected Visitors and Unwanted Guests*
Book 7: *Dark and Deadly Demons*
Book 8: *Phantoms, Apparitions, and Ghosts*
Book 9: *Alien Strangers and Foreign Worlds*
Book 10: *Ghastly and Grisly Spooks*
Book 11: *Secret Schemes and Conspiring Cabals*
Book 12: *Freaks, Fiends, and Evil Spirits*

Please visit us at www.visibleinkpress.com

True Tales from Across America

PREFACE

How This Book Came to Be
by Michael A. Kozlowski

I was in the gym, working off my penchant for Pepsi and snacks instead of working on the *Unexplained Mysteries* book whose deadline was beginning to loom large, when I received an email from Roger (the owner of the publishing house who would soon be expecting a draft about aliens, and cryptids, and mysterious geographical anomalies, and any number of other paranormal phenomena). Surely, he was going to ask about my progress.

Yikes...

I already had one book published with Visible Ink Press (Roger's company), a book about haunted places that was doing well. Although I cut my teeth writing horror fiction, both Visible Ink and I were excited about my venture into this different, though certainly overlapping, genre. *American Ghost Stories* had, in less than a year, outperformed my entire catalog of horror fiction in terms of sales and general buzz. Not to imply that I was breaking records or winning awards with the book (the bar to surpass my other publications was pretty low), but *AGS* was earning royalties that had numbers *before* the decimal place! I had been interviewed on radio and podcasts and was planning some signing events.

You'd think I'd be burning up the keys on my laptop, working on the next book, but, for a variety of reasons that I won't go into here, it was slow going. Research was going well, but I was having trouble finding my usual time in front of the screen and getting into the flow of the book. I wasn't panicking or anything—this is kind of how I work and not much different than how the writing of *American Ghost Stories* went—but you can only tell your publisher that "research is going well" so many times before he might start getting nervous about the actual writing bits.

As it happened, the email wasn't about the mysteries book, or the ghost stories book—for that matter, it was about an entirely *new* book. On my phone, I hadn't

True Tales from Across America

been able to see the subject line. It read: Another project (soley on Bigfoot)?

Alright, alright, alright. This was interesting. But it seemed a little strange. After all, the mysteries book was going to have a section dedicated to hairy hominids. Roger and I had talked about some of the main topics that would be included.

To be fair, Roger did seem to have an inkling toward Bigfoot books. He'd mentioned that being a popular topic more than once in the past, when we were brainstorming some ideas for the *American Ghost Stories* follow up, sort of hinting that I might consider a book dedicated to the subject.

I was less enthusiastic than he was. It seemed to me, a relative newcomer to the world of what I'll call "paranormal & mystery" research and writing (it's a catch-all term for the sake of brevity; please don't send nasty emails LOL), that the whole Sasquatch, Yeti, Bigfoot thing had been done to death, and, really, how much was there to really dig into?

I know, I know, I'm an idiot. But stick with me here: Eventually, I'll get to the point (probably).

I was also nervous about getting in the weeds with the vast Bigfoot community of researchers, hunters, spotters, abductees, lovers.… It's a huge community, and I was afraid of trying to break in as a newcomer or of not being taken seriously for my lack of experience.

But I was intrigued and, honestly, excited at the thought of getting an unsolicited offer to sign another book contract. Little victories. So, I popped into the "members lounge" (it's just Planet Fitness, but that sounds kinda cool, right?), where it was quieter and phoned Roger.

As you may have guessed by now, particularly if you're already a Jim Willis fan, the pitch was for this book, a co-authorship with Jim. That sounded promising. A collaboration with an established author in the genre?

Hell, yeah!

Bigfoot Sightings

Preface: How This Book Came to Be

Unfortunately, before I could even get through that whole thought in my head, Roger told me that Jim had recently passed. He had been working on this book when he took ill and, literally, one of his last wishes was for this book to be completed and published. I'm certain that directive was more as a favor to his publisher, and friend, than it was for any sort of legacy or posthumous accomplishment for Jim's sake (he was more than set in that regard).

I've said I'm a newbie in this realm, and I make no bones about it. I've always had an interest in the "unexplained," but I'd never thought to take a run at the investigative journalism side of it until the *American Ghost Stories* opportunity came up.

Of course, it didn't take long to come across Jim Willis' name once I began "running in those circles." But as a newbie, I wasn't especially familiar with him or his work. I would learn that it was certainly my loss in both cases.

Roger offered to send me what Jim had written so far. It wouldn't be polished, but there was a fair bit of volume. I said I'd look at it and give it a few days' thought. Then I went directly to the locker room, grabbed my gym bag, and headed home to google Jim Willis (that sounds like some weird euphemism, but it's just an internet search).

If you're smarter than me, you already know that Jim has written 20-some books on religion, the apocalypse, spirituality, arcane culture, lost civilizations, out-of-body experiences, and psychics.… Jim was an ordained minister with a master's degree. He was a college professor, a lecturer, and a musician. I think it would be fair to call Jim a Renaissance Man.

I'm writing this introduction as I begin the final draft of this book. I've spent the last five months with Jim – well, with his words. While that can't compare to knowing the man in person—to being able to ask him questions and discuss the work with him—it's still an intimate thing. And I think I have a good sense of the man not just from his published works but from working with his notes and his rough drafts.

True Tales from Across America

Jim was a person who was clearly fascinated with the world around him; helpless but to wonder and question, driven to explore and research. He had what I like to call a "yearnin' for learnin'."

And Jim wanted to share that thirst for answers, and the knowledge acquired in the never-ending effort to quench it. He wasn't the type to "tell you how it is," but rather one who would share his fact finding and his opinions and conclusions. He did so conversationally, ready to be challenged, willing to entertain other viewpoints and change his own if the evidence warranted it.

Obviously, I was excited to have the opportunity to co-author a book with Jim. I already had some of my own notes on hairy hominids for the expected section in the "unexplained" book I'd been working on. I had even visited some of the locations that we touch on in this book (spoiler: I didn't find Bigfoot). With Jim's partially completed rough draft, the flow of the thing came together pretty quickly.

Rather than another book that's little more than a list of Bigfoot sightings, Jim aimed to explore the phenomenon more broadly. As I said, Jim (like me) was, more than anything else, curious. It wasn't enough to simply explore the current state of Bigfoot research and evidence; it was necessary to try to understand as much about the subject as possible.

In an effort to answer the question of whether or not Bigfoot exists, we need to first ask ourselves, "What is it? Where did it come from? How does it survive? And why is the mystery so difficult to solve, one way or the other?"

I didn't have the opportunity to ask Jim his opinion on the whole Bigfoot subject, but the following preface, written by Jim, makes it fairly clear. I would describe myself as an optimistic skeptic when it comes to most things: open to believing but a hard sell most of the time. And while Jim was also one to rely on facts and evidence to form an opinion, I feel he wasn't just open to believing but that he wanted to believe.

This book is a true collaboration between Jim and I, with each of us contributing portions to each chapter.

Preface: How This Book Came to Be

In some cases, I've edited and modified Jim's words. In others, I left whole sections unchanged from the way I found them. A lot of the time, as we go along, I suspect you'll know who is doing the heavy lifting in a particular section (I'll even tell you now and again), but most of the time I hope you won't.

By necessity, the "voice" of the book is mine, but the "soul" of it is ours. As I worked on it, I could feel Jim's presence through his words, and sometimes it seemed as though he was sitting right next to me at my writing desk. As the "optimistic skeptic," I can't say that he was.

But it's what I want to believe, and maybe that's enough.

Anyway, welcome to our Bigfoot book. Thanks for being here, Hopefully, I'll see you at the end, and we'll all have learned something and had some fun along the way.

Michael A. Kozlowski
Detroit, Michigan
December, 2024

True Tales from Across America

PREFACE
A Personal Experience
by Jim Willis

In the Fall of 2008, I retired to the woods of South Carolina. Although I didn't know it at the time, the piece of land I was about to call home was once used by the first people of the American Southeast as a seasonal meeting ground. I've written about this place in other books, so I won't repeat myself here, but my reasons for coming are probably best summed up in this paragraph from my book *Cosmo and Me*:

> *In many ways I'd lived a fulfilling life and done pretty much everything I ever dreamed of doing. But when I retired from it all there was one more thing I wanted to accomplish. It had always been my goal to live for one year in the woods, cut off from people in general, so I could watch the leaves change colors with the passing seasons ... That one year turned into more than a decade, so far.*

That Fall, I hadn't yet built a house. I lived in a small travel trailer and had constructed a wooden deck out front. The surrounding area was considerably wilder than it is now. It would take a good three years of clearing paths, cutting out acres of greenbrier and vines, gently pruning the forest, and getting to know the rhythm of the seasons while acclimating to the silence of the woods around me before the place reached the point of civilized comfort that it now boasts.

I still needed to build a long driveway from the one-laned gravel road that connected me to the outside world, drill a well, install a septic system, and bring in underground electric and telephone wires.

Now everything has changed, probably for the better, but I miss those rugged days. The county has paved the road that leads to my homesite. I even have a hot tub, for heaven's sake! Because of fiber optic cable—however that works—I am regularly interviewed by podcasters and radio hosts, sometimes talking to thousands of people at one time, whereas a classroom or auditorium where I once conducted college classes, church services, and seminars, held, at best, a few hundred people. I find it extremely ironic, but there it is. On the one hand, I live surrounded by miles and miles of uninterrupted state forest. A week might go by without my seeing half a dozen people. On the other hand, I am now more connected than ever. That connection is technological rather than physical, but it's still there.

When I first moved in, with no TV and nothing between me and the woods, I felt a peace that I often must work to restore nowadays. Even my current front porch, screened in as it is, offers a barrier that I never would have imagined simple screening could impose.

On a warm Fall evening, however, during my sixty-second year on earth, I experienced something that gives me chills to this very day.

Before I describe what happened, I need to set the geographical stage a bit. This might seem like a detour around a story about a possible Bigfoot sighting, but bear with me. It's important. I want to set the stage for considering the possibility of my woods being, before civilization claimed its inevitable toll, Bigfoot territory.

South Carolina's western boundary is the Savannah River, and three distinct bands of country run from southwest to northeast across the countryside.

The top band just barely clips the Blue Ridge Mountains in the upper-left corner of the state. The next band, running parallel to the first, is a wide strip called the Piedmont. What's left is the widest strip of them all: the Coastal Plain. A narrow swath of land called the Sandhills separates the Piedmont from the Coastal Plain, and its boundary on the southern side is called the Fall Line.

The Blue Ridge in South Carolina is a thin strip on the edge of the Appalachian Mountains. Way up there is where the headwaters of the Savannah begin. Snow and rain from up in the mountains make their way, via hundreds of streams and tributaries, into two main rivers,

Preface: A Personal Experience

the Tugaloo and Seneca, which empty into what is now called Lake Hartwell.

The Appalachians are beautiful now, but they must have been spectacular when they were formed, following an ancient collision with Africa. When the underlying North American tectonic plate collided with the African plate more years ago than I can get my brain around, it pushed up the Appalachians. Back then, they were bigger than the Swiss Alps, dwarfing even today's Rockies. Geologists call this kind of mountain building an "orogeny," so the epoch to which I now refer is called by the delightfully named Alleghenian Orogeny.

There is a seasonal stream that flows through the back of my property, a remnant of a large body of water that once drained into the Savannah River, and then down to the sea. The Piedmont was then the east coast of what would one day become known as America.

Coasts are known for their sand dunes. That's exactly what the Sandhills are. They are a strip of ancient beach dunes that would have marked prime real estate back then if there had been anyone around to speculate in such things. This occurred during the epoch we now call the Miocene. If you're lucky and sharp-eyed, you can still find beach fossils along the front edge on the eastern side of the hills. Living where I do right now, I just missed being rich. Imagine what I could have sold my place for 20 million years ago. Beachfront property!

The Coastal Plain was underwater back then. It was once ocean, and it still hides fossil evidence of its former role in the great picture. But shores are higher than oceans, obviously. There is always a drop-off below the water off the beach. And that's what the Fall Line is. It marks the place where the beach ended and the ocean began. Below this line, the river broadens out and forms larger flood plains.

All the great rivers of South Carolina and Georgia cross over this Fall Line. It marks the dividing line between two completely different ecological systems and runs northeast all the way to Washington, D.C. From the Blue Ridge to below the Fall Line, there is a drop in elevation of more than 1,500 feet. It's historically important

True Tales from Across America

because the resulting waterfalls were the prime attraction for early, indigenous people, who camped there to trap fish that swam upstream to spawn in the Spring. Before the first people arrived, it would have been prime habitat for animals of all kinds, including any primates that might have been part of the local ecosystem.

Later, Europeans built their mills at these locations because they used the falling water to power water wheels that in turn drove the machinery needed for commerce. Cities such as Augusta and Columbia owe their very existence to the waterfalls along the Fall Line.

The Europeans most definitely changed the landscape around here, but in some ways the Indians beat them to it.

Like all the area east of the Mississippi, the ancient habitat tended toward what is called a climax forest. Mosses led to grass and shrub, which led to pine and spruce, which led to oak and maple and other hardwoods, depending on current climate variables. As the trees grew tall, they shaded out the lower-growing plants. Left to itself, with no outside influence other than naturally occurring soft rain and sunshine, that's the way nature works.

When hardwood trees grow up and out, they will eventually space themselves with their trunks some 30 feet apart, providing a lush over-story of leaves that shut out the sun. It looks just like a park.

But the thing is, that hardly ever happens. It would lead to a pretty boring, sterile environment if it did. There would be nothing for the fauna to eat. Deer would go hungry staring at leaves way up where they couldn't get to them. Turkeys might like it, but there would be no cover for them except for when they fly up to roost at night. Bigger mammals would all depart for greener pastures.

Early humans saw all this. Most wild animals do best where there are "edge" environments—trees for cover, clearings for low-growing vegetation, brush to hide in, and food down low. Mother Nature knows this even better than we do. And sure enough, that's what hap-

Preface: A Personal Experience

pens when she is left to herself. A mature tree dies and falls, letting sunlight strike the forest floor. Low growing plants spring up. When a drought occurs and the dry tinder on the ground is struck by lightning, it often causes a forest fire. The understory—and sometimes the over-story as well—is burned, fertilizing the loam of the woods with ash. The process begins anew. As grass grows in, deer and antelope play once more, and so do buffalo and elk and rabbits, and the foxes and coyotes and wolves and bears that feed on them.

Early inhabitants of South Carolina, like humans everywhere, sometimes helped the process along. They set fires deliberately but without malice. To them, fire was a tool, plain and simple. If they burned a climax wood, the grass started to grow right away. Then came buffalo and elk, to say nothing of deer. Even better, gardens grew more bountiful in the replenished soil. Enriched by potassium from the ash, they were free to luxuriate in the open sun.

When the first Europeans arrived on the scene in the sixteenth century, they were amazed to find open prairies all along the Savannah River. They described buffalo grazing in great herds. Elk were abundant. The place was teaming with life. It was a paradise.

And it was all managed by human hands that had been caring for it with fire, stone ax, and hoe for thousands of years. Europeans, thinking they had come to an undiscovered, "virgin" territory, suffered under the delusion that this was "natural." But the land was already old. It had been under cultivation and care since the first people showed up thousands of years ago.

The Europeans soon discovered that the prairie grew fine crops. Tobacco became the money maker of choice, followed shortly thereafter by "King Cotton." The trouble is, tobacco and cotton deplete soil very quickly. At best, you can hope for four or five years of decent production. But that was okay because all they had to do was burn more forest.

Then, beginning in the late '50s, the Army Corps of Engineers built a series of dams that harnessed the Savannah River, creating a series of lakes that brought

True Tales from Across America

both electrical power and increased tourism to the area. The whole watershed became much more civilized. Gone were the wide-open spaces and quiet forests with few visitors, except for some hunters and fishermen. Wildlife must have noticed the difference. They were gradually pushed back into small conclaves, memories of what was once bountiful wilderness.

The point of this geography lesson is that for thousands of years the area in which I live offered plenty of land rich in resources and varied in habitat. I wasn't necessarily aware of all this when I sat on the front deck outside my trailer, enjoying the soft dark of a Fall evening many years ago. It wasn't that I didn't know any of this history. I just wasn't thinking about it. I had spent the day working in the woods and was tired. It was pleasant to watch the darkness deepen and listen to the sounds of the forest around me.

The fact that I was living at the end of an era never entered my mind. The knowledge that I had, even in a small way, contributed to it, and that flora and fauna, both large and small, were even then moving north toward the relative safety of the northern Appalachians, fleeing incipient climate change and encroaching civilization, was something that totally escaped me.

Then I heard the sound of wood knocking on wood coming from the creek bed below my house. It's hard to describe exactly what the sound was like. It was as if two hollow, hardwood tubes were being whacked together.

The next morning, when I went out to inspect the scene of the night's disturbance, I tried to replicate the sound by picking up various sticks and banging them on trees. The best I could produce was a kind of "thud." Last night's sound was an almost musical "tonk."

Later that evening, I sat in the darkness listening for more sounds and eventually heard footsteps. They were heavy footsteps and could be heard clearly in the autumn leaves. Needless to say, I began to get a little nervous. The footsteps seemed to move up the hill, from east to west, about 50 yards into the woods. They didn't approach me. It was as if they were just passing through and I was in their way.

Preface: A Personal Experience

Nevertheless, I felt it was time to take action. I went inside and grabbed a handy flashlight from its place by the door. I had been slowly sipping a little liquid courage imported from the great state of Kentucky to the north, but back-up is always welcome, so I pocketed a .38 caliber revolver I kept handy for just such occasions. Besides, the blue-steel of the short barrel complemented the color of the jeans I was wearing. I also woke up my dog, Rocky, who was sleeping in his accustomed place on the floor beside my bed.

Thus, armed, accompanied by a big dog who was always ready for an adventure, and dressed to kill and outfitted for the night, I went back to the porch.

But there was nothing more to hear. The footsteps had stopped, the leaves on the forest floor didn't even rustle, the night insects and tree frogs sounded normal, and Rocky didn't even sniff the night breeze.

I slowly walked from south to north, hoping to cut the trail of whatever I had heard, but ... nothing. Rocky didn't growl, as he surely would have if it had been a person or large night animal such as a bear or feral hogs. As a matter of fact, he just eyed me as if I had brought him out on a fool's errand. He showed absolutely no interest at all in what he had probably hoped was going to be an adventure of some kind.

When I returned to the trailer, he just "humphed" at me and went back to bed.

I didn't sleep well that night. I kept waking up at the slightest sound coming through the open window. But the "strange" sounds were done for the night, and I never heard them again to this very day.

Since then, I have pondered what happened. Seldom does a week go by, even 15 years later, that I don't try to make sense of the event.

Did I imagine the whole thing? I don't think so. Years later I would learn that "tree-knocking" is common to those who search for Bigfoot, or Sasquatch as it is also called. They believe it to be a kind of warning—a shot across the bow of any intruders—a way of saying, "I'm coming through. Keep your distance." That might have

True Tales from Across America

been the source of the "tonk" in the night. But back then I didn't know anything about such things.

I've wondered if it was a coon hunter, returning home from a night's hunt, but I had heard no dogs that evening, and Rocky would surely have reacted to the presence of coon dogs in our neighborhood, just as he reacted to coyotes or the stray dog that wandered by from time to time. In the same way, he would have barked like crazy if a person was out there just like he did when someone came unexpectedly to the door.

So, what was it? Was it anything?

I didn't tell people about the incident. I wasn't even sure it *was* an incident. I'm still not. But the memory lingers, sharp and vivid, to this day, even though it's never been repeated. Sure, there have been times when I was alone in the woods and felt as though I was being watched, but I'm a fully educated—some might even say overeducated—liberal, academic, former college professor and minister, facing my eighth decade on earth. I just chalk it up to normal, healthy paranoia.

Still, I find myself drawn to the hundreds of YouTube videos, newspaper articles, books, and magazines devoted to such things. As a matter of fact, it has become a bit of an obsession even when—and maybe especially when—the authors debunk eyewitness accounts with plain and simple scientific facts and analysis. I'm not interested in perpetuating a hoax or a misguided superstition, but I'm not interested in sweeping what might be the biggest discovery of a generation—or even multiple generations—under the rug, either.

If an unidentified primate, secretive species of human, or even a metaphysical entity of some kind is or was out there and has been hiding from what we call progress for perhaps thousands of years, sparking untold thousands of eyewitness accounts, I want to know about it.

That is the inspiration for this book. It's a mystery story. Join me in the hunt.

Jim Willis

INTRODUCTION

High above the hiking trail, on the eastern face of the mountain, the morning sun sparkles off the dew-tipped branches of the conifers as if the stars of the night sky had settled here to sleep the day away. A creature strides among the trees through the tall grass and saplings of a clearing. It doesn't have the grace of a mountain cat and is too large to be a deer. It must be a brown bear, the observer thinks, it might even be large enough to be a grizzly.

At this distance, it's not much more than a hairy, brown blob, but the zoom lens on the camera brings the viewer closer, slowly zeroing in on the animal's location. It's clear now that it's standing on its hind legs, possibly reaching for a meal in the branches above it. And then it moves, loping like an awkward teenager, limbs too large for its body, but upright, taking long steps like a human. A blurry, grainy image on film—convincing but far from conclusive—is all that documents the encounter.

This is a typical telling of an encounter with North America's most infamous cryptid. Known most commonly as Bigfoot or Sasquatch and thought to be a relative of the Himalayan Yeti, this creature has captured the minds, imaginations, and even hearts of the public. While it's true that not everyone believes in Bigfoot's existence, some of the most hardened skeptics of the paranormal and unexplained allow a little more doubt to creep into their voices and chip away at their convictions when discussing the possibility.

In the following pages, we will explore the physical, circumstantial, and anecdotal evidence supporting the existence of Bigfoot. We'll review ancient texts, oral tradition, mythology, and folklore that suggest these creatures have lived along and among *Homo sapiens* since our ancestors first appeared on the African continent. And we'll dissect sightings not only on the North American continent but around the world, indicating that this may not just be a small population of an elusive crea-

True Tales from Across America

ture residing in the woods and forests of Canada and the United States, but perhaps it is a species that has populated the globe.

I am writing these words having completed the final draft of the book and having sent the pages on to my publisher. I won't claim to have conclusively proven that Bigfoot does or does not exist, but I promise to give you plenty of information to help you form your own opinion. I hope, above all else, that you will be entertained.

And maybe, just maybe, this book will fall into the hands of someone who finds that the information within it drives them to learn even more. Maybe they will have the curiosity and bravery to venture into the forest in search of that piece of undeniable evidence. Maybe they'll find tracks to follow, hear the whooping and whistling sounds the creature is said to make, and discover nests and tree structures that can't be attributed to any other known animal. Maybe they will be able to put an end to the argument once and for all.

If they do, I hope they give me a call. I'd love to write that story.

Michael A. Kozlowski
Detroit, Michigan
February, 2025

WHAT'S IN A NAME?

Before we get into whether a gigantic, hairy hominid exists anywhere in the world, we must settle some linguistic issues. First and foremost, what are we going to call this thing?

One of the first names I recall for a large, apelike, human-ish hominid was the Abominable Snowman—mostly because of Bumble, from the *Rudolph the Red-Nosed Reindeer* Christmas TV special, who was actually called the Abominable Snow Monster, but I was a kid, and they might as well have been the same thing. Back then, I still thought *abominable* meant "big."

Maybe it was the 1957 British movie *The Abominable Snowman* that gave the name some permanence. These days, you don't hear the term much, and when speaking of the creature of the Himalayas, we typically refer to it as *Yeti*. Yeti is the pronunciation of a Tibetan word that means roughly "bear-like" or "rocky bear." The name was coined for use in English by journalist Henry Newman in 1921.

Newman was a writer for an Indian English-language newspaper called *The Statesman* when he interviewed members of the British Mount Everest Reconnaissance Expedition. They sought a route to Everest and then on to the mountain's peak, but they found more than they expected. During their mission, they discovered large, unidentifiable footprints. The expedition members' native guides attributed the tracks to *Metoh-Kangmi*.

Metoh roughly translates to "man-bear" and *Kangmi* to "snowman." And right now, if you've ever watched

True Tales from Across America

What's in a Name?

South Park, you're looking up how to say *pig* in Tibetan, so you can say *manbearpig* in another language. Well, don't mess it up, like Newman did. He mistranslated *Metoh* as meaning "filth." He thought "Filthy Snowman" a little gauche for a proper British writer—the irony being that the "proper British writer" misinterpreted the word in the first place—so he opted, instead, for *Abominable*.

And there ya go.

The Nepalese people hold that the Yeti is a large hominid living high in the Himalayas.

The native people of Nepal, in the Himalayan mountains, maintain a traditional belief that the Yeti is a human-like creature that lives high above the snowline. We can track the oral history back to at least the time of Alexander the Great (356–323 B.C.E.). When the conqueror heard the story of the Yeti, he wanted to see one but was told it could not survive at low altitudes.

In his *Naturalis Historia*, Pliny the Elder wrote of the mysterious Himalayan being: "In the land of the satyrs, in the mountains that lie to the east of India, live creatures that are extremely swift, as they can run on both four feet and on two. They have bodies like men, and because of their speed can only be caught when they are ill or old."

The myth is not only old but also enduring. Today, Sherpas of various Himalayan population groups, famous for their mountaineering skills, accompany expeditions intent on a conquering of their own—the high summits such as Everest. Many insist they have seen the Yeti, and reports of footprints are rather common.

The Yeti is typically described as an ape-like, bipedal creature. It's large, up to 15 feet tall, sometimes described as having sharp teeth, and covered with hair. Although various sightings have noted the creature's hair as brown or gray, and within Tibetan lore subsets

Bigfoot Sightings

What's in a Name? 3

of the creature are described as having black or reddish-brown hair, we most often think of the Yeti as having white hair. Like a polar bear. And if the Yeti is the polar bear version of the giant, bipedal hominid we're searching for, then Sasquatch is the grizzly.

In North America, there is a linguistic group of Native American tribes called the Salish. Their traditional homelands stretched from current-day British Columbia down through the present-day American states of Washington, Idaho, and Montana—an area that makes up the bulk of what is commonly referred to as the Pacific Northwest.

While there have been sightings of large, hairy, hominid creatures in many places, it could be argued that this is Ground Zero of the Bigfoot mythology, and it is, without question, the area most active for sightings.

Within this area, in the shadows of the northeastern slope of Mount Keenan (once known as Mount Morris), lies the reservation of the Confederated Tribes of the Chehalis. Back in 1925, when the land was known as the Chehalis Indian Reserve, an Irish expat named John Walter Burns (1888–1962) became the "Indian agent" and the reservation's schoolteacher.

Burns was well liked by the natives and became friends with a prominent medicine man in the tribe. Eventually, this friendship and respect translated into trust, something rather rare for the Chehalis to bestow upon outsiders. They recognized Burns's genuine interest and, more importantly, his open-mindedness toward the myths and legends of the First Nation, and they shared some of their most guarded secrets. This included stories of "hairy giants" that the Chehalis people believed had inhabited the land from time immemorial. Burns would compile those stories for an article in *Maclean's* titled "Introducing B.C.'s Hairy Giants: A Collection of Strange Tales about British Columbia's Wild Men as Told by Those Who Say They Have Seen Them."

That's a mouthful.

We'll revisit some of these earliest North American stories later. The piece of information that we're most

True Tales from Across America

interested in at the moment is that the Chehalis called these "hairy" and "wild" beings *Sasq'ets*, rendered in English as *Sasquatch* and pronounced "SASS-quatch."

So, we have the Yeti and the Sasquatch, but most people are far more familiar with the creature's colloquial title: Bigfoot. It's a catchy name, and we Westerners have a bit of a thing for nicknames, so often this is the name that's used for the North American creature these days. Even when discussing similar creatures in other parts of the world, it's normal to hear them described as "Bigfoot-like" beings.

Andrew Genzoli (1914–1984) is credited with coining the name. A writer for the *Humboldt Times* (later the *Eureka Times-Standard*) daily newspaper in Eureka, California, Genzoli was a noted historian and an authority on the history of Humboldt County, California. In September 1958, he received a letter from one of his readers about Northern California loggers who claimed to have discovered mysteriously large footprints in the woods. Genzoli thought it quite humorous and, to meet a word quota in a piece he was writing, posted a copy of the letter and floated the idea that "maybe we have a relative of the Abominable Snowman of the Himalayas."

As he didn't take the matter seriously, he was quite surprised at the enthusiastic reactions he received from the readers of what he had called "a good Sunday morning story." Some of those contacting him even claimed to have seen such a creature.

Knowing a good thing when he saw it, Genzoli and a colleague, Betty Allen, published a series of follow-up articles about the footprints and the being that supposedly left them. The loggers had used the name "Big Foot" to describe the creature, so that was the name Genzoli and Allen used in the paper. News services across the country picked up the story, and within a short time, the Bigfoot legend became part of North American folklore.

> *The loggers had used the name "Big Foot" to describe the creature, so that was the name Genzoli and Allen used in the paper.*

What's in a Name?

This creature has been called Yeti, Sasquatch, Bigfoot, Yeren, Skunk Ape, Wood Booger, and other names. Is it the same species, or is it several related species?

As a writer, I find it particularly pleasing to think that the Bigfoot name—and, really, the whole North American phenomenon—started because a journalist was trying to meet a word count.

At the beginning of this chapter, I mentioned that Bumble, the "Abominable Snow Monster of the North," was my first encounter with the giant, hairy hominid folklore. Well, that classic Rankin/Bass *Rudolph* TV special, which debuted in 1964, was capitalizing on the popularity of the Bigfoot legend. The interest in Bigfoot inevitably led people to stories of the Himalayan Yeti.

Throughout the centuries, tales of a hairy humanoid creature have been surprisingly prevalent, which adds a bit of substance to claims that such a creature exists today. After all, if so many cultures have tales of such a creature, how can they be easily dismissed? That seems like an extraordinary coincidence.

In China they're called *Yeren*, the folklore of Australia's aboriginal people tells of the *Joogabinna*, and the *Almas* stalk the mountainous regions of Mongolia and central Asia.

So many ape-like hominids, so many names. While Bigfoot and Sasquatch are broadly used in North America, we still manage to have regional monikers for what seem to be close relatives of the Pacific Northwest's Bigfoot, if not the same creature, in other parts of the country. There's the Skunk Ape of the Everglades and the Fouke Monster of Arkansas. Is the Dogman of Michigan a relative? Or the Wood Booger (a name any inner child will snicker at) of Virginia?

Throughout this book, *Bigfoot* and *Sasquatch* will be used most of the time, as deemed appropriate in the moment—or because I get bothered by using one or the

True Tales from Across America

other too frequently—but there's one last bit of linguistic pondering we need to cover.

It seems that *Sasquatch* and *Yeti* can be used as both singular and plural ("I saw a Sasquatch" or "I saw a family of three Sasquatch," for example), but what is the plural of Bigfoot?

Bigfeet?

Bigfoots?

Maybe it's best to ruminate on that one a bit longer. Meanwhile, we will use *Bigfoot* as the plural.

We can proceed with the understanding that the giant hominids, if they exist today, are likely related in the same way that Caucasians, Asians, Hispanics, and the rest of humankind are related. The appearances may be different enough to note, but they are likely the same species. We can use *Bigfoot* or *Sasquatch* in much the same way we use *human* or *people*.

Bigfoot is often confused with Sasquatch. Yeti doesn't complain.

Bigfoot Sightings

THE ELEPHANT IN THE DARK

There is a parable that originated in the ancient Indian subcontinent, the earliest versions of which are found in Buddhist, Hindu, and Jain texts and that dates to *at least* 500 B.C.E. The story has several variations in which the protagonists are either blind, blindfolded, or in a dark room. The main point is that they are unable to see when they are introduced, in one manner or another, to an elephant.

The men try to ascertain what this animal, previously unknown to them, might look like. During their investigation, each man touches a different part of the elephant and comes to a different conclusion about its physical appearance. The first man feels the elephant's trunk and assumes it must resemble a thick snake. The second man touches the elephant's leg and concludes that it is like a tree trunk. The third man places his hands on the animal's side, arguing that the elephant is like a wall. The fourth man grabs its tail and thinks the creature is rope-like. The fifth man feels the elephant's tusk and states that the beast is obviously hard and smooth, like a spear. The sixth man grabs the elephant ear and exclaims that it is clearly like a big fan.

In some versions, the men collaborate to ascertain the full scope of their experiences and "see" the elephant properly. In others, a sighted man describes the elephant to them. The parable has been used to explore the nature of truth, the behavior of experts in contradicting theories, the need for deeper understanding, and a respect for different perspectives. Broadly, the story is an illustration of ontological reasoning, succinctly demon-

True Tales from Across America

strating that, while one's subjective experience is true, it is inherently limited and may not account for other truths or the totality of truth. Simply put, it's easy to misinterpret things because you can't see the larger picture.

While the idea of what Bigfoot looks like does not vary as widely as the blind men's individual conclusions on the appearance of the elephant, there *are* some significant differences in witness descriptions from around the world and even from within the same region. And the thoughts about what our furry friend actually *is* can vary even more wildly.

Some people believe that the Bigfoot are extraterrestrials. While this may be a fringe theory, it *has* gained traction in the last decade or so, especially as Bigfoot hunters have reported encounters with floating, orange orbs in areas associated with the creature.

As floating lights are often associated with UFOs, it's not an enormous leap to make. Some people believe the orbs serve as some sort of portal or interdimensional transportation beam. This would very conveniently explain away the conspicuous absence of physical evidence that most skeptics point out.

Others believe that Bigfoot are entirely supernatural beings or shape-shifters with psychic and magical abilities. Or they claim that the creatures are similar to demons. In 2022, an Oklahoma man claimed that he killed his friend because he believed the friend had summoned Bigfoot and that he was going to be sacrificed to the creature.

Even among the often-colorful community of Bigfoot researchers, these theories remain on the fringe. Two less exotic, and more scientifically plausible, ideas dominate the narrative. Most people believe that Bigfoot, or Sasquatch, are either an "officially" undiscovered species of ape or a distinct species of human, a long-lost "cousin" of *Homo sapiens*.

First, let's touch on the undiscovered ape theory. Some speculate that Bigfoot is a descendant, or even a remaining population, of the largest ape known to exist

The Elephant in the Dark

Gigantopithecus blacki was a huge ape that lived in southern China during the Early and Middle Pleistocene.

on earth, *Gigantopithecus blacki*. This cousin of the modern orangutan was twice the size of the largest modern apes. *G. blacki* lived in southern China, appearing about 2 million years ago. Until recently, it was believed that the species went extinct around 100,000 years ago due to changes in habitat. Recent research by paleoanthropologists at the Chinese Academy of Sciences in Beijing push that date to 200,000 to 300,000 years ago. As fossil records of *G. blacki* are very limited, estimates of its size vary, ranging from 9 to 12 feet in height and weighing as much as 660 pounds.

Originally, it was hypothesized that there was a direct line from *Gigantopithecus* to the Javan ape *Meganthropus* (then believed to be a human ancestor) and eventually to Aboriginal Australians. As scientists learned more about human origins, they concluded that any shared ancestor between modern humans and *G. blacki* was very distant (12 to 15 million years ago), and while humans fall in the subfamily of *Homininae* (along with gorillas), *Gigantopithecus* is a member of the *Ponginae* subfamily (whose only nonextinct member is the orangutans).

In 1960, zoologist Wladimir Tschemezky, describing a photograph of alleged Yeti tracks in the journal *Nature*, concluded that the creature making the footprints walked like a human and was similar to *Gigantopithecus*. This was around the same time that Andrew Genzoli was coining the name Bigfoot. Subsequently, there was a burst in scientific attention given to both the Yeti, in Nepal, and Bigfoot, in the United States. Several authors published in *Nature* and *Science*, but the interest was short-lived in the broader scientific community. This was, however, a significant moment for the monster-hunting community that developed around the creatures.

The idea that populations of *G. blacki* survived to the present day was quickly dismissed by most, but a few

True Tales from Across America

continued pushing the idea of a connection between the extinct, giant ape and Bigfoot. Individuals like anthropologist Grover Krantz (1931–2002), whom we will discuss more later in this book, championed the theory.

Could a small group of *G. blacki* somehow have survived to the present day? Or could the Sasquatch be a descendant of this greatest of apes? A cousin of the orangutan? After all, the orangutan itself was a relatively new discovery. The first scientific description of orangutans was less than 300 years ago.

Given human expansion and exploration of the world, it might seem ridiculous to think that there would be a large primate wandering in the wild without us being aware of it. Yet the bonobo, historically known as the pygmy chimpanzee, wasn't discovered until 1929. And as recently as 2017, a distinct species of orangutan was identified in Sumatra. Would it be so far-fetched that a large, fairly intelligent species of great ape could have managed to exist in small pockets of largely undisturbed wilderness?

Bonobos, a close relative of the chimpanzee, were not discovered until 1929 in central Africa.

Okay, okay … I can hear it already. And I'm with you. It's one thing to discover a species that is more or less just a variation of a species we're already aware of—something that a casual observer might not be able to differentiate from a known species. This occurs in science journals and on nature shows all the time. A new "species" of, say, a bee is discovered, but the thing that makes it a different species is rather minor, like a slight genetic variation that causes it to be larger than other bees that may otherwise look and act the same. Often, a layperson wouldn't even be able to recognize these differences, which require scientists to take deep dives to discover.

It's another thing altogether for something as unique as what we believe Sasquatch to be to avoid detection all this time. A being the size of Bigfoot, unique in its physiology from what we ascertain from witness testimony, would have a hard time staying hidden. At least that seems to be the logical reaction. But discoveries like these are not unheard of in modern times. There is likely much more we *don't* know about the world we inhabit than we *do*.

The "kraken" of Norwegian folklore and the giant squid featured in Jules Verne's *20,000 Leagues under the Sea* were thought to be mythical beasts, known only by rumor and scant evidence. It wasn't until 2012 that the giant squid was caught on camera, in its natural habitat. Hundreds and hundreds of years of sea travel and exploration, and not until this century did we have a fairly clear understanding of what the creature was.

Is Bigfoot terra firma's version of this elusive, giant squid? A new creature to be discovered? Or perhaps what's left of great apes we thought to be extinct?

In 2023, a mammal called the long-beaked echidna, thought to be extinct, was rediscovered in the mountains of Indonesia. It has the spines of a hedgehog, the snout of an anteater, and the feet of a mole, but the weird creature managed to escape observation for hundreds of years.

> *It's currently estimated that there are anywhere from 10 million to 100 million undiscovered species on Earth. A study conducted by marine ecologist Boris Worm, of Dalhousie University in Halifax, Nova Scotia, estimates that 85 to 90 percent of species on Earth remain undiscovered.*

There are many more examples, but the point is that we are still discovering (or rediscovering) species we thought either never existed or that we "knew" to be extinct for thousands of years.

It's currently estimated that there are anywhere from 10 million to 100 million undiscovered species on Earth. A study conducted by marine ecologist Boris Worm, of Dalhousie University in Halifax, Nova Scotia, estimates that 85 to 90 percent of species on Earth remain undiscovered.

Now, granted, many of those are microbes and insects (and probably, fittingly, worms). And a significant portion are presumed to exist in the deep biosphere, beneath the earth's crust. It's further suspected that, given the very minimal amount of ocean exploration we've managed, some 91 percent of ocean-dwelling species remain unknown to us, just like the giant squid had been for so long.

Still, there are places like the Amazon rainforest that provide a vast, unexplored area where thousands, perhaps millions, of undiscovered animals are suspected to live. According to *National Geographic*, there are so many undiscovered species in the Brazilian rainforest that scientists in 2017 were discovering a new Amazonian species every other day. Let's not forget the vast, frozen landscapes at the poles and high elevations that have, thus far, proved too inhospitable for intense exploration. They are a prime location for a Yeti population.

If Bigfoot turned out to be a new species of bear or ape, it would be fairly exciting, but as we've noted, that kind of thing happens with surprising regularity: It would be both exciting and disappointing.

Honestly, most of us don't believe Bigfoot is just a species of monkey that stands a bit taller than those we already know about. Or walks more upright.

Bigfoot hunters and Sasquatch researchers believe these creatures are more than just another animal that is exceptionally elusive. Most Bigfoot believers consider the creature to be closer to human than ape or a sort of missing link between the two.

This might lead skeptics to believe that the existence of Bigfoot is even more unlikely. For many people, the idea that a distinct species of large animal existing beyond our knowledge is hard to fathom. There has only been one significant discovery of megafauna (large animals) since the early 1900s. An entirely unique creature, such as that described by those claiming encounters with Bigfoot, is an even further stretch.

But should it be?

The differences in genome (the genetic information of an organism) that make a species unique from another is rather miniscule. The aforementioned bonobo is

The Elephant in the Dark

Located in the Bashelaksky Range of the Altai Mountains in Siberia, Russia, Denisova Cave is the site where the Denisova hominin was discovered in 2008.

only genetically different from a chimpanzee by about 0.3 percent. Modern-day humans are less than 2 percent different from either of them. It would be a minor difference in genetic development that would result in a larger, hairier version of ourselves.

High above the Anuy River in Siberia lies the Denisova Cave. The August 22, 2018, issue of the *New York Times* reported the work of Carl Zimmer, who discovered in the cave the remains of a 90,000-year-old female who was unquestionably the daughter of a Neanderthal mother and a Denisovan father. The cave has a history of having sheltered humans and other species for 120,000 years. It now appears certain to have attracted humans of differing species who apparently had no problem getting to know one another on a personal level. The research of Svante Pääbo, a renowned geneticist at the prestigious Max Planck Institute for Evolutionary Anthropology in Leipzig, Germany, confirmed the result.

Denisovan DNA has now been found all over the world, including in many Native American tribes. So who were they?

The Denisovans were a large species of early human ancestors. Anthropologists call them "robust." Individ-

True Tales from Across America

uals of 8 and 9 feet or more were not uncommon. Given the amount of DNA evidence they left behind in the genomes of modern human population groups found everywhere from Siberia to Asia, Australia, and North America, they got around, and they were usually made to feel welcome.

Judging from the beautiful jewelry they made, they were intelligent. They were extremely old on the land. Current evidence suggests they emerged nearly 300,000 years ago—around the same time as *Homo sapiens* (us) but well after Neanderthals. Neanderthals seem to have disappeared from the fossil record about 40,000 years ago, just when the explosion of art in the caves of western Europe burst on the scene. Denisovans were thought to go extinct about that time as well, but some evidence suggests they may have still been around as recently as 25,000 years ago. Did they, like the Neanderthals, blend into modern human populations by the simple act of assimilation? In other words, did they become us? DNA evidence indicates this was at least partially the case.

It's clear that Denisovans lived side by side with Neanderthals and modern humans. There is a large amount of Denisovan DNA found in modern American Indian tribes such as the Ojibwa, who lived around the Great Lakes, so it's clear there was intercourse between the species. The Ojibwa are also the keepers of many leg-

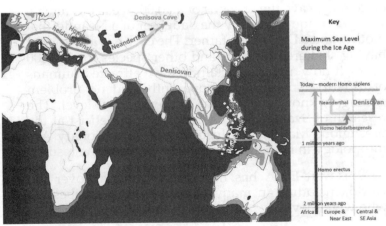

The Denisovans existed during the same time as Neanderthals and Homo sapiens, making their way into Siberia and Southeast Asia.

ends involving ancient giants who were familiar to their ancestors.

Do stories about giants, Sasquatches and other Bigfoot-type creatures carry echoes of real and "robust" Denisovans who once lived on the land? Are these just "memories" of beings who were absorbed by the modern human population, or did a distinct line descending from the Denisovans survive the evolutionary fate of the many other close relatives of *Homo sapiens*? Has a self-sustaining population of Denisovans managed to survive in various secluded pockets around the globe and now make up what we call Yeti, Sasquatch, and Bigfoot?

Let's not get carried away just yet. That would be too broad a claim, given the lack of evidence. But here's the point. Denisovans existed. They were thought to have gone extinct 40,000 to 250,000 years ago, but their DNA is a fact. The few remaining bones we have discovered are a fact. Their artifacts are a fact.

Physical evidence of their existence is sparse. We know more about Denisovans from DNA evidence than physical remains. Until a decade ago, no one knew they existed. There were no identifiable remains or bones to examine.

Or were there?

There has been anecdotal evidence reported for years about giant bones being discovered and even photographed. Much of that evidence is now unavailable for examination because museums such as the Smithsonian have rightly returned boxes and boxes of indigenous people's remains due to the Native American Graves Protection and Repatriation Act (NAGPRA) enacted on November 16, 1990. This act requires all agencies that receive federal funds to return any and all "cultural items," including bones, to their descendants. This is a good thing but possibly a roadblock to certain research.

If the Smithsonian *was* hoarding giant bones without realizing what they were, those potentially revealing remains are now, at least officially, reburied in Indian graves. Were they the bones of Bigfoot that no one thought to examine for DNA? We just don't know.

True Tales from Across America

When we consider the recent possibilities and ongoing studies, the ramifications are almost staggering. According to current thinking, the Neanderthals and Denisovans split from each other between 300,000 and 500,000 years ago. Modern humans didn't appear until 200,000 to 300,000 years ago.

Denisovan brains were as big as ours. They could think and reason as well as us. They were biologically compatible enough to interbreed with both Neanderthals and our Cro-Magnon ancestors. They could craft fine implements such as bracelets, beads, needles, and tools. They made the world's first bird-bone flutes. They apparently invented pressure flaking in the creation of sharp stone tools. There is compelling evidence that they were sophisticated astronomers with an in-depth knowledge of eclipse cycles, and perhaps they were the first to understand calendar-based cosmological systems that would eventually be incorporated by religions around the world. Why should we assume that given that amount of time, more than *we've* had so far, they wouldn't do the same thing we did—go forth and multiply?

Distribution of Denisovan DNA in Melanesians, Aboriginal Australians, and Filipino Negritos suggests that Denisovan populations were spread across Asia. The first fossil to be identified as a Denisovan was found in what is now known as the Denisova Cave in south-central Siberia. The cave, and subsequently a whole species of human, is named after a Russian hermit, Denis (Dyonisiy), who lived there in the eighteenth century.

The fossil is that of a finger bone from a juvenile female hominin, and extracted DNA was found to be genetically distinct from Neanderthals and modern humans. Additional fossils were found on the Tibetan plateau in China and a Laotian jungle. So we know the Denisovans existed in multiple locations.

And what of the Denisovan DNA found in North American tribes?

The Bering Land Bridge was exposed more than a few times during recurrent ice ages. We understand the migration pattern of early humans and know that they

The Elephant in the Dark   17

During the last Ice Age, sea levels fell, creating a land bridge between what are now Alaska and Russia.

used this bridge to cross over from Asia to the Americas. The prevailing theory has been that this migration occurred around 14,000 B.C.E., but recent discoveries in the Chiquihuite Cave in Mexico suggest that humans occupied that area as early as 33,000 years ago.

Considering the distance from Alaska and the Bering Land Bridge to north-central Mexico and the Chiquihuite Cave, coupled with the pace of early human migration, it seems logical that, if the dating in the Mexican cave is accurate, human populations in North America would have existed even earlier.

Further, based on records of estimated global temperature and sea level, scientists have speculated that the Bering Land Bridge could have been exposed some 70,000 years ago. While the prevailing scientific winds assume that Denisovans and Neanderthals were assimilated by *Homo sapiens* before the human migration from Asia to North America—that they died *in* to us rather than *out*—it's also possible that Denisovans could have migrated across the Bering Land Bridge as modern humans were just beginning to move out of Africa. In fact, they might have been here to watch the first struggling bands of *Homo sapiens* move across the landscape and decided to keep their presence a secret, as much as possible.

Maybe they existed side by side with the first humans in North America, until our inevitable ferocity made the "Bigfoot race" decide to retreat to the mountains to which they were so genetically well-suited to survive. Since then, it might have been a game of cat-and-mouse that exists to the present day.

The only thing standing in the way of that theory is the lack of such hard evidence as living sites, bones, scat, and other telltale signs, but that evidence may have been hiding in plain sight all along. It's just so old we didn't understand what we were looking at.

True Tales from Across America

Whether we posit that Bigfoot populations are surviving Denisovans, descendants thereof, or some other as-yet-unknown species of human, the question remains: Where are they?

Even if they were actively hiding from us, we humans have shown that we're exceptionally skilled at getting around. We have an unquenchable thirst for exploration, which is not always fueled by the best intentions. We've shown that we rarely respect the autonomy, or even the right to existence, of members of our own species, let alone that of others. Certainly, by now, with such modern advances as airplanes and satellites, we'd have stumbled across a whole other race of people, right?

It's one thing to not have discovered a small population of arctic cat, or some species of ant on the rainforest floor, or even a large, toothy, glow-in-the-dark sea creature in a trench deep below the ocean's surface. It's another thing to have missed a population of *people*. Particularly a population of really, really *big* people. Right?

Well …

There may be hundreds of tribes in isolated places such as the Amazon and Indonesia who have never been exposed to modern civilization.

Bigfoot Sightings

The Elephant in the Dark

There are more than 100 uncontacted tribes around the world that we are *aware* of. Most of these are in the Amazon region of South America, but populations also exist in Indonesia and on the Indian subcontinent. Our interaction with, and knowledge of, these tribes is miniscule. In some cases, we *literally* only know that they exist and have had only one or two sightings of them, even when we've made concerted, but cautious, attempts to observe them.

There are several islands and inhospitable areas around the globe that remain unexplored—even mountains yet to be summited. There are large swaths of forest floor that remain untrod by the foot of man (as far as we know) and areas so vast and dense, but sparsely populated, that a small tribe of people, or a number of nomadic family units, escaping detection is not only possible but probable.

If you were to hear that a small community was found to have been living off the land, deep in the Appalachian Mountains, for the last few generations, you probably wouldn't be especially doubtful of that. It's the sort of thing we've seen in documentaries, not to mention the kind of scenario that shapes some of our own most frightening myths and legends that seep into books and horror movies.

That's not to say that Sasquatch are an inbred population of backwoods cannibals with poor dental hygiene. It's just to give some perspective regarding our perceptions.

The "more than 100" uncontacted tribes is just an estimate. This is because the smartest people in those sorts of matters are relatively certain that there are tribes that we're not aware of yet. They just assume they exist.

So, does that mean that Bigfoot is just a lost tribe of *Homo sapiens* that has the good sense to avoid the rest of us, but that we occasionally stumble across—Perhaps while they're wearing clothing that they've made from black bear hides, since it is documented that areas with known black bear populations yield an increased number of Bigfoot sightings?

True Tales from Across America

Not necessarily. And given the consistent descriptions of Bigfoot-like creatures, and how those descriptions differ from that of all known *Homo sapiens*, not likely. The point is that, while we will consider various explanations for what Bigfoot may or may not be, the overwhelming opinion in both academic and folkloric circles is that Bigfoot is neither an alien nor ape but rather a taller, stronger, slightly wilder, and dramatically less ambitious member of our family tree, just a branch or two over. Some would suggest they are the "missing link" between apes and humankind. Others would say they are a large race of humans that had lived side by side with our not-too-distant ancestors. And many are desperate to find them.

Whatever the origins or lineage of Bigfoot may be, we do not need to look millions or hundreds of thousands of years into the past for our purposes. What we want to know is whether a giant, hairy, humanlike creature lives among us *today*. It's exceptionally unlikely that we will prove this unequivocally by the end of this book, but we can hope to tip the scale of probability more in one direction or the other. Rather than searching the fossil record to speculate about the existence of Sasquatch or their ancestors before the spoken word, let's continue our search with a look to the relatively recent past of oral and written history.

Bigfoot Sightings

ONCE THERE WERE GIANTS

The most defining characteristics of Bigfoot are that they tend to be hairy and that they are *big*—often reported to be anywhere from 9 to 15 feet. A giant! And if we are going to assume that they are hominids, our relatives, let's first ask if there is any reason to believe such large humans could exist. I mean, we have some professional basketball players topping out over 7 feet, and the world's tallest man, Robert Wadlow, was just a whisker below 9 feet. Look at a photo of him—that's a *big* dude! But he would be on the short side for a Sasquatch. Could a race of giants have survived beyond some fossilized past and lived alongside modern humans?

Here is a photo of eight-foot-eleven Robert Wadlow next to his average-size father, and on the next page is my 6' 3" friend Haisam Rahal standing next to a replica of the "Alton Giant," as Wadlow was known.

Well, there is some compelling evidence that just such a thing happened. And not just that they lived with "modern" humans in the

Robert Wadlow stands next to his average-size father in this c. 1935 photograph.

True Tales from Across America

sense of when *Homo sapiens* first emerged into the historic record some 300,000 years ago, but also in the relatively recent times of our recorded history. A time that in the broader context of human existence we could arguably deem "the present."

One of the earliest mentions of giants occurs in the New King James Version of the Bible, in the book of Genesis, chapter 6:

> *There were giants on the earth in those days, and also afterward, when the sons of God came in to the daughters of men and they bore children to them. Those were the mighty men who were of old, men of renown.*

The author's friend, Haisam Rahal, stands next to a dummy of the "Alton Giant."

In this passage, the original Hebrew word for "giants" is *nefilim*. Many believe the proper interpretation would be something like "fallen warriors" based on the Hebrew root word. However, early Greek translations of the Bible rendered the word as *gigantes*, who were beings of great strength and aggression in Greek mythology (though not necessarily of great size).

The Vulgate, which was one of the earliest Catholic translations of the Bible into Latin, transcribed the Greek term rather than translating the original Hebrew. The Vulgate became the dominant Bible text and was affirmed as the official Latin Bible at the Council of Trent (1545–1563).

In fact, most ancient biblical translations interpret the word to mean "giants," though some call them "fallen ones," "violent ones," or "the ones falling [upon their enemies]."

Once There Were Giants

At some point, the *n* was capitalized and what may have been a verb or adjective became a noun: Nephilim. The consensus was that a specific race of beings was being described, and with the influence of the Greek translation, that race was believed to be a people of abnormal size.

When the suspected root word (meaning "fall") is considered at all, it is usually said to convey that the beings were the offspring of humans and fallen angels. Due to the ambiguity of the text, though, some would argue that it means that the Nephilim were the actual "sons of God" who mated with humans, rather than the offspring of those unions.

Here, our "giants" are again being considered supernatural or, at least, supernatural adjacent. It's clearly inferred that the "genes" of their heavenly fathers are what contribute to their abnormal size. This "godly" stepparent motif is common in classic mythology and would no doubt have influenced early biblical writers.

Giant humanoids would have been quite a sight to ancient peoples, and the few references in biblical texts seem to regard them with a certain measure of awe. It's not surprising that a relatively uneducated populace would see them as a species separate from themselves and explain their differences as being due to supernatural means.

The Nephilim are referenced again in the book of Numbers, chapter 13, verse 33. Moses sent a group of spies to scout the land of Canaan, which was believed to be the land that God had promised the Israelites. There were 12 spies, one chieftain from each of the 12 tribes of Israel, and they were to report on the geographic features, the potential and current performance of the land, the inhabitants and their strength and numbers, and whether the population lived in camps or cities.

Ten of the 12 spies returned with negative reports, mostly because what they had seen had frightened them and they didn't believe they would be able to conquer the land, even with God's help. Consequently, it was this slandering of God's promise that led to the Israelites wandering lost in the desert for the next 40 years, while

True Tales from Across America

God waited for that generation of men to die because he was mad at them for doubting his promise. Only Joshua and Caleb would see the "promised land," as they were the two spies who had returned with positive reports.

In the Numbers verse, the spies report seeing a tribe they called the Anakites, who were a Rephaite tribe, said to be the descendants of the Nephilim. The Rephaites are mentioned in Deuteronomy and also in non-Jewish texts, and they were said to be a people of greater-than-average height and stature.

The Israelite spies would have also seen the great walls of the Canaanite cities, some as thick as 18 feet. Some argue that these walls and large structures, built with massive limestone boulders, are what led the Israelites to believe giants lived in Canaan, and not the actual sighting of gigantic beings. The argument is that the Israelites would have thought that only giants could accomplish such things. This idea would certainly dilute the impact of the biblical references to giants, but it dismisses much of the Israelite experience at that point in history.

The exact origin of the Israelites, while a bit murky beyond the biblical narrative, is as descendants of Jacob and his 12 sons. It's believed they emerged from groups of indigenous Canaanites, and the first nonbiblical reference to "Israel" is in an ancient Egyptian inscription from about 1200 B.C.E. If we're to believe the Exodus story, that the Israelites were enslaved in Egypt, the biblical chronology tells us that they escaped slavery around 1300 B.C.E., which seems to line up with the timing of their mention in the Egyptian inscription. And, as we're talking about the biblical reference to giants in the first place, the actual historical accuracy is less important than the overall story as told in the text.

In 1300 B.C.E., the Giza Pyramid complex, with the Great Pyramid and the Great Sphinx, would have been over 1,000 years old. The Luxor Temple would have been constructed during the Israelites' time in captivity. They could even have been laborers on the project. The temple complex at Karnak could have been constructed with the use of Israelite slaves. Large and complex structures of stone would not have been foreign to them.

Once There Were Giants

A statue of a fallen angel in Madrid, Spain. Certain interpretations of the Bible say that stories of giants—the nefilim—*were actually about angels of enormous size.*

While in Egypt, they would have seen plenty of them and understood and helped with their construction. So the spies' reports of giants would not have been inferred from the architecture of Canaan but more likely have been a direct observation of the beings.

There is a third reference to the Nephilim in the book of Ezekiel, but it is likely a misinterpretation. It is a reference back to the original Nephilim: the "old, mighty men of renown" in the Genesis verse.

If we *are* to accept the Bible as a historically accurate text, we might question how the Nephilim of Genesis would have managed to have descendants at all in the time of Moses. After all, everyone other than Noah and his family should have been wiped out in the Great Flood, which would have occurred between the account in Genesis and the events in Numbers.

That might be fodder for another book, but just to address it briefly, stories of a Great Flood exist in several ancient religious and mythological canons. Science doesn't support a global flood event, but ancient peoples may have exaggerated local events that were devastating enough to leave a cultural scar.

What's important to us is the mention of "giants" in a text considered "ancient" but that, in the grand scheme of our species' existence, was practically written yesterday.

It's important to differentiate between a race of large hominids and the occasional larger-than-life (pun intended) individuals who stalk the world's myths and legends. Goliath, the "giant" Philistine warrior slain by

True Tales from Across America

David in the Bible story, is said to have been either six feet, nine inches or nine feet, nine inches tall, depending on the text. However, it's clear that he is just an abnormally large Philistine and not a member of a seperate race, such as the Nephilim.

The stories in the Bible are often thought to be historical, nonfiction accounts, as opposed to the stories of "dead" religions or mythologies. Still, across all these beliefs and legends, giants are common. Giants in Norse mythology possessed supernatural powers and fought battles against the gods. Remember the Greek word used in the translation of the biblical verse? *Gigantes*?

In the biblical story of David versus Goliath, the giant was clearly just a very large Philistine and not one of the Nephilim.

In addition to meaning "large being," it was also the name of a *race* of large beings who fought the Olympians. Stories of giants are found in folklore around the world: African, Chinese, Australian, Gaelic, and more.

There's much in oral tradition, folklore, legends, and historical texts to suggest that one or many races of exceptionally large people existed—recently—alongside our ancestors. The problem is, we've already agreed that, in the same way that we're not talking about other types of apes, we're also not talking about taller versions of ourselves. Bigfoot is something in between.

This doesn't mean that the giants of these stories weren't ancestors of today's Sasquatch. In much the same way that ancient people would assign supernatural characteristics to things that science has since explained otherwise, it would not be beyond them to take a creature they didn't understand and try to fit it into a box that made sense to them. This would be no different than the first people to see gorillas or orangutans describing them as another race of humans.

Once There Were Giants

The stories of giants provide us with circumstantial evidence that some other species of hominid—of great size and intellect, very similar to ourselves—existed in our recent past, even though we don't see them today. Beyond the Bible, we've already discussed a couple of other legends of man-ape-type creatures, but there are many more examples in history.

There are mentions of the Persians using creatures with descriptions similar to Sasquatch as ferocious battle animals. The translated account of Greek admiral Nearchos tells of his Macedonian troops encountering a race of primitives along the Persian Gulf shore that "were hairy, not only their heads but the rest of their bodies; their nails were rather like beasts' claws; they used their nails as if they were iron tools; with these they tore asunder their fishes, and even the less solid kinds of wood; everything else they cleft with sharp stones.... For clothing they wore skins of animals...."

Native Americans, from the Chehalis in northern reaches of present-day British Columbia to the Seminoles in the deep southeastern swamplands of the United States, almost universally told tales of big, hairy, bipedal giants. Their stories are often incredibly similar in details, such as the sulfuric odor of the creature, but also varied enough to cast doubt. To some, the being is a benevolent spirit; to others, it is a dangerous, man-eating giant, which they warn children about so they don't stray too far into the wilderness on their own, or a malevolent shadow being that can cause paralysis and insanity and that molests women and causes negative thoughts and evil to befall men.

> *Native Americans, from the Chehalis in northern reaches of present-day British Columbia to the Seminoles in the deep southeastern swamplands of the United States, almost universally told tales of big, hairy, bipedal giants.*

Northern Paiute oral history tells of an enemy tribe called the Si-Te-Cah that the Paiutes fought with. Members were described as having red hair, as sometimes being cannibals, and, in some versions of the legend, as giants. The Paiutes defeated this enemy tribe but it

True Tales from Across America

is unclear whether they completely exterminated them or drove them away.

It would seem rather strange that cultures across the globe would all come up with stories of races of human-like beings of abnormal size if there wasn't something to it. But then, most cultures develop some idea of a creator being and an afterlife, and many would argue that these are just made-up stories that *also* lack any conclusive evidence.

Much like the defense many make regarding a god and an afterlife, if the stories weren't true, why would they bear such similarities? Why would cultures across great distances, both physically and chronologically, have stories that seem to reinforce those of each other? There must be *some* truth within them.

A carving of a Bigfoot stands outside the International Cryptozoology Museum in Portland, Maine. If there were no such thing as Bigfoot, why are there so many similar stories of the beast around the world?

Or ...

Could it just be in our nature, in our storytelling DNA, to come up with an extra-large version of ourselves that exists somewhere between us and the supernatural gods we create (which, coincidentally, also tend to be exaggerated versions of ourselves)?

Prior to the development of the written word, stories were passed on through memorization and the tradition of oral storytelling. It has been argued that the similarities in the stories of various cultures result from the fact that we all come from the same place originally, and the stories of those first ancestors color all subsequent stories. The unique experiences each culture encounters as it migrates away from the original "source material" accounts for the differences in the stories. We can see this in the way cultures assimilate the stories and beliefs

Once There Were Giants

of other cultures that they may conquer or merge with. You might call this the "Origin of *Stories* Out of Africa" theory.

A somewhat similar theory is that, since we are so alike in our genetic makeup and our neurology, we tend to seek answers to the same big questions, such as, Why are we here? Where did we come from? While we may be unique individuals, we're remarkably the same and rather predictable as a species. So, there should be no surprise that our efforts to answer those questions, to fill in the gaps, and to create gods to worship and monsters to fear would look much the same across cultures, even if we had no contact with one another. We might call this the "Vulcan Brain Meld" theory.

We can see that stories of Sasquatch and related creatures have been pervasive and prolific in both our distant and recent past. Some would argue that's compelling evidence of their possible existence today.

But ...

There are approximately 800 versions of the classic Cinderella fairy tale, with some dating as far back as 1,200 years, spanning various cultures. That doesn't mean we take it for granted that magical godmothers are flitting about turning pumpkins into buggies and doling out glass slippers.

However, given the scientific evidence of such large hominids as the Denisovans, which we know lived hundreds of thousands years ago, and the proliferation of more recent stories of giants—specifically, hairy hominds—we must admit that the continued existence of such a creature seems more plausible than, say, mice turning into coachmen.

Admittedly, this doesn't eliminate the fact that there is no direct evidence that Sasquatch, Yeti, or Bigfoot really exist. In the end, the thousands of sightings may simply be related to an unknown primate, or even glimpses of bears or other animals.

We've been unable to verify firsthand accounts, and some are so outrageous that they do more harm to the argument than good. Could it all be some sort of mass

True Tales from Across America

There are hundreds of amateur and scientific Bigfoot hunters across the United States alone. However, the many scams over the years have caused the belief in the cryptid ape to diminish.

hallucination? Or perhaps sightings are influenced by the power of suggestion and a bias to believe.

There is an active community of amateur "hunters" and scientific researchers dedicated to proving or disproving the validity of Bigfoot sightings and the creatures' existence or nonexistence. Unfortunately, regardless of their passion, dedication, and intentions, they are often viewed as "crackpots." Scientific studies are considered "fringe," at best, and are typically lumped into the cryptozoology pile, with other creatures of folkloric and paranormal origin, rather than treated as mainstream scientific research.

Most people don't believe Bigfoot exists. Surveys estimate that only 10 to 30 percent of North Americans believe that Bigfoot is a real, living creature. The hundreds of misguided hoaxes don't help. Whenever charlatans are unmasked, it puts the whole study back and undermines any legitimacy and public trust.

The hunters and researchers are a tenacious community, however, and not easily dissuaded by failure or ridicule. It seems that tenacity may be bearing fruit in opening others to the possibility of Bigfoot's existence.

Bigfoot Sightings

While belief in alien life appears, thus far, to have peaked with Gen X, the expressed belief in Bigfoot shows strong growth among Gen Z.

As long as truthful researchers (in efforts to prove or disprove) go about the task using modern, scientific methods and carefully document their research, opening their work to peer review, it at least offers the possibility of new discoveries. After all, most of the things we've learned through the scientific method were, when first speculated, met with doubt or derision.

Let's look at what research, studies, and evidence exist beyond stories about big people written in ancient languages or passed on through oral tradition.

LET'S GET PHYSICAL!

It's probably a safe bet that the field of Bigfoot studies produces more hoaxes than any other area of research. Scientists hate hoaxes, so many of them steer clear of the subject because they don't want to be branded as kooks and charlatans.

It's hard to deduce why so many people take perverse pleasure in trying to deceive the public. Perhaps just because *they* don't believe in the possibility of an unknown primate species, they are trying to make those who do appear foolish. But many supposed hoaxes cannot be proven false, and since no one has stepped forward to take credit for them, it's hard to put *all* sightings, pictures, footprints, and other evidence in the category of deception. It's less difficult to cast doubt on them, however, and that's because many of the people who report such sightings are considered reputable. Friends and family often describe them as people who would *never* believe in ghosts, UFOs, or Bigfoot. They're often well-educated, successful, average citizens who are hesitant to share their experiences because of the fame and potential ridicule that may follow.

There have been many Bigfoot hoaxes over the years, including fake footprints and people in costumes.

True Tales from Across America

They are clearly impacted and moved by what they saw. They are often shocked or frightened, and the encounters they describe have sometimes changed their lives and their view of the world. They are not nutcases, despite some nonbelievers' attempts to discredit them by attacking their character or intelligence. A few people who report strange experiences that happen at night can be written off as overly zealous or thrill seekers who want fifteen minutes of fame. But there are too many reputable accounts to ignore.

Still, there is that *one* argument against the existence of such a creature, and it's a fundamental one: Where is the physical evidence?

In this case, the large number of eyewitness accounts works against itself. If so many people, scattered across the world, have seen a Yeti, Sasquatch, or Bigfoot, doesn't it seem plausible that at least *some* solid evidence would have been discovered by now?

> *We've found the bones of dinosaurs that have been extinct for over 60 million years, even the complete skeleton of a Scelidosaurus, but we're to believe we haven't stumbled across even one Bigfoot body?*

Skeptics often ask why a carcass, a skeleton, some bones, or other artifacts have been discovered by now. If so many people are *looking*, given today's technology, why isn't anyone *finding*? We've found the bones of dinosaurs that have been extinct for over 60 million years, even the complete skeleton of a *Scelidosaurus*, but we're to believe we haven't stumbled across even one Bigfoot body?

Nick Redfern, in his 2016 book, *The Bigfoot Book: The Encyclopedia of Sasquatch, Yeti, and Cryptid Primates*, suggests that the answer could be because of an association that some believe exists between Bigfoot and alien activity. There have been occasional reports of UFOs, orbs, and other such oddities associated with Bigfoot. Redfern claims this explains the lack of physical evidence. After all, UFOs, or UAPs (unidentified aerial phenomena) as they are now called, also have pictures and eyewitness accounts, but we have yet to examine a real flying saucer, unless you believe the government is covering up

Let's Get Physical!

such evidence (again, fodder for another book).

Arguably, more people believe in, or are willing to accept the possibility of, aliens from outer space or parallel dimensions than in Bigfoot. Yet, there's not an abundance of evidence available to support "Martians" any more than there is to support belief in Sasquatch.

It's hard to believe, though, that a big, hairy, reclusive primate would be popular with aliens who possess the technology to fly here from another planet, and it requires another leap of logic to come up with a reason *why* an alien civilization would have a particular interest in Bigfoot carcasses and, seemingly, in *every* Bigfoot carcass that might die in plain sight. Or that Bigfoot is, itself, an alien race.

Those who believe say there is plenty of evidence. There are photographs and films, but they are usually (conveniently or not, depending on your perspective) rather grainy or blurry. That might be understandable, though, given the settings and circumstances under which the images are captured. Bigfoot, obviously, can't be expected to show up for a photoshoot under studio conditions.

A less far-fetched possibility is that Bigfoot is not just a simple animal but also an intelligent hominid. We know that even our most primitive ancestors had burial practices for their dead. It was recently discovered that a tree-climbing, Stone Age hominid known as *Homo naledi*, a primitive species at the crossroads between apes and modern humans, buried its dead.

Whether it developed as a matter of practicality that minimized filth and disease and kept scavengers away, or showed a measure of

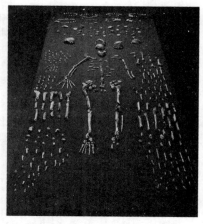

Quite a few bone specimens of the Homo naledi *have been discovered, a species from the Middle Pleistocene that is believed to have buried its dead. Perhaps the Sasquatch buries its dead as well?*

True Tales from Across America

reverence and even a belief in an afterlife of some sort, intentional burials have been a human ritual for most of our existence. The burying of one's dead is often recognized as a sign of higher intelligence and social development, such as with elephants who bury their dead calves.

Who's to say that Sasquatch don't bury their dead? Would it be easy for us to find the relatively few buried bodies of what we presume is a rather small population that lives in the most remote of areas? Heck, some of our best forensic specialists and enforcement investigators can't locate the remains of murder victims, even when they have a rough idea of where to look and only a shallow grave concealing the body.

> *Who's to say that Sasquatch don't bury their dead? Would it be easy for us to find the relatively few buried bodies of what we presume is a rather small population that lives in the most remote of areas?*

According to the NamUs database, an average of 600,000 people are declared missing each year, and about 1 percent—or 6,000 people—remain missing. That's a pretty big number of people we can't find, just in the United States, who we *know* existed and had a starting place from which to begin the searches. Imagine a population of 6,000 Sasquatch in the United States. This is certainly enough to maintain a population but, apparently, few enough that they could go undetected by our best investigators.

Remember those Stone Age *Homo naledi* mentioned earlier? We only found their remains in 2023. Granted, they were buried about 100 feet underground in a cave system, but still ...

At any rate, there are no exhibits of Bigfoot in public museums, unlike extinct animals such as mammoths or saber-tooth cats. To date, no remains of Bigfoot have been located, which makes it hard to argue in favor of its existence.

Could it be possible that we do have physical evidence but we just don't know it?

Let's Get Physical!

According to the most recent information gathered by anthropologists, there have been more than 20 hominin species that are part of our family tree. That's a lot of ancestors. But here's the amazing part. More than half of these species were deduced by fossils discovered only in the last 30 years.

Think of it! All those ancestors, and no one knew about most of them until the last few decades. To think that most of these discoveries happened in the twenty-first century is rather startling. Suddenly, the idea of a previously unknown human cousin still roaming the earth doesn't sound nearly as far-fetched as it once did.

In the same way that we ask why we haven't found any carcasses of recently deceased Sasquatch, we'd also have to ask why we haven't found anthropological evidence of these creatures. If any number of Sasquatch exist today, then their ancestors must have existed. Even if there are *no* living specimens today, if they *ever* existed, there should be some fossil record. Why haven't we found it? As we stated in the previous chapter, there doesn't seem to be a lineage to follow that would lead to Bigfoot today.

The answer is, maybe we have found such evidence and we just didn't know it at the time. Because Bigfoot's presence was unknown and unsuspected by most specialists, bones and related material that could have been evidence of the creatures were often placed in boxes and

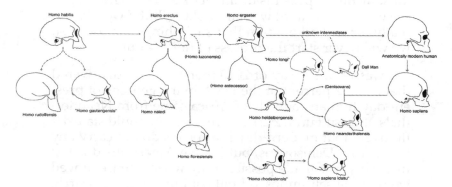

Some of the many hominin species are shown here, along with how they are linked on the evolutionary scale.

True Tales from Across America

sent off to various museums for future study. Between not knowing *what* to look for and not knowing *how* to look for it, potential evidence sat, literally collecting dust, until a new technology called DNA analysis was invented, coming to the fore in 1986.

When these boxes began to see the light of day, in some cases after decades of neglect, new revelations burst onto the scene. We are not alone. We have ancestors in our family tree that only DNA evidence could conclusively prove.

Anyone who has ever seen the first *Indiana Jones* movie about the Ark of the Covenant remembers the final scene, when the ark is boxed up and delivered to a huge warehouse for storage after Jones was told by FBI officials that "top experts" were studying it. That was, of course, fiction, but apparently it isn't as far removed from reality as it might seem. Perhaps the fictional ark was stored right beside a very real box of bones that were assumed to be those of early *Homo sapiens* but were actually a different species altogether.

This brings us back to the Native American Graves Protection and Repatriation Act (NAGPRA) of 1990, which required all agencies that receive federal funds to return all "cultural items," including, of course, bones, to their descendants to be reinterred in various Native American burial places throughout the country. But perhaps more evidence is still sitting in a box somewhere, right next to the fictional Ark of the Covenant, waiting for someone to peek inside and look at it with fresh eyes. We won't know until we start looking, but if we have already formed an opinion that such things cannot exist, we will never start the process of finding out.

It wasn't until May of 2010 that scientists discovered that up to 2 percent of the DNA in the genome of present-day humans outside of Africa came from Neanderthals. It wasn't until 2021 that researchers could state definitively that modern-day Europeans do not carry any DNA from Denisovans, but Native Americans do. The discovery was made possible only when science moved beyond the self-imposed limits of Eurocentric research. It's entirely possible that DNA evidence of Bigfoot exists, and we just haven't bothered to look at it.

Let's Get Physical!

Analysis of DNA samples back in 2010 has revealed that humans carry some Neanderthal genes in them, which of course means that our two species mated with each other at least occasionally.

In 2012, a study released by Melba S. Ketchum made news when she claimed her research indicated that a "five-year-long DNA study, currently under peer-review, confirms the existence of a novel hominin hybrid species, commonly called 'Bigfoot' or 'Sasquatch,' living in North America. Researchers' extensive DNA sequencing suggests that the legendary Sasquatch is a human relative that arose approximately 15,000 years ago." Her information suggested that this species had sex with modern human females that resulted in hairy hominin hybrids.

It's a rather common trope in mythology that various species (angels, gods, Sasquatch) are literally "sexed" out of existence by *Homo sapiens* women. This speaks more to the patriarchy (and probable perversions) of "civilized" society than it does to any sort of actual scientific evidence. It can be seen in other supernatural and paranormal fields, as well, such as the extensive mythology of women having sex with demonic entities or the regular belief that aliens are coming to steal women for breeding purposes.

Media picked up on Ketchum's research, and for a while the Bigfoot seekers' community expressed considerable glee, but things soon turned in a different direction. Some in the scientific community were highly dubious about Ketchum's report. Claims of tainted hair samples, a peer review that never materialized, suspicious collection procedures, and more soon halted the excitement.

In March 2021, a team brought together to film a TV series called *Expedition Bigfoot* for the Discovery Channel announced some interesting results taken from the vast forests of the Appalachian Mountains in Kentucky. The series follows the work of Bryce Johnson (expedition operations), Dr. Mireya Mayor (primatologist),

True Tales from Across America

Russell Acord (ex-military/survivalist), and Ronny LeBlanc (Bigfoot researcher).

It makes for good television, certainly, which needs to be considered.

The team produced such standard Bigfoot fare as recorded vocalizations and massive 16-inch footprints, but while involved in one search, they came across what some call a Bigfoot nest. From this they extracted soil samples, hoping to find eDNA (environmental DNA) left behind by whatever creature used the nest. This is a relatively new technique.

The samples were sent to Miroslava Munguia Ramos, a project manager at the UCLA California Environmental DNA program. After analysis, she issued a report that included these findings:

> *What we're looking at are the unique organisms that we were able to identify. Our software does what's known as metabar coding. So, it'll match up all the DNA sequences that we were able to detect and try to cross reference them with the thousands of genomes that have been published, and it's pretty common that when we're looking at environmental DNA samples, we detect humans, because there's going be human traces almost everywhere.*

> *But what I found very interesting was that, yes, we have detected human DNA in these areas, but we're still seeing different primate DNA. There wasn't just one human primate, there are several different primates, some sort of primate relative that exists in the data. ... Finding what appears to be a very large structure, seemingly created with intention and requiring great strength as well as foresight, is interesting. It is not unheard of for primates to stack sticks or rocks, although for me, the jury is still out as to what that was. There is no guess work in science. It is great in that eDNA was collected from that site.*

Let's Get Physical! 41

That may give us the answers we are looking for.

Yes, that sounds like a whole lot of words without a whole lot of substance. Essentially, it's giving us a big, fat "maybe."

Other such stories often wind up debunked after initial public interest begins to wane. The problem is that the evidence that drove the initial interest often remains as accepted "fact" long after the time the stories are analyzed and shown to be false or inconclusive. What we're left with is some people putting a lot of weight on shoddy evidence that they might not even realize has been shown to be, at best, questionable. The skeptics—who, frankly, tend to get deeper in the weeds—are then able to point out the holes in the research and render it suspect.

The gears of science move slowly, while the Internet is almost instantaneous. When people want to believe something, they can usually gather plenty of hearsay-type evidence before that evidence crumbles under scrutiny. Bigfoot DNA is only one such example.

On the other hand, even the most skeptical scientists must admit to the existence of a pattern of closed-loop thinking that says: "Bigfoot does not exist because there is no evidence, and we will not waste time and resources looking for such evidence because Bigfoot does not exist."

Might DNA research eventually discover that Bigfoot is some type of hominin hybrid species?

Academic prejudice is a real thing. But so is popular enthusiasm. Right now, all we can do is wait and accept that, for now, there is no conclusive DNA evidence that has been pulled from the bones of the dead to support the existence of Bigfoot. There is, however, another piece of physical evidence regularly presented as "proof."

Hair.

True Tales from Across America

In 2014, Bryan Sykes, a genetics professor at the University of Oxford, analyzed some 30 samples of Bigfoot hair donated by museums and enthusiasts. By far the largest number of them point to bears, possibly a new species of bear. Examples from India and Bhutan, for instance, show an unknown species that could be a distant cousin of the polar bear, or a brown bear hybrid. Sykes, who died in 2020, said, "If these bears are widely distributed in the Himalayas, they may well contribute to the biological foundation of the Yeti legend."

The same results are often found in North America, although hairs from deer and elk often enter the picture. In Texas, DNA analysis revealed that one clump of hair belonged to a hairy human. Rarely do hairs pass the Bigfoot challenge, but when they do, they cause quite a stir. The problem is a simple one. There is no Bigfoot hair with which to compare samples taken in the field. Just because a hair doesn't match any other known samples doesn't mean it belongs to a Sasquatch.

Dr. Esteban Sarmiento, now famous in the Bigfoot community for his appearances on the *Monster Quest* television series, is a primatologist and biologist. He is scrupulously honest, even while talking to those who want him to confirm the possibility that Sasquatch is out there somewhere. He noted, "My comments on all the Sasquatch hair I have seen, that is of organic origin and purported to be of a Bigfoot, is that it is degraded hair or one that lacks a distinctive morphology."

That's not very encouraging.

Probably the most exhaustive analysis of possible Bigfoot hairs was released in August 2014 by the National Library of Medicine's National Center for Biotechnology Information. It didn't offer much hope for Bigfoot believers either. It said:

> *With the exception of these two samples, none of the submitted and analyzed hair samples returned a sequence that could not be matched with an extant mammalian species, often a domesticate. While it is important to bear in mind that absence of evidence is not evidence of absence and this survey cannot*

Let's Get Physical!

refute the existence of anomalous primates, neither has it found any evidence in support. Rather than persisting in the view that they have been "rejected by science," advocates in the cryptozoology community have more work to do in order to produce convincing evidence for anomalous primates and now have the means to do so. The techniques described here put an end to decades of ambiguity about species identification of anomalous primate samples and set a rigorous standard against which to judge any future claims.

While it's true that the academic and scientific communities do not throw a lot of effort or resources toward Bigfoot research, it wouldn't be correct to argue that *nobody* is looking. That often seems to be a sort of defense for Bigfoot enthusiasts, falling back on the "absence of evidence isn't evidence of absence" crutch and claiming that Bigfoot's existence would be easily proven if only the effort was taken seriously.

Only recently, we've learned what was long suspected: that the U.S. government has been conducting research into UFOs and the existence of extraterrestrials for decades. In 2021 the U.S. intelligence community released a report on its knowledge of flying saucers and the like. Troves of files and documents have been released since. And while the government hasn't provided any concrete evidence of alien existence, it has shown that it believes strange sightings by Navy pilots and others deserve legitimate scrutiny.

It has only been within the last couple of years that the U.S. government has acknowledged UFOs are a thing. What if they have also been concealing what they know about Bigfoot?

So if there's something worth investigating, the U.S. government is probably looking into it. In June 2019, *New York Times* reporter Liam Stack said that the FBI did, indeed,

True Tales from Across America

The International Cryptozoology Museum was founded in 2003 in Portland, Maine, by Loren Coleman.

finally release the results of a study it had been conducting since the 1970s into the possible existence of Bigfoot. It consisted of 22 pages of documents and soon became an exhibit at the International Cryptozoology Museum in Portland, Maine.

In 1976, Peter Byrne (a name we will revisit) was the director of the Bigfoot Information Center and Exhibition in The Dalles, Oregon. He wrote to Jay Cochran Jr., the assistant director of the FBI laboratory division, seeking confirmation of the rumor that the FBI had been testing possible Bigfoot hair samples.

At that time, Bigfoot research was just beginning in the United States. The famous Patterson-Gimlin film, which we will soon study, had taken the country by storm. Eyewitness accounts were beginning to stream in.

The U.S. intelligence community wasn't considered the most transparent of entities. It didn't help that D. B. Cooper had just disappeared, parachuting into the night with a small fortune after hijacking a plane, and the FBI was accused of covering up the facts of the crime. Additionally, the FBI hadn't yet recovered from either the Roswell incident or its supposed cover-up of the John F. Kennedy assassination.

But Cochran replied right away. He revealed that the FBI had tested hair samples. "However," he wrote, "we have been unable to locate any references to such examinations in our files."

Byrne revealed that he had a sample of 15 strands of hair attached to a small piece of skin that was "the first

Let's Get Physical!

that we have obtained in six years which we feel may be of importance." Byrne later reported that he and two men from the U.S. Forest Service had spotted an unidentified creature in the Pacific Northwest and, subsequently, recovered this tuft of hair.

Since the agency could not locate the results of a previous examination, he suggested, perhaps they might be willing to conduct another. Somewhat to Byrne's surprise, Cochran agreed.

> *Why was the FBI conducting research into the possibility of Bigfoot activity in the first place? And why had it been covering it up for so many years?*

According to Byrne, in a 2021 interview after the release of the 22-page report, he had heard nothing more from the FBI or Cochran. Yet the report notes a letter to Byrne, from Cochran, that seems to have gotten "lost in the mail." In the letter, Cochran wrote, "It was concluded as a result of these examinations that the hairs are of deer family origin."

One would think that would have been the end of it, but by 2021, the FBI was soundly ensconced in the web of conspiracy theorists. The fact that they reported nothing of interest was unacceptable to those who distrusted them. Just the existence of the report threw gasoline on the fire of some Bigfoot enthusiasts.

The thing about conspiracy theorists is that when something comes along that pulls the rug out from under them, they just chalk it up as additional evidence of the conspiracy. Why was the FBI conducting research into the possibility of Bigfoot activity in the first place? And why had it been covering it up for so many years? Could this new study be believed any more than the FBI's explanations of the Kennedy assassination or the Roswell incident?

Even with copies of the original letters of the 22-page report in public view at the International Cryptozoology Museum, there are people who refuse to believe them. Such is the nature of suspicion.

Thus, we remain in a stalemate of sorts. There are those who are certain that the evidence of Bigfoot exists and is either not being probably reviewed or is being covered up, and then there are the skeptics pointing to the lack of evidence or to evidence that has been debunked as "proof" that Bigfoot is no more than a creature of folklore and legend.

But no Bigfoot hunter worth his hiking boots and night vision goggles would be dissuaded by something like a lack of DNA evidence or some misidentified hair samples. Many would argue that there is still plenty of evidence that the Sasquatch ... the Yeti ... Bigfoot is out there.

TO WALK A MILE IN THEIR FOOTSTEPS

Perhaps the most prolific "evidence" of Sasquatch consists of plaster casts and pictures of footprints. They also represent the greatest number of hoaxes. Thousands of casts have been collected and analyzed—far too many to document here. A Google search on the Internet will reveal far more than can ever be studied in one person's lifetime. A solid week of watching YouTube videos will barely scratch the surface.

Because of the ease and possibility of fakery, plaster casts tend to not be taken seriously. There are even Internet sites that offer templates for producing your own replicas.

It's a troubling loop. You really can't document Bigfoot prints without a plaster cast, but plaster casts tend to be viewed with suspicion. A hoaxer with even limited artistic ability can create the resemblance of a big footprint along a muddy path to convince the most ardent believers.

The supposed Bigfoot tracks do raise an interesting point, however, that might be more convincing than any detailed study of the casts themselves.

Many of them were observed and recorded in territory that rarely sees any human presence. Years might go by without anyone traveling through such rugged country, even to hike, hunt, or camp. Why would someone go to the trouble of backpacking into such formidable wilderness to strap on a pair of Bigfoot shoes and make prints, hoping that someone might stumble along and "discov-

True Tales from Across America

er" them someday? Unless, of course, the "maker" and the "finder" were in cahoots.

In some cases, tracks were found protected by bushes that would have to have been brushed aside when the tracks were made and then discovered by accident when a hiker came through and did the same thing. If not a coordinated effort, it begs the question, "Who would fake such a thing?" It seems illogical if only because the fake would seem so unlikely to be discovered in the first place.

The science of Sasquatch anatomy, especially as it applies to footprints, is exacting and technical. Suffice it to say that the prints that draw the most attention are quite different from those left behind by humans.

First, there is the matter of weight, which translates into depth. A Bigfoot or Yeti is understood to be a large animal, estimated to weigh as much as 500 pounds (226 kilograms) or more. That much weight translates into deep prints.

The stride of a Bigfoot is bigger than most humans as well. A creature that stands up to 9 feet tall covers much

Outside the Willow Creek China Flat Museum in California is this bronze cast of a reputed Bigfoot footprint. Analyzing how genuine these prints are is a rather detailed science.

Bigfoot Sightings

To Walk a Mile in Their Footsteps

more ground with each lumbering stride than the average human.

Experts on Sasquatch prints have established what they claim to be tell-tale signs of an authentic Sasquatch footprint. "Real" Bigfoot prints generally display a flattened arch, wide heel, and double ball, as well as uniformly sized and nearly squared-off toes, sometimes featuring a toe that angles off from the rest.

A double ball is a feature found at the base of the big toe. In a human foot, a single bulge is found at the forward end of the first metatarsal bone. In a Bigfoot track, there are often two distinct bulges, one behind the other. The metatarsals are the longest bones in the forefoot. If this region is shortened, the base of the first metatarsal is moved forward, so that its two ends will be in the proper positions to form the double ball as seen in many Sasquatch footprints.

> "*Real*" *Bigfoot prints generally display a flattened arch, wide heel, and double ball, as well as uniformly sized and nearly squared-off toes, sometimes featuring a toe that angles off from the rest.*

Bigfoot prints are also quite flat. There is no instep, or what podiatrists call a longitudinal arch. This is understandable, given the weight the foot must support. The interesting thing is that in smaller prints, supposedly made by immature Bigfoot young, there *is* such an arch. It seems to disappear with age and size.

Bigfoot develop flat feet as they age. This is a fairly obscure fact, and it is doubtful that hoaxers would deliberately set out to reproduce this feature.

There are many other technical differences specialists look for, involving gait and muscle development. Needless to say, legs that have evolved to propel creatures of an immense size are quite different from those of a typical human, and this translates to the footprints left behind. The foot lifts off the ground differently as well, leaving behind a unique impression.

Put all these attributes together, and it becomes obvious that fooling a foot specialist involves more than

True Tales from Across America

simply strapping on a set of Bigfoot shoes and walking off through the forest or using your best mold-making techniques to shape a large footprint in a patch of mud.

Are there hoaxes that have fooled such specialists? Probably, but they usually don't last very long before an expert blows the whistle.

Even if footprints, or the casts, are not convincing evidence of Bigfoot's existence, they are important for another reason. Beyond personal accounts of encounters, which could easily be dismissed, footprints represent the earliest evidence of the fascination with the idea of an undiscovered, giant, ape-like human relative walking the world with us.

Explorer David Thompson is sometimes credited with first discovering Sasquatch footprints in 1811. Thompson was a surveyor and pathfinder who worked for the Hudson's Bay Company and the North West Company. He is credited with traveling over 100,000 kilometers by canoe, horseback, and foot throughout western North America between 1785 and 1812.

In the winter of 1810–11, Thompson followed the Athabasca River to the site of present-day Jasper, Alberta, and then to the mouth of the Whirlpool River. Although the exact location is unknown, Thompson's find occurred somewhere just above the mouth of the Whirlpool. From his journal:

> *January 7, 1811 Continuing our journey in the afternoon we came on the track of a large animal, the snow about six inches deep on the ice; I measured it; four large toes each of four inches in length; to each a short claw; the ball of the foot sunk three inches lower than the toes, the hinder part of the foot did not mark well, the length fourteen inches, by eight inches in breadth, walking from north to south, and having passed about six hours. We were in no humour to follow him; the Men and Indians would have it to be a young mammoth and I held it to be the track of a large old grizzled bear; yet the shortness of the nails, the ball of the foot, and its great*

Bigfoot Sightings

To Walk a Mile in Their Footsteps

> *size was not that of a Bear, otherwise that of a very large old Bear, his claws worn away; this the Indians would not allow.*

Over 100 years later, mysterious footprints in America's Pacific Northwest—and the fantastic story that accompanied them—would be credited for launching public interest in Bigfoot within the United States.

On the southeast side of Mount St. Helens, in Washington, there is a gorge called Ape Canyon. The name comes from the story told by a group of prospectors who, in 1924, claimed to have come across a group of 7-foot ape-like creatures in the wilderness. As their tale goes, one of them shot at the creatures, striking one of the beasts three times. The wounded creature tumbled into an inaccessible canyon and the others fled, only to return in the night to attack the prospectors' cabin with large stones and try to enter their cabin. Surviving the night, the prospectors ventured out in the morning to survey the damage, finding 14-inch-long footprints left about their camp.

Ape Canyon near Mount St. Helens in Washington state got its name from a 1924 report of Bigfoot sightings.

The story caused quite a local hullabaloo and spread quickly. It took hold of the public's imagination, creating such an uproar that U.S. Forest Service rangers William Welch and J. H. Huffman were sent to investigate the site.

The rangers descended into the "inaccessible" canyon, finding nothing. They demonstrated how the footprints around the cabin could have easily been faked. But even with the story debunked, it was repeated and spread. Perhaps the "apes" had retrieved the body of their fallen comrade. Even if the footprints *could* be faked, it didn't mean they *were*.

True Tales from Across America

The Ape Canyon story inspired various theories and further claims of sightings. After all, if we have learned anything over the last decade or so, it's that the last people conspiracy theorists are going to believe is the government.

The discovery of Sasquatch and Yeti footprints seems to have been particularly rampant from the 1950s to the 1970s, coinciding with a vigorous interest in mountaineering and a significant increase in the dissemination of information through newspapers, radio, and television. More people were looking and finding, and those findings were being heard or read by more and more people.

During a Mount Everest reconnaissance expedition, mountaineer Eric Shipton captured photographic evidence of what he believed to be Yeti footprints in the snow.

A year later, explorer Edmund Hillary discovered prints high in the Himalayas and a scrap of skin with blue-black hair that his Sherpas claimed was that of a Yeti.

Eric Shipton's famous 1951 photograph of a Yeti footprint discovered by Michael Ward on Mt. Everest's Menlung Glacier.

Bigfoot Sightings

To Walk a Mile in Their Footsteps

Edmund Hillary (left) with his Sherpa, Tenzing Norgay.

The Hillary prints were described as if having been made "by naked human feet—size elevens or even fifteen, broad across the instep, fallen arches, and a big toe that protruded inward." Hillary dismissed them as being made by snow leopards or a type of wolf. A later study concluded that they were made by a smaller creature but, having melted back under the heat of the sun, appeared larger than they were when originally laid down. Still, the native Sherpas remained convinced that they belonged to the Yeti with which they had been familiar since childhood.

Don Whillans was a plumber by trade and a colorful character by reputation. A resident of Manchester, England, he was a short, scrappy man who learned early in life to defend himself, both with his eloquent tongue and always-ready fists. Many of his stories wound up with his trademark line, "So I 'it 'im."

He was often compared to the colorful cartoon character Andy Capp, not only because of his ability to rough things up but because of his ever-present hat. Indeed, it was no coincidence that he was called "the 'ard little man in the flat 'at."

In the 1950s, Whillans partnered with legendary rock climber Joe Brown. The two became famous for making many first ascents and pioneered routes of many rock formations. His greatest claim to fame, however, was

True Tales from Across America

the first reported western sighting of a Yeti.

In 1970 he was at a base camp on Annapurna, the tenth tallest mountain in the world and a difficult ascent—some consider the climb up Annapurna to be harder than Mount Everest. Earlier that day, he had seen and photographed what, in hindsight, might have been Yeti footprints. Later that night, in bright moonlight, he spotted an ape-like creature about a quarter of a mile away. He watched it through binoculars for a good 20 minutes. He would later report the creature as "a powerful animal, bounding along on all fours, and headed straight up the slope in the absolutely bright moonlight. It looked like an ape. I don't think it was a bear."

In the morning, his stash of Mars candy bars had disappeared. I can't say that Yetis have a particular yearning for chocolate bars but, really, who doesn't? In any case, Whillans felt it was a significant piece of the puzzle to include in his retelling. Who am I to argue?

Along with some Sherpa guides, Whillans climbed to make a full reconnaissance above the base camp. Apparently, he really wanted those Mars bars back. Also, he wanted local experts to look at whatever tracks they could find.

The Sherpas' behavior surprised him.

> *I thought I'd see their reaction at the point where I'd photographed the tracks the day before. The tracks were so obvious that it was impossible not to make any comment, but they walked straight past and didn't indicate that they'd seen them. I had already said that I had seen the Yeti, not knowing exactly what it was, but they pretended they didn't understand and ignored what I said. I am convinced that they believe the Yeti does exist, that it is some kind of sacred animal which is best left alone; that if you don't bother it, it won't bother you.*

Footprints were not relegated to only the snowy mountainsides of the Himalayas. On the other side of the globe, the Pacific Northwest region of North Ameri-

To Walk a Mile in Their Footsteps

> *The moment when the shift of focus from the "abominable snowman" of the Himalayas to the Sasquatch of North America began can be traced to August 27, 1958. While California is well known for its seasonal wildfires, a spark on that day would light a different kind of blaze.*

ca was producing a fair number of photographs and plaster casts of its own.

The moment when the shift of focus from the "abominable snowman" of the Himalayas to the Sasquatch of North America began can be traced to August 27, 1958. While California is well known for its seasonal wildfires, a spark on that day would light a different kind of blaze. A full-fledged inferno of interest in Bigfoot was about to begin. We can see a direct line from that day to every kitschy Sasquatch souvenir found across the country today, like the gunpowder trail to a pile of TNT in an old western movie.

On that day, Jerry Crew drove out to his remote job site in northwest California, near the borders of Humboldt and Del Norte counties, in what is known as the Bluff Creek area. Jerry's crawler-tractor was waiting for him to continue the work of pushing a new lumber-access road into the uninhabited area.

When Jerry went to start up his machine, he noticed a series of footprints that seemed to approach the tractor, circle it, and then move away into the wilderness. Given the number of men working on the site, these might not have roused any interest, but they appeared to be those of a barefoot person and measured 16 inches long.

Jerry—by all accounts an honest, levelheaded man—thought the prints must be a prank. There had been talk of a crew in another area having found similar footprints earlier in the year. Jerry assumed some "outsider" had made the prints over the weekend, while he was home with his family.

Following the tracks, Jerry measured the stride of the prints to range from 46 to 60 inches. That was roughly twice Jerry's own stride. Though most of Jerry's fellow workers dismissed his find, a few of them eventually looked for themselves. While many said they had seen or heard of something similar, their interest waned quickly.

True Tales from Across America

A month later, more footprints appeared, and again some weeks after that. In September, the wife of one of the workers contacted the local newspaper, the *Humboldt Times*, whose editor, Andrew Genzoli, was mentioned earlier. Initially, he ran the story of the mysterious footprints as a lark—nothing more than a Sunday morning entertainment piece.

In October, the "Bigfoot" creature, as it was by then being called, returned and left prints over a three-night period. Jerry Crew was ready for it this time. Using plaster of Paris, he made a series of casts of both right and left feet. When he later visited Eureka, he took the casts to show a friend. Genzoli was alerted to Jerry's presence and that of his casts, and met with him to see them. Knowing a good story when he saw it, Genzoli ran a front-page story that was picked up by the wire services and run in almost every major paper in the country.

Ivan T. Sanderson was a biologist and cofounder, with Bernard Heuvelmans, of the field of cryptozoology.

In 1959, noted expeditionist, zoologist, and author Ivan Sanderson wrote a story about Crew's find for *True* magazine. Sanderson had, by this time, cemented himself, for better or worse, as a leading figure in the new field of cryptozoology. The name for the study of unknown creatures was, in fact, coined by Sanderson.

Sanderson's story would elaborate on Crew's find, tying it to the century-old story of the Sasquatch of British Columbia and adding the corroborating stories of Ray and Wilbur Wallace.

Ray Wallace was the owner of the construction company that Jerry Crew worked for. Ray stated that, when he heard about the things his men were claiming to see in the woods, he worried that someone was trying to scare his workers and disrupt the operation. However, Ray's brother, Wilbur, who worked for him, claimed he saw the tracks with his own eyes. Wilbur also said that several objects too heavy for an average man to move—such as a 250-pound tire, an oil drum, and a length of 18-inch, galvanized steel culvert—had been carried off from job sites.

Sanderson's article also referenced a number of reports from the "common citizenry" of discovering Bigfoot tracks, finding human-like piles of feces but of a volume similar to a horse, and actually glimpsing the creature itself.

The most significant impact of Sanderson's article may have been that it was read by Roger Patterson, who later stated that it was what first piqued his interest in the Bigfoot legend. Sanderson's subsequent book, the encyclopedic *Abominable Snowmen: Legend Come to Life*, was published in 1961. Patterson said this worldwide survey of accounts of Bigfoot-type creatures, which included recent track finds such as those in the Bluff Creek area, only heightened his interest in the creature.

Sanderson's book claimed that there were four types of abominable snowmen creatures scattered over five continents. While the book was roundly criticized by the scientific community for its low standards of evidence and lack of scientific methodology, it was influential among amateur researchers such as Patterson.

In 1962, Patterson visited Bluff Creek himself to interview believers in Bigfoot. Two years later he saw tracks at Laird Meadow that further drove his desire to prove Bigfoot's existence and bask in the fame and fortune such a scientific breakthrough would bring. Investing thousands of hours and dollars into his quest, and soliciting funds through his Northwest Research Foundation, Patterson wound up leading several expeditions.

Patterson published his own book, *Do Abominable Snowmen of America Really Exist?*, in 1966. Money earned from the book and lectures helped further fund Patterson's hunt for the elusive, hairy hominid. And while many of those who initially joined his search dropped out as each expedition fell short of providing proof of Bigfoot's existence, Patterson would go on.

True Tales from Across America

In 1967, Patterson set out to film a docudrama in which flashback scenes would recall the 1924 Ape Canyon incident, and live footage would follow their efforts to track Bigfoot on horseback. This effort led to the most famous 30 seconds of Bigfoot film footage ever recorded. We turn to this, as well as further photographic and video evidence.

Arguably the most famous, and certainly the most influential, Bigfoot image ever produced is from the 1967 film shot by Roger Patterson and Bob Gimlin in Northern California. Frame #352 has become the iconic Bigfoot image. It has even inspired a name—Patty—after Patterson.

The Patterson-Gimlin film was shot with a 16mm camera rented from Sheppard's Camera Shop in Yakima, Washington, operated by photographer Harold Mattson. A rarely mentioned tidbit: Patterson kept the camera longer than he had contracted it for and had a warrant issued for his arrest that was exercised within weeks of his return from the expedition that produced the film. Upon returning the camera in working order, the charges against Patterson were dropped.

According to the filmmakers, the recording was made on October 20, 1967. The footage of the alleged Bigfoot walking lasts less than a minute, with most of the film showing men and horses in a forest. It was filmed alongside Bluff Creek in the Six Rivers National Forest, about 25 miles northwest of Orleans, California, 38 miles south of Oregon and 18 miles east of the Pacific Ocean. Bluff Creek, you will recall, is where Jerry Crew discovered those infamous footprints.

It was no accident that Patterson chose this location for his "pseudo-documentary" about hunting Bigfoot. He had been pointed to the area by the corroborator of Crew's story, Ray Wallace.

True Tales from Across America

Known as the Patterson-Gimlin film, this footage, taken in 1967, is considered to be one of the most convincing visual images of Bigfoot.

The premise of the film Patterson set out to make was that some cowboys, led by an old miner and a wise Indian tracker, are on the hunt for Bigfoot. The storyline entailed the cowboys and the Indian tracker (Robert Gimlin in a wig) recalling stories from the 1924 Ape Canyon incident—filmed as flashback sequences—as they tracked Bigfoot, on horseback.

The other actors and assistants were volunteer acquaintances. The filming took place over the course of three days.

The shaky, grainy piece of work shows imagery of the forest and the men on horseback. As the camera pans the tree line along the creek, it zooms in, and the filming becomes very erratic. This is when Patterson and Gimlin claim to have rounded a turn in the creek and a large, uprooted tree. Then coming upon a logjam left from previous flooding, they spotted the creature crouched on the other side of it. Patterson stated that he took about 20 seconds to get out of his saddle and control his horse.

It's at that point in the film when a dark, bipedal creature can be seen walking across, and slightly away from, the camera's field of view. It's evident that the cameraman—Patterson—then begins running toward this creature. He pauses, roughly 80 feet from the creature, gets it in frame, and films for about 30 seconds—half of

Smile! You're on Candid Camera!

which is fairly clear footage of the creature walking at a brisk pace away from him. The creature does not seem especially hurried or alarmed and, at one point, glances over its shoulder at Patterson.

"Clear" footage is a relative assessment, as the entirety of the film is rather low quality.

The suspected Sasquatch disappears behind some trees for 14 seconds. Patterson moves for a better vantage point and relocates the creature on camera for another 15 seconds or so. The film runs out as the creature fades into the trees, about 100 yards away from Patterson.

Gimlin then followed the creature at a distance, on horseback, for another 300 yards, until Patterson called him back. Patterson said he felt vulnerable on foot, and without a weapon, should the creature's mate be in the vicinity.

Patterson then grabbed a second roll of film and recorded the tracks left by the creature. The group tried tracking the creature for a mile or two but lost the trail in the heavy undergrowth. Back at camp, they retrieved plaster and returned to the site of the initial encounter. They measured the creature's stride and made both right- and left-foot casts of the best prints.

> *Although it is still far from perfect, specialists claim to be able to see muscle definition, moving fingers, arm movement, and flexing feet that appear distinct from humans.*

With technological advances, it has become possible to clean up parts of the Patterson-Gimlin film. Although it is still far from perfect, specialists claim to be able to see muscle definition, moving fingers, arm movement, and flexing feet that appear distinct from humans. Meanwhile, those who say it's difficult to tell if it's anything more than someone in a costume can certainly be forgiven given the quality of the footage.

Despite decades of study and declarations from people that they were in on the hoax, the film has technically proficient supporters who believe it to be the best evidence ever produced to prove the existence of Bigfoot.

True Tales from Across America

Jeffrey Meldrum is a professor of anatomy and anthropology at Idaho State University. He is one of a few qualified academics to openly study Sasquatch. Meldrum is also an adjunct professor in the Department of Physical and Occupational Therapy and the Department of Anthropology. He is considered an expert on foot morphology and locomotion in primates.

Meldrum is well known for his interest in cryptozoology and, in particular, his research on Bigfoot, which he believes exists. In 2006, Meldrum published *Sasquatch: Legend Meets Science* (though the book was largely criticized as not distinguishing "good research from bad" or "science from pseudoscience"). If there is an expedition, significant finding, evidence to be considered, or conference or television show discussing the legitimacy of the Bigfoot myth, Meldrum is almost certain to be involved.

To be clear, Meldrum is highly educated and has published numerous academic papers on topics ranging from vertebrate evolution and bipedal locomotion in modern humans to the plausibility of the Sasquatch phenomena. He attained a B.S. and M.S. from Brigham Young University (Meldrum is an active member of the Church of Jesus Christ of Latter-day Saints), and he earned his Ph.D. in anatomical sciences from Stony Brook University.

> *Regarding the Patterson-Gimlin footage, Meldrum says he is "as confident as I can be [that the film is real], short of standing on the sandbar with Roger and Bob and witnessing it myself."*

He is not a "blind" believer, having come out against the authenticity of alleged footprints belonging to the Siberian Snowman "found" in a cave in the Russian city of Kemerovo.

Regarding the Patterson-Gimlin footage, Meldrum says he is "as confident as I can be [that the film is real], short of standing on the sandbar with Roger and Bob and witnessing it myself. It's all so easy to say, 'Obviously that's a man in a fur suit.' Until you see [the film] up against a man in a fur suit."

Smile! You're on Candid Camera! 63

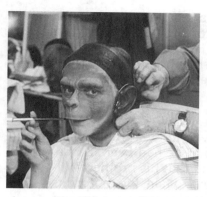

Actress Kim Hunter undergoes her makeup transformation for the 1968 Planet of the Apes *movie. Even if Patterson had hired a gifted artist to create a Hollywood-style Bigfoot, it would not have fooled an expert.*

Meldrum uses the *Planet of the Apes* movies in his argument to skeptics who dismiss the Patterson-Gimlin footage as a "man in monkey suit." The first movie of the series was released in 1968, one year after the Patterson-Gimlin film was shot. It used state-of-the-art technology and trained actors to make advanced human-like apes look believable, and it even won an Oscar for makeup. But, according to Meldrum, "they look like big, hairy, Pillsbury Doughboys."

If Hollywood, with its big budgets, couldn't produce convincing film apes, how could two cowboys from Northern California pull it off?

Meldrum continues: "Start at the head and [you] can see the trapezius ... the deltoid ... erector spine down the back ... shoulder blades moving under the skin ... the quads contract when they're supposed to contract. None of which ever show up in a cheap, off-the-shelf costume."

Nevertheless, costume manufacturer Philip Morris claimed he sold just such a costume to Patterson. And it would stand to reason that, if the intent was indeed to shoot a docudrama chronicling a hunt for Bigfoot, there would likely be a climax in which the protagonists would discover the creature. Of course, for such a finale, a costume would have been necessary.

Over the years, many have discredited the film, calling it an elaborate hoax. They note that, despite having several volunteers with them, only Patterson and Gimlin were present when the encounter occurred. They point out inconsistencies in the stories the two men later shared. They question their motives and highlight other problems in their behavior. Even family members discredited the film, but only long after Patterson had died.

True Tales from Across America

Patterson seems to have been a self-promoter bent on fame and fortune. The legend of Bigfoot appeared to hold a particular draw for him. He had previously shot film about Bigfoot believers and had tried unsuccessfully to sell it to Hollywood—he even contacted cowboy movie legend Roy Rogers.

Patterson was directed to the location by Ray Wallace, but Wallace was later proven to be a fraud. After his death, his family revealed that he had been in possession of large, wooden feet and that his brother, Wilbur, and a nephew had used these to fake the footprints around Northern California. Ray also created hair and fecal "samples" to be left for Bigfoot researchers to find.

Patterson's neighbor Bob Heironimus claimed that he was hired to don a gorilla costume and paid $1,000.

Bob Heironimus, a neighbor of Patterson, claimed that Patterson offered him $1,000 for one day of shooting. He was to wear a monkey suit, a football helmet, and shoulder pads. He said he went to California, shot the famous scene, and returned to Yakima, where his mother and two brothers both claimed they saw the suit in the trunk of his car.

Bob Gimlin, the only other eyewitness to the shooting of the film, remained silent for years. He finally began to speak publicly at conventions after Patterson died but insisted that if Patterson pulled off a hoax, he fooled Gimlin as well. Although he and Patterson had a falling out because Gimlin believed Patterson had profited from the experience and he had not, the two reconciled in the end.

"I strongly believe that if a real [Bigfoot] walked in the house and sat down at a table—or, the best it could—they'd say no, it's a fake. It's somebody in a suit. That's how naive they are," Gimlin said. "So that's just the way I'd tell them until the day they spank me in the face with dirt."

Bigfoot Sightings

Smile! You're on Candid Camera! 65

The stories later told by the two men don't agree as to dates and circumstances. But believers say this only proves the reality of the situation. If the whole incident had been a hoax, why wouldn't the two have agreed beforehand to concoct a credible story? Recollections and memories are often faulty or murky, especially in hindsight. Add in the gravity of the situation in the moment and a lack of ability to recall some of the finite details, and it is more than understandable.

There are many who swear by the film. They point out that Bigfoot's gait has never been duplicated. If "Patty" is just a guy in a gorilla suit, they claim, it is the greatest hoax of all time. "Patty," for instance, has unmistakable breasts. Why go to that trouble if you are simply perpetuating a hoax? It seems unlikely.

To date, the film has neither been proven to be an authentic sighting of an actual Bigfoot creature nor conclusively debunked.

We may never *know* the truth, but this film remains the single best photographic evidence that Bigfoot exists. That might be enough to question its authenticity. Even now, with a camera in everyone's pocket and much improved picture clarity, and with technology like drones, the best footage of Bigfoot we have mustered is a couple minutes of 60-year-old grainy footage?

In any case, it has become iconic. The still frame of the creature in stride, arms wide, looking over its right shoulder, is *the* image of Bigfoot—the first conjured in one's mind when the creature is mentioned.

Now, just because we don't have *better* photos or videos of a legitimate large, hairy, bipedal creature, that's not to say there *aren't* any others. Some of the most notable that have been produced since 1967 include the following (a few which we will discuss in more depth later):

- In 2001, Jim Mills was camping with his youth group in the Marble Mountain Wilderness of California when he filmed what appears to be a Bigfoot moving stealthily along a nearby ridge. Seven long minutes later, he captured

True Tales from Across America

what is now the longest video of an alleged Bigfoot sighting. Like all Bigfoot film, it is grainy (maybe Bigfoot has a magical power that causes poor quality imaging).

- In 1994, former U.S. Forest Service patrolman Paul Freeman took some shaky video of what seems to be a whole Bigfoot family in Washington's Blue Mountains.
- The Independence Day film, produced by an unknown filmmaker in an unknown location, is much clearer. It seems to be a female Bigfoot carrying a baby. But many skeptics claim that there is a visible seam that indicates a gorilla suit.
- In 2007, a famous Bigfoot image was captured on film by a trail camera set by Rick Jacobs, a hunter in Pennsylvania's Allegheny National Forest. The camera also took pictures of bear cubs. It is perhaps the clearest picture ever recorded, but skeptics claim the subject is simply a bear with mange.
- Twice in Provo Canyon, Utah, different groups claim to have captured a Bigfoot on film in 2012. In one incident, the Bigfoot stood up and began to throw rocks at the cameraman.
- Josh Highcliff, of Mississippi, took some pictures while hunting on his property. He posted the image on YouTube, asking for help identifying what the creature is. If it was a prankster, he said, he asked him to step forward and confess.

All this evidence seems to have produced a sort of Bigfoot Rorschach Test. Those inclined to believe Bigfoot exists see one in these images. Those who don't, well, don't.

As mentioned earlier, now that almost everyone carries a cell phone capable of taking high-quality pictures and video, it would seem to be only a matter of time until a definitive image is captured and verified, if these creatures do exist. But every day that goes by without

Smile! You're on Candid Camera!

Forget "Where's Waldo"; the real master of hiding from people is Bigfoot!

such an image coming to light only strengthens the opinion of those who don't believe such a creature is out there.

Those who *do* believe argue that the creatures are essentially the champions of Hide and Seek. They are highly intelligent beings that are actively working on *not* being discovered, and they stick to otherwise uninhabited, inhospitable areas, where few people ever venture. The researchers and "hunters" who consider themselves the most ethical conduct their searches while trying to minimize their intrusion upon these areas and seeking minimal contact with the creatures, like those who observe uncontacted civilizations such as the Sentinelese. Given what's befallen some who have tried to interact with such tribes, that's probably smart thinking.

And if the Sasquatch population is small—remember, Neanderthals are now thought to have only numbered a few thousand individuals at most—stumbling upon them might be more difficult than we imagine.

Still, it seems suspicious that in the 70-odd years of intense interest in the Sasquatch and Yeti, a still frame from a low-quality video shot in the 1960s remains our best video or photographic evidence of their existence. While hopes remain high that technology will soon produce something more significant, for the time being, Bigfoot continues to remain tantalizingly just out of frame.

True Tales from Across America

Tantalizing DNA discoveries about our ancestors and others who have walked this planet. Grainy video and blurry photos. Plaster casts of footprints and the occasional "inconclusive" tuft of hair. These are as close as we've come to actual physical evidence that a large, hairy, bipedal primate—that may or may not be related to *Homo sapiens*—continues to share this world with us.

We cannot conclusively say such a creature exists based on this evidence. Of course, we can't say it doesn't either, but the burden of proof rests on those who make a claim, not on the skeptic. What we've covered so far is not enough evidence to prove Bigfoot exists, even though there are certainly people who believe more fantastical stories with even less proof.

So what else is there that we can look to in an effort to build the argument? In a court of law, prosecutors typically follow their presentation of physical evidence with the less concrete, but often very convincing, circumstantial evidence.

Benjamin Radford is deputy editor of the science magazine *Skeptical Inquirer* and the "Bad Science" columnist for *Live Science* magazine. He covers psychology, urban legends, unexplained or mysterious phenomena, and the like. The headline of his November 18, 2011, article in *Live Science* reads "Yeti 'Nests' Found in Russia?"

In the article, Radford recounts the claim by Bigfoot researcher and biologist John Bindernagel that his re-

True Tales from Across America

search group had found evidence of nests made by the snow-loving species of Bigfoot. According to Bidernagel, "We didn't feel like the trees we saw in Siberia had been felled by a man or another mammal."

In October of 2011, Bindernagel was one of a small group of scientists who visited Siberia to examine evidence of the Yeti. He noted that similar structures had been observed in North America. The Siberian group also located a few strands of hair and, despite scant evidence, issued the bold statement that it had "indisputable proof" of the Yeti's existence.

Such structures dot the landscape of North America, from upper New York State to California, and have long been claimed as evidence of Bigfoot. Experts are almost unanimous in saying that these structures were not made by bears or other known animals. Generally, the branches, some of them quite large, are broken and torn by force, seemingly by something stronger than humans. They are just the right size for a big, hairy primate to crawl inside of, lie down, and wait out inclement weather in a safe, dry place. These nests could also serve as a measure of protection from predators or other threats for Bigfoot young—which presumably, like most mammalian babies, would be fairly helpless when born.

The twisting of trees, also known as splintering, regularly occurs near ground level, though some are found with breaks and bends considerably higher, and even at the tops of trees. Researchers point to these taller structures as stronger evidence that they are not man-made, claiming only a Bigfoot-like primate would be able to climb to those heights *and* have the strength to twist, bend, and break the trees and branches. In some cases, large branches or trunks of trees have been lifted and placed into the structure, even suspended off the ground. This feat would seem, if not impossible, certainly difficult for most humans.

A tree structure whose construction has been attributed to Sasquatch (photo courtesy Nick Redfern).

Victims of Circumstance

Sometimes called beds or shelters, they are typically circular or oval-shaped constructions, sometimes reinforced and insulated with forest debris like leaves and pine branches, consisting of interwoven sticks and branches. They are rather large, ranging up to 8 to 10 feet in length and 4 to 5 feet in width.

They are not haphazardly piled or loosely assembled. The sticks and pine branches are carefully woven together, creating a sturdy, basket-like structure. To accomplish this requires a certain amount of manual dexterity. Planning such a design goes beyond the capabilities of most known animals.

> *The consistent size, shape, and construction of these nests, found across different regions and habitats, suggest a species-shared cultural practice, perhaps passed down through many generations from an "ancient" source.*

On occasion, a clear, body-sized impression has been found in the center of the structure, indicating that a large creature had slept there. The materials lining these impressions can include smaller twigs, leaves, grass, and even moss, creating a relatively comfortable surface for resting.

While great apes, such as gorillas and chimpanzees, do construct nests, they are usually located in trees rather than on the ground. And, of course, there are no known great apes in the wilds of North America.

The consistent size, shape, and construction of these nests, found across different regions and habitats, suggest a species-shared cultural practice, perhaps passed down through many generations from an "ancient" source. This wouldn't be any different from humans' ability to build shelters or make fire.

Skeptics, of course, argue that unless we observe the building or use of these structures, it's too early to attribute them to a Sasquatch. As with many pieces of evidence presented to prove Bigfoot's existence, easily identifiable hoaxes often enter the mix, which only serve to cast doubt on any legitimate finds.

In the case of the Siberian nest, even other scientists who participated refused to sign the group's statement

True Tales from Across America

of "indisputable proof," two of whom who called the whole thing a hoax.

Sharon Hill, of the *Doubtful News* blog, and Jeffrey Meldrum, whose credentials we discussed previously, were both vocal in their opinions that the nest was a fake and that the whole expedition was more publicity stunt than scientific endeavor. Meldrum noted that tool-made cuts were evident on some of the branches and that the structure itself was conveniently located just off a well-traveled trail, an unlikely place for the notoriously shy creature to build a nest.

While cold water may have been thrown on the Siberian expedition, a compelling find from the Olympic Peninsula in Washington state, far from any established paths or human activity, raised eyebrows even among some skeptics.

In 2010, a team of researchers called the Olympic Project discovered a series of some 20 nests all near each other. They were of the typical construction of others considered to be Bigfoot nests, with intricately woven branches and sticks forming large, circular structures. Some of the nests were built high up in trees, suggesting a skillful level of climbing ability.

A display at a Kirov region, Russia, exhibit shows a Yeti in a kind of forest nest.

Victims of Circumstance 73

The area in which they were found required a lot of off-trail hiking through dense, rugged terrain. It would require the most dedicated of hoaxers to have chosen such a remote area. The nests were typically 8 feet long and 4 feet wide, and the consistency of their construction techniques indicated that they were built by individual members of a common species, possibly even working together.

The investigations into nests and bedding areas raise some additional, interesting possibilities in the scientific efforts being employed in the search for Bigfoot. While potentially lending a certain level of credence, circumstantial as it may be, to the possibility that such a creature exists, these investigations might provide samples that can be tested by the relatively new science of environmental DNA (eDNA) studies. Soil samples taken from such nest sites, for instance, are ideal candidates for such analysis.

At the Washington site, soil, hair, and scat samples were collected from in and around the structures. The sheer number of samples points to a group of creatures, rather than an individual. Some of the collected material could not be matched to any known animal species in the region. Of course, the lack of identification doesn't prove the samples come from Bigfoot any more than a lack of scientific knowledge about the universe proves the existence of God, but it's certainly interesting and can drive the efforts of further research and investigation.

> *The tree nests, as opposed to the ground nests, may prove to be especially interesting. Canadian researchers have found nests like the arboreal platforms built by great apes like gorillas and chimpanzees.*

Although no footprints were found at this site, a similar number of ground nests were discovered near a series of 16-inch human-like footprints found in the Blue Mountains of Oregon, a hot spot of suspected Bigfoot activity.

The tree nests, as opposed to the ground nests, may prove to be especially interesting. Canadian researchers have found nests like the arboreal platforms built

True Tales from Across America

by great apes like gorillas and chimpanzees. But what would gorillas and chimpanzees be doing in Canada?

The Salish people, from whom we get the "Sasquatch" name, told stories of wild men who wove large baskets and constructed hut-like shelters from branches to serve as sleeping refuges from the elements. Similar stories can be found in the oral traditions of other Native American cultures across North America, ranging from the Lummi of Washington state to the Seminole of Florida. Tales of hairy, man-like beings building primitive dwellings in the forest have been passed down through generations. It's from these stories, reinforced by the creature's current elusiveness, that we've come to understand Bigfoot as a shy, reclusive creature, more interested in avoiding humans than in engaging with them.

Nests are not the only building projects that interest researchers. They also point to the existence of tree structures. These typically consist of saplings, sometimes up to a foot or so in diameter, and even whole trees, that are pulled together into an arch and held down by other trees, branches, or rocks. These rarely have the same "finished" look of nests, lacking insulation or bedding materials.

Where Bigfoot aficionados see deliberate structure, skeptics see deadfalls and naturally occurring wind damage. However, it's clear that natural causes can't explain all these discoveries.

In some cases, the construction is obviously deliberate. As with the nests, the twisting, tying, and bending of the trees appear to require a certain level of intelligence. Further to the apparent planning ability, be it instinct or intelligence, the structures also utilize skillful manipulation and construction, suggestive of a creature with an opposable thumb, like a primate.

The purpose of the structures is as speculative as the identification of the builders. Some First Nations tribes believe that these structures mark territory or the birth of a Sasquatch family member. Some suggest they could serve as navigational aids, places for food storage, or, if covered by foliage, shelter. They may be multiuse. The structures may also be incomplete, abandoned before

Victims of Circumstance

being finished as if the creatures were frightened away from the site.

What *is* obvious, in many cases, is that they are created with intent and require great strength or cooperation to complete.

The fact that some of the structures presented for inspection have shown evidence of tool marks, such as those found on the branches of the Siberian nest, does not particularly help skeptics' argument that these are not man-made or deliberate hoaxes. Bigfoot researchers counter that this is only further evidence of the creatures' intelligence, suggesting that they may have located and used common hardware tools misplaced or discarded by humans.

A particularly compelling find was documented on the Discovery Plus television series *Expedition Bigfoot*. The show, which debuted in 2019, features a team of Bigfoot researchers exploring suspected Bigfoot habitat, with all the latest technology, to prove the creature's existence. The team consists of an operations manager, a primatologist, a Bigfoot researcher, and an ex-military survivalist. Renowned Bigfoot scientist Jeffrey Meldrum makes regular appearances to evaluate the evidence the team discovers.

A team of researchers collected DNA samples in the Appalachian highlands of Kentucky and discovered nonhuman primate DNA.

During filming in Kentucky's Appalachian highlands, the team collected DNA samples from beneath a tree structure they had found. The samples were analyzed by UCLA California Environmental DNA Program project manager Miroslava Munguia Ramos.

The findings noted both human and primate DNA. In fact, according to Ramos, several different primates seemed to be evident in the samples. Of note was over 3,000 reads of the *Pan*, or chimpanzee, genus. Unless we're talking about the *Planet of the Apes* movie franchise, there isn't a community of chimpanzees living wild in the United States. Could this be the DNA of an as-yet-unknown chimp relative?

Now, this information should be taken with a grain or two of salt. The DNA evidence, at this point, is not robust enough to draw any real conclusions. More samples and a broader database will be required. It should also be noted that reality TV may not be the most trustworthy source. They make these shows for ratings, after all, and a group of people walking through the woods *not* finding possible evidence of Bigfoot would probably not survive a pilot episode, let alone six seasons.

Environmental DNA (eDNA) has been used to detect endangered wildlife existing in an area, even though they were unseen. Even microscopic species have been detected using this analysis. The process allows for identifying and studying species without requiring samples collected from a living being. Soil, permafrost, freshwater, and seawater are various macro environments from which eDNA samples have been extracted.

While the process is relatively new, it is being widely utilized and perfected. Of particular interest to Bigfoot researchers is the many ways, and environments from which, eDNA samples can be gathered. In 2021, researchers demonstrated that the eDNA can be collected, and used to identify mammals, from the very air we breathe. DNA from snow track samples have been used to identify the presence of such elusive and rare species as polar bears, arctic fox, lynx, and wolverines. Imagine the possibilities as more suspected Sasquatch prints are found. DNA sampling of such prints certainly promises to offer more insight than a plaster cast.

This research is also able to detect ancient DNA, preserved in sedimentary archives, fossils, and the like. In 2022, two-million-year-old eDNA genetic material was discovered and sequenced in Greenland, the oldest DNA discovered. Environmental DNA could help us not only discover an existing species of hominid roaming the snowy peaks and old growth forests of the world but also map the lineage of such creatures.

Bigfoot Sightings

There are a few more things that witnesses mention when retelling their stories and that researchers say are typical of Bigfoot encounters. These are not quantifiable evidence but rather typical claims that establish a pattern.

Often accompanying sightings of Bigfoot are reports of the sounds they make, such as howls, shrieks, chattering, and whistles. Often, however, those who have claimed to hear these vocalizations have come away shaken, describing the calls as frightening and threatening, as if being made as a warning to anyone getting too close.

The Society of Jesus, or Jesuits, is a religious order of men in the Catholic Church. Its founders include Ignatius of Loyola and Francis Xavier. Although the Jesuits have founded many high schools, colleges, and universities around the world, their original primary goal was to educate people about Catholicism, stop the spread of Protestantism, and convert people to the "true faith."

Among their many accomplishments is the first recorded instance of a Bigfoot yowl. It happened in 1721 in Natchez, Mississippi.

A priest was working with an indigenous Natchez tribe that was terrified by sounds they heard emanating from a nearby forest. "These are folks that live in the woods," he wrote, "so it was something clearly different. They called it a monstrous beast."

Sixteenth-century Spanish explorers and Mexican

True Tales from Across America

settlers had told tales of the *Vigilantes Oscuros* ("Dark Watchers"), who were large creatures said to stalk their camps at night. The priest reported stories of hairy creatures in the forest known to yowl loudly and steal livestock. But one night, "there came a big scream and a noise in the woods. A ruckus. A ruckus," he wrote.

Thus it was that Bigfoot's yowl came to be part of the records of the Catholic Church.

In 1971, a group of hunters claimed to have encountered a mysterious group of creatures in the Sierra Nevada mountains of California—between Lake Tahoe and Yosemite National Park—while at their deer camp. They said they heard the creatures make "horrific, intimidating" sounds. One man reportedly fled the camp in terror.

Upon returning from the trip, one of the hunters, Alan Berry, who was also an investigative reporter for the *Sacramento Bee*, contacted his friend, Ron Morehead. Berry told Morehead he saw large, human-like footprints near the deer camp. The men agreed to return to the woods with a small group for further investigation.

Their first expedition back to the camp was fruitless, but their second yielded exciting results. Once at the camp, the men began to hear sounds from the same nearby ridge that the deer-hunting party had heard the original vocalizations. The creatures whistled, screamed, whooped, chattered, and made guttural grunts and low growls, which the two men caught on audio recordings.

Berry and Morehead spent the next year returning to the site to record audio and take plaster casts of footprints, but they were unable to catch anything more than the briefest glimpse of the creatures. The supposed Bigfoot were stealthy and evasive and able to avoid the camera traps that were set. They didn't seem to notice the microphones attached to bushes and hanging from tree limbs, however, and a trove of audio recordings were made. The recordings came to be known as the Sierra Sounds, and Bigfoot researchers consider them some of the earliest, and best, evidence of Sasquatch vocalizations.

Bigfoot Sightings

Howl at the Moon!

Berry stated that he was initially skeptical and that his intent was to disprove the Sasquatch theory and expose any fakery. He said he always felt that proving how the deception had been achieved "would have made the story even more interesting," but he never found proof he was being tricked. Berry died in 2012.

Wentworth Military College professor and retired Navy crypto-linguist R. Scott Nelson analyzed the tapes. He was considered an expert in analyzing foreign and unknown languages. He concluded that the sounds exhibited the patterns and structure of a spoken language, though he couldn't identify the source. He referred to the vocalizations as "Sasquatch language," concluding that the language is twice as fast as that of any known dialect and would need to be slowed down to transcribe.

> *R. Scott Nelson analyzed the tapes. He was considered an expert in analyzing foreign and unknown languages. He concluded that the sounds exhibited the patterns and structure of a spoken language, though he couldn't identify the source.*

Nelson's subsequent paper, "Sasquatch Phonetic Alphabet and Transcription Standard," is either a work of genius or madness. We could consider the jury still out at this time.

The recordings also underwent a yearlong evaluation at the University of Wyoming. In analyzing the speed of the language, it was concluded that the original recordings were neither sped up nor slowed down. Dr. R. Lynn Kirlin, a professor of electrical engineering, opined that the vocalizations were beyond the lung capacity and physical capabilities of the average human and that the "format frequencies were clearly lower than for human data."

As with most proposed evidence of Bigfoot, the Sierra Sounds are viewed with skepticism by the broader scientific community. Nelson was a translator in the Navy, fluent in four languages, but being a self-proclaimed crypto-linguist is not the same thing as being an actual linguist, like Dr. Karen Stollznow. Writing in *Scientific American* in 2013, she concluded that the portions of the recordings that sounded like a language were likely human-made hoaxes. Convincing replications by humans can be found online.

Additionally, the 90 minutes of Sierra Sounds do not sound like other recordings that claim to capture Sasquatch sounds. The "language" on the Morehead/Berry tapes has only been captured in the one small area of the Sierra Nevada mountains that the men visited. The differences among these recordings is problematic.

A species tends to produce a consistent range of vocalizations, and the various Bigfoot recordings, as noted by paleontologist Darren Naish, are "phenomenally diverse." Writing in *Scientific American*, he said, "There's nothing approaching homogeneity of the sort present across known primate species."

Paleontologist and author Darren Naish is noted for his skepticism of cryptozoology.

The sounds of the Sasquatch have been likened to those of a howler monkey but also like the midnight wailing of a fox or coyote. A howl recording in Ohio by *Expedition Bigfoot*'s Matt Moneymaker is often used by other researchers as a Bigfoot call. The shrieks and screams of Bigfoot are described as "evil" and "demonic," while "chatter" is a quieter, close-quarters vocalization like a fast conversation being played in reverse.

A bit less common than shrieks and howls are reports of Bigfoot whistles. Several recordings have been made that claim to capture the sound, not dissimilar to a human whistling. It sounds similar to a pursed-lips whistle rather than the high, shrill tweet made by using one's fingers. There is no consensus on what the whistling means, but many believe it's an effective way for the creatures to communicate with each other over distance.

It should be noted that if Bigfoot does whistle, that would indicate a specific similarity with humans. No

Howl at the Moon!

animal or primate on the planet can whistle the way humans do. We are the only species capable of shaping our mouths in such a way as to produce the high-pitched noise.

One final note on vocalization recordings. Morehead and Berry spent three years acquiring these recordings. In some cases, the sounds seemed to be near their location, but they never produced even a poor-quality piece of photographic or video evidence. None of the other supposed recordings of Bigfoot, Sasquatch, or Yeti managed to provide an image of one of the creatures on film making a noise either.

What Bigfoot hunters *do* manage to capture on their videos are rocks or sticks being thrown. According to believers, throwing rocks to intimidate or harm unwanted visitors is standard Bigfoot practice. In some of the earliest accounts of Bigfoot encounters, such as the Ape Canyon story, the creatures are said to have thrown pebbles, rocks, or even boulders.

The logic of believers is that other than humans, there are no other beings in the Pacific Northwest, the Appalachians, or the snowy summits of Nepal that can throw rocks with any sort of velocity or accuracy. It's the whole opposable thumb thing.

So, it must be Bigfoot.

Again, the lack of videos or photographs documenting an actual Bigfoot throwing rocks is problematic. The creatures continue to prove that they are—even at 7 to 10 feet tall and weighing several hundred pounds—masters of camouflage.

A video taken in 2021 in Provo, Utah, reveals a Bigfoot emerging from a fairly sparsely wooded area alongside a split rail fence near a path or road. The exceptionally poor quality of the film clip is surprising given the modern capabilities of the most basic cell phone or camera.

The videographer is walking along the path and captures the large, brown, hairy creature walking down a slight slope toward an open area of high brush and grass. It pauses, seeming to attempt to take cover behind the only tree between it and the cameraman. As filming

True Tales from Across America

continues, you can see that the wooded area ends at the path and an expanse of short, green grass. It looks like this encounter is occurring at the end of the filmmaker's driveway, in his backyard.

The creature seems to wind up and throw a rock in the general direction of the camera. Since the creature doesn't look like it searched for the rock, the being must have been carrying it. The creature hunches down again, and that's where the film ends.

The only audio is of the cameraman saying, "What the...?," upon spying the creature, and maybe the rock striking a tree. The rest is wind and leaves rustling. No vocalizations. No warning the person to go away. No aggressive hoots, whoops, or growls to intimidate, which you might think would be a first course of action, rather than throwing the rock.

The video can be found on YouTube. It is considered one of the best examples of video showing Bigfoot throwing rocks.

If one dares to ignore the screeches and howls that may be early warnings from afar for those encroaching on Bigfoot habitat or long-distance communications between members of the tribe or clan, and if one is not scared off by sticks and rocks being thrown by unseen hands from the cover of the trees and brush, they may encounter another of the tell-tale signs of the presence of Bigfoot: the smell.

Approximately 10 to 15 percent of witnesses report a foul smell when encountering Bigfoot. This odor has been described as smelling like rotting meat, horse manure, and skunk—the last being responsible for the name of the southeastern United States' "Skunk Ape."

Reports of the creature's stench, vocalization, or penchant for throwing things at people don't prove the existence of Bigfoot. More important is the general consistency of these attributes as described by witnesses in multiple sightings over vast geographical areas.

While we're mostly wrapping up our initial review of physical and circumstantial evidence, let's touch on some Sasquatch mannerisms and observations regarding evidence and belief.

While the shrieks, howls, and chattering are the vocalizations most often heard during Bigfoot encounters, the beings are also said to be fond of whistling. Further methods of communicating—among themselves and when attempting communication with humans—include hitting pieces of wood together, clapping, and knocking on wood. These are behaviors that would be familiar to anyone who has spent time observing chimpanzees.

Speaking of chimps, famed primatologist Jane Goodall isn't necessarily a believer in Bigfoot, but she is open to the idea and even hopeful that the creature's existence would be proven. She visited a remote village in Ecuador where she had asked the people if they had ever seen a monkey without a tail. Three hunters replied that they had. "They walk upright and they're about six foot tall," the hunters told her. She noted that they knew nothing of Bigfoot legends.

Jane Goodall, famous for her work with chimpanzees, has said that she is open to the idea that there might be some kind of yet-undiscovered primate species like Bigfoot.

True Tales from Across America

"Every single country has its version. Yeti, Yowie in Australia, Wild Man in China. So I don't know if it's perhaps a myth that stems from maybe the last of the Neanderthals," Goodall said. "But then is the last of the Neanderthals still living in these remote forests? I don't know. But I'm not going to say it doesn't exist and I'm not going to say people who believe in it are stupid."

"I guess I'm romantic," she concluded. "I don't want to disbelieve."

Another famous, if perhaps less trustworthy, believer is Russian president Vladimir Putin. In 2016, Putin claimed to have spotted three Yetis while flying in a helicopter over a remote area of Siberia. He reportedly saw what appeared to be a family unit—an adult male and female, with a smaller child. The creatures were said to have been covered in thick gray hair and took long strides. "Far bigger than a man," according to national park wildlife expert Dmitry Ivanov, who accompanied Putin.

Russian leader Vladimir Putin has claimed that he has personally seen three Yetis.

Belief in the Yeti is common in Russia. You'll recall the expedition to Siberia we discussed earlier. Local branches of the Russian government have funded several such expeditions, and consideration has been given to founding an institute devoted to the study of Yetis.

In North America, 21 percent of Canadians think the creatures exist, and nearly a quarter of Americans say they believe in Bigfoot.

The greatest number of sightings of Bigfoot occur in the Pacific Northwest states of Washington, California, and Oregon. Appalachia sees many reports as well. Kentucky has made a substantial claim as a hotbed of Bigfoot activity. But Bigfoot is likely to show up in nearly

Bigfoot Sightings

Don't Stop Believin'

any location that has a decent amount of forested land.

Even if there's no forest, the Bigfoot species appears to be adaptable to whatever secluded habitat is available. Internationally, large, hairy, hominid creatures can be found in Australia (the Yowie), South America (Mapinguari), and Malaysia ("oily man").

It seems these creatures are everywhere.

Does this mean there are many more of these creatures than we might imagine? Could it suggest that they're migratory and can travel great distances? Maybe they are more nomadic than we might have imagined. They may travel great distances for food, preferred climate, or mating.

Many species have extended ranges due to migration. Caribou have round-trip migratory patterns of nearly 750 miles. A Mongolia gray wolf is known to have traveled over 4,500 miles in a year.

Doubters quickly point out that primates tend not to migrate seasonally, but that foolishly dismisses the habits of our own ancestors. Native Americans traveled with the migrating bison they relied on for food and clothing. Typically, the Native People would have summer and winter camps.

Since we haven't stumbled upon any Sasquatch villages, we can safely assume they would maintain a hunter/gatherer lifestyle. This makes seasonal migration not only likely but also necessary.

> *Ivan Sanderson claimed that four types of abominable snowmen existed, spread over five continents. These days, some claim there are at least 12 different types just in North America.*

It seems there are as many types of Bigfoot as there are locations of Bigfoot, though they mostly resemble each other in the same way humans in Mexico, China, Switzerland, and Nigeria resemble each other. Their differences are largely products of their environment and genetic lineage.

It was previously mentioned that Ivan Sanderson claimed that four types of abominable snowmen exist-

True Tales from Across America

ed, spread over five continents. These days, some claim there are at least 12 different types just in North America.

The Bigfoot-type creature of Cherokee legend was thought to be a magical beast, capable of reading people's minds. Even today, many claim that Bigfoot is a supernatural being that can cause people to lose track of time or erase their memories of an encounter. On occasion, they say, Bigfoot will use its powers to cause people to strip naked and go crazy.

Bears live in habitats similar to many Bigfoot, and even their omnivorous diets might be the same.

Bigfoot is sometimes depicted as a large, gentle beast that just wants its privacy and, at other times, as a ferocious animal capable of great violence. Legends and folklore that speak of Sasquatch-type beings often hold them responsible for killings.

In line with that violent nature, some people have claimed the creatures are maneaters, but the widely accepted theory is that Bigfoot is an omnivore, eating both plants and meat. In fact, rather than being an opportunistic predator, it's generally assumed that Bigfoot's diet is primarily plant-based with meals of meat being a matter of opportunity.

Given that Bigfoot is typically sighted in habitat suited to bears, it would make sense that it has similar feeding habits. Forested areas, where the creature is most often seen, contain ample vegetation—fruits, nuts, and vegetables. These would provide essential vitamins and minerals. Meals of fish may become more frequent during spawning periods, with small, easily caught mammals making up the bulk of the creature's carnivorous fare. Larger mammals, like deer or elk, would be less frequent as, like us, Bigfoot isn't a particularly well-suited hunter without weaponry.

Bigfoot Sightings

Don't Stop Believin' 87

Of course, the opposite could be said for other habitats, such as the snowy mountaintops of the Himalayas or the arid desert of the Australian interior. In these spaces, the creature may be more predatory due to a lack of vegetation. Additionally, eyewitnesses have claimed to see Bigfoot actively hunting deer, hogs, and fish.

Again, this predatory behavior would be reminiscent of bears. And, as it seems that Bigfoot doesn't hibernate, a predatory diet may help it survive harsh winters, when vegetation is scarce.

The diet of the hairy "hominoid" is likely dependent on where they live. In the United States alone, Bigfoot is thought to inhabit the forested Pacific Northwest, where a diet of berries, nuts, mushrooms, and the like would make sense. Bigfoot living in the swamps of the Southeast would have to adjust their diet and rely on the more available aquatic plants and fish.

Given the size of Bigfoot, whatever it's eating would need to be in abundant supply. Nutrition would be critical for the creatures to maintain physical health and energy levels. Life in the wilderness is harsh, and Bigfoot would burn a lot of calories roaming its territory.

Humans require between 1,600 and 3,000 calories per day. Gorillas consume up to 8,000 calories in a day, eating as much as 40 pounds of foliage. Bigfoot are, presumably, larger than both. There would have to be a lot of whatever it's eating going in, and that means a lot coming out.

> *Scat analysis, the process of identifying and quantifying the components of Bigfoot's big poo, could help to conclusively establish what it is eating. Studies of suspected Bigfoot scat have shown it to contain plant matter, animal hair, and bones.*

Scat analysis, the process of identifying and quantifying the components of Bigfoot's big poo, could help to conclusively establish what it is eating. Studies of suspected Bigfoot scat have shown it to contain plant matter, animal hair, and bones. Many times, however, supposed Bigfoot scat has turned out to be that of a bear or another animal, and that has muddied the findings of such analysis.

True Tales from Across America

We've covered some of the most substantial and common claims of Bigfoot researchers. We've looked at the history of giants and the idea that a race of prehistoric creatures may have survived, in hiding, alongside our *Homo sapiens* ancestors up to modern times. We've reviewed physical evidence such as DNA analysis and hair samples. We've looked at available video and photographic evidence. We've entertained circumstantial evidence, such as nests and tress structures.

The truth is that the only thing that is likely to convince a hardened skeptic that Bigfoot exists would be if it is caught in a trap or shot by a hunter. Many claims have been made, but the evidence, which would undoubtedly be welcomed by zoologists and anthropologists, is severely lacking.

The field of study would be easier to navigate were it not for hoaxers. Skeptics are a good thing—they keep harmful claims at bay—but hoaxers can taint the whole body of research and evidence. Even if only one or two accounts are true out of every 100 scams, that leaves a lot of evidence that needs to be followed up and studied. If Bigfoot is someday proven to be a fully substantiated species, it would be big news.

The most difficult evidence to dismiss is that of an eyewitness. Even a skeptic cannot help but be moved by the

While there might not be much physical evidence to offer for proof, there are literally thousands of eyewitness testimonies concerning Bigfoot.

Bigfoot Sightings

Don't Stop Believin'

emotion that shakes many witnesses who have reported a real encounter with Bigfoot. In many cases, it changes their whole lives. Rather than immediately talk about their experience—which one would want to do if trying to fool a gullible audience—many, if not most, people try to keep their experience quiet. Some take years to tell anyone because they are afraid of drawing ridicule from friends and family. To hear such a story, perhaps for the first time, is to be drawn into a close, personal, privileged encounter, not to be taken lightly.

As Carl Sagan used to say, absence of evidence is not necessarily evidence of absence. We simply cannot write off thousands of eyewitness accounts and a rich oral history that extend far into the distant past. Can all these encounters be the ravings of lunatics and attention seekers, or simple cases of mistaken identity?

To that end, we turn now to some actual stories, beginning in the motherland of the Yeti: the Himalayas.

True Tales from Across America

Most of us will never get an opportunity to travel to the Himalayas and search for Bigfoot, but we must begin there because that's where many of the legends began. Even before Bigfoot stories began to circulate among the pre-European, indigenous tribes of North America, the mysterious Yeti haunted the high mountain lore of Nepal, China, Pakistan, Bhutan, and India.

Ancient rishis from India coined the term *Himalaya*, a Sanskrit term formed from *hima* (snow) and *alaya* (abode). Although many North American stories about Sasquatch feature supernatural activities, the Yeti has *always* been associated with the religious and spiritual mythology of this region. It is not worshipped as a god, per se, but is certainly viewed as a supernatural being, with magical powers, by Sherpas and others who dwell in the high peaks, many of which offer views of Mt. Everest, the world's highest mountain. Perhaps the majestic views from their mountain homes imbue a certain inclination toward the mystical.

Another reason for beginning with the Yeti stories, however, even though the majority of those reading these words come from North America, might prove to be the most important one. If we examine a world map, with human migration history at the forefront of our minds, we find some interesting similarities between early human migration routes, especially Denisovan and Neanderthal, and what is believed to be their African genesis. *If* Yeti and Bigfoot prove to be an unknown human ancestor, it would make sense that they

The members of the 1921 Everest expedition included (standing left to right) Guy Bullock, Henry Morshead, Oliver Wheeler, and George Mallory; (seated left to right) Alexander Heron, Sandy Wollaston, Charles Howard-Bury, and Harold Raeburn.

followed a similar path of migration and expansion. Like our earliest *Homo sapiens* ancestors, the ancestors of the Yeti (and subsequently the Sasquatch and Bigfoot creatures) may have originated in Africa and made their way into the Himalayas, across Europe, west to Siberia and an early exposure of the Bering Land Bridge, and then to North America. There is considerable evidence that both Denisovans and Neanderthals did just that. North American DNA research seems to prove this conclusively. Yeti and Bigfoot may be long-lost cousins of these two species, and us as well, *or* they were early primates who blazed the trail for human species to come, *or* an earlier hominid species with which our ancestors could have crossed paths in their travels.

Regardless of its origin and migration path, there is no doubt that the Asian Yeti, a creature shrouded in religious mysticism, has long been part of the oral history and belief system of the native people of the high peaks. These stories surfaced and became widely distributed beginning in 1921.

At that time, the "sun never set on the British Empire." They ruled almost a quarter of the land on the planet,

Back to the Beginning

and India had been firmly under the British Crown since 1757. In the early twentieth century, India's Himalayan foothills had become a popular adventure destination among Brits for hiking, hunting, and mountain climbing. Imagine gazing up at the snow-capped peaks, fantasizing of being the first among your peers to reach the top.

The sight of such majesty alone could inspire such an undertaking—a challenge irresistible to the explorer, the adventurer, the risk taker. As George Mallory answered, in 1924, when asked why he would want to climb Mount Everest:

"Because it's there."

Three years prior to the uttering of those famous words, Mallory was a member of the British Mount Everest Reconnaissance Expedition, which set out from India to forge a route to the vicinity of Mount Everest, the largest mountain on Earth. Although the mission was successful, it did not result in an ascent of the mountain. Most interesting for us is that, upon their return, the team was interviewed by journalist Henry Newman and passed on reports of large footprints they had found in the snow.

Expedition leader Charles Howard-Bury was convinced that the prints had been left by a wolf. The local guides and porters, however, assured him that they were evidence of *me-toh-kangmi*—the genesis of the term that would soon become famous around the world: the *Abominable Snowman*.

Expedition leader Charles Howard-Bury believed that the footprints they found were merely those of a large wolf.

Subsequent encounters and reports pointed to three types of Yeti recognized by the natives of this area.

True Tales from Across America

- The *dzu-the* is probably the most terrifying of them all. It is said to be as much as 8 feet tall when it stands on its hind legs, but it prefers to walk on all fours and has been known to kill a yak with one mighty swipe of its claws.
- The *chu-the* is much smaller and is found in the forests of Nepal. It features red hair, walks on two legs, and has very long arms.
- The *meh-the* looks most like a man. It has orange-red fur and is known to deliberately attack humans. This is the beast most often depicted on monastery wall paintings in the area.

Examples of Yeti "scalps" are venerated in various village monasteries in Nepal. Usually, they are sealed off from human contact, displayed in glass boxes or cases that are only opened on special occasions.

The famous mountaineer Sir Edmund Hillary was allowed to borrow one usually housed in a small village monastery in northeast Nepal. The priests there claimed it was 300 years old. After some convincing, he was allowed to take it to be inspected by independent zoologists in Paris, Chicago, and London, but they were not impressed, and it failed to pass inspection. The scientists agreed the scalp was a fake, made from the skin of a serow, which is a goat-like creature found in the Himalayas.

At the monastery in Khumjung, Nepal, you can find this display of a purported Yeti scalp.

Hillary later wrote in *Stars and Stripes* that "I have never believed in the existence of the snowman. Pleasant though we felt it would be to believe in the existence of the Yeti, when faced with the universal collapse of the main evidence in support of this creature, the members of my expedition could not in all conscience view it as more than a fascinating fairy tale."

Back to the Beginning

The popularization of the Yeti legend probably began in 1889 in Northern India, sparked by Scottish explorer Major (later Lieutenant Colonel) Laurence Waddell. Waddell is sometimes called the inspiration for the movie hero Indiana Jones.

Laurence Waddell was an Indian Army surgeon, a professor of chemistry, pathology, and Tibetan, an amateur archaeologist, and — some say — the inspiration for the fictional character Indiana Jones.

Waddell was a professor of both Tibetan culture and chemistry. He was also a surgeon and an archaeologist who had roamed Tibet in disguise, searching for substantiation for his theory that all civilization began with Aryan, blond, blue-eyed Nordics originating from early Sumerians. The German Nazis later picked up his theories, which led to their expedition to Tibet in 1938 and 1939. Today, Waddell's books, which were soundly rebuked even at the time of their publication, are most commonly referenced by White Supremacists and conspiracy theorists.

While exploring in northeast Sikkim, Waddell discovered a set of large footprints that his servants said were made by the Yeti, a beast that was highly dangerous and fed on humans. In Waddell's words:

> *Some large footprints in the snow led across our track and away up to the higher peaks. These were alleged to be the trail of the hairy wild men who are believed to live amongst the eternal snows, along with the mythical white lions, whose roar is reputed to be heard during storms* [perhaps these were avalanches].

He thus became the first Westerner to report the discovery of Yeti tracks.

True Tales from Across America

Tibetans, of course, had longed believed in these creatures. Later scientists would claim that the "hairy wild men" of the Himalayas were probably a species called *Ursus isabellinus*—the great yellow snow-bear. But the spark ignited by Waddell would grow into a flame 70 years later.

Earlier we noted that Hillary doubted the existence of the Yeti. This raises an interesting question. If he didn't believe in the existence of the Abominable Snowman, why pull together an expensive hunt to go looking for it?

The Himalayan brown bear (Ursus isabellinus) *has a blond coat and can be over seven feet long. It is found in the western Himalayas of Pakistan, India, and Nepal.*

Ed Douglas, author of *Tenzing: Hero of Everest*, thinks the whole project used the Yeti stories as a headline-grabbing tool to get funding for a monumental expedition. "The yeti was a useful marketing tool," said Douglas. "I doubt Hillary really believed in it except when he was talking to PR people."

It's important to remember that in the 1950s and early 1960s much of the European and American world was caught up in what might be called Yeti mania. It makes sense that Hillary might capitalize on this. According to Graham Hoyland, author of *Yeti: An Abominable History*, "The yeti wasn't considered mythical in the early '60s."

It was even the law of that region that a Yeti could not be killed except in self-defense. The Abominable Snowman was considered a real, flesh-and-blood creature that fascinated the public conscience—so much so that a U.S. State Department memo dated December 10, 1959, reminded would-be mountaineers and researchers in Nepal of the regulations relating to Yeti hunting. There were three at the time.

- A 5,000 rupee fee was required for a permit from the Nepali government.
- Yeti, if discovered, could be photographed

Bigfoot Sightings

Back to the Beginning

or caught alive but not killed, except in the case of self-defense. Any photographs and any creature, alive or dead, were to be surrendered to the Nepali government.

- Any reports as to the existence of the creature were to be submitted, and vetted, by the Nepali government and could not be released to the press without government permission.

This was an age when news had begun to travel the globe in a matter of minutes rather than days, when there was a newspaper on every doorstep and a TV in every home. The world was still recovering from World War II and the Korean War, but those wars had introduced new and exotic lands to a public clamoring for safe, vicarious adventures. Places such as the South Pacific, Eastern Europe, North Africa, and Russia had been seen by what Tom Brokaw later called "The Greatest Generation" who had fought the good fight for world freedom. With the horrors of the war that had consumed those locations behind them, Westerners clamored to learn about and visit these "exotic" locations.

The race to conquer Mount Everest had heated up in the 1950s, so the number of alleged Yeti sightings grew apace. Western audiences were hooked. Despite Darwin's *The Origin of Species* being published in 1859, the evolution debate in America really didn't extend beyond academic and intellectual circles until the 1930s. By the time stories of an ape-human hybrid began circulating in the 1950s, the public thirsted for the discovery of a new, evolutionary creature that was halfway between man and beast. They bristled with excitement to think that there were beings beyond comprehension who survived at the ends of the known wilderness. It was exciting, even comforting, for the armchair explorer to think that there were still wild places left in the world that other brave souls would explore and bring to the common man's living room through the media of the day.

Eric Earle Shipton had photographed so-called Yeti footprints in 1951, which captured so much attention in his day that years later, in 2014, Christie's Auction house in London sold the original photo for nearly $5,000.

True Tales from Across America

Eric Earle Shipton had photographed so-called Yeti footprints in 1951, which captured so much attention in his day that years later, in 2014, Christie's Auction house in London sold the original photo for nearly $5,000.

When Edmund Hillary set off in search of the Abominable Snowman, he wasn't simply following a wild conspiracy theory. He might not have been a believer himself, but undoubtedly some who accompanied him hoped to encounter a Yeti in the wild.

So it was that, on the morning of September 10, 1960, the famous Hillary expedition set out into the Rolwāling Valley, chosen because Sherpas had reported Yeti sightings in the area and it was close to Makalu, the world's fifth highest mountain. The idea was to spend the next nine months searching for the illusive Snowman while studying the effects of long-term exposure to high altitudes on human fitness.

The expedition featured a stellar line-up. Peter Mulgrew and Wally Romanes had accompanied Hillary on his 1955–58 expedition to Antarctica. American space physiologist Tom Nevison and glaciologist Barry Bishop were along to conduct scientific tests designed to measure effects of long-term altitude exposure. Marlin Perkins—who would later go on to television fame hosting *Mutual of Omaha's Wild Kingdom* from 1963 to 1985—was, at the time, the director of the Lincoln Park Zoo, and Dr. Larry Swan was a self-described "Himalayanist," who brought practical expertise to the hunt.

English mountaineer Eric Shipton photographed Yeti footprints in 1951.

It was thus a serious, well-funded, professional expedition, backed by no less than the *World Book Encyclopedia*. Their avowed mission was to prove, once and for all, whether there was anything to the legends. They intended, at least according to press releases, to "capture a live Snowman."

But was it a real goal or a public relations stunt? Whatever the motives of the individuals involved—and they were undoubtedly mixed—the lack of success led to a gradual thawing of public interest, and the Yeti trend began to wane. That is until Don Whillans breathed new life into the legend.

We recounted Whillans's story, at length, in Chapter 5: "To Walk a Mile in Their Footsteps." He was instrumental in bridging the gap between the Himalayan Yeti and North America's Sasquatch.

Now that we're crossing that bridge ourselves, this is an excellent time to move from history and the folklore of the past to see if we can understand how not just the idea of Bigfoot, but the physical being, could have made that journey—and just what it is that we think is stalking the uninhabited regions of our own continent.

True Tales from Across America

HOW DID WE END UP HERE?

We've looked back into the past at some possible ancestors of Bigfoot and the lore from multiple ancient cultures, even prior to written history, which might suggest that this creature has been living and evolving right along with us the whole time. There's no question that the first stories of a giant, hairy, human-like creature of the wild—particularly as they pertain to what we currently think of as the Yeti, Sasquatch, or Bigfoot—originated in the pre-Buddhist beliefs of the Himalayan people and made their way into the Buddhist beliefs of Tibet and Nepal.

As Western explorers and adventurers began to frequent the region, their stories of bipedal, apelike creatures and large, strange tracks and footprints began to spread. The frequency of reports increased in the twentieth century, as mountaineers attempted to scale the many mountains in the area. With information spreading wider and farther than ever, through newspapers, telegraphs, and then radio and television, it's no surprise that such stories would capture the imagination of people around the world. Nowhere has that been more the case than in North America.

As confidently as we can trace the origins of the Bigfoot lore back to the snowy peaks of the Himalayas, we can assert that the cultural phenomenon of that lore today is rooted in the stories from the North American continent. Before we get into those stories and the legends and beliefs of the continent's original peoples that might support them, we should narrow our focus going forward.

True Tales from Across America

Regardless of the creature's origins, lineage, or evolution, what do we think of *today* when someone asks us if we believe in Bigfoot or Sasquatch? And, if such a creature exists on a continent that, to the best of our knowledge, has no indigenous primates other than us humans, how did it get here?

So two questions to address before moving on:

- What is it? Or, I suppose, what do we *think* it is?
- If such a creature exists, and assuming it originated in Africa like other apes and hominins, or possibly Asia, given the prevalence of Yeti myths, how did it get to North America in the first place?

The questions may be simple, but the answers range from difficult to unknowable. Let's tackle the second question first.

When humans got to North America, whether that was 16,000 years ago or 135,000 years ago, the country was teaming with wild game. That begs the question: Unless they evolved here, how did *any* animals get to North America?

Bears, for instance, originated in Africa from one large, ancient species called *Ursus minimus*, found in present-day South Africa. The giant, short-faced bear—almost twice as big as today's brown bear—once lived

Ursus minimus *was a species of bear that lived about two to five million years ago.*

Bigfoot Sightings

in the Americas. It was among the largest mammalian carnivores that ever existed. How did *it* get here?

The standard answer is that they migrated, over the course of many millennia, to Asia, and then, some 500,000 years ago, over a previous Bering land bridge. Eventually, through the process of evolution, they became what we now know as the North American black bear. Their habitat stretches from the Alaskan tundra to the hills of Kentucky and the wilds of Maine to the tropical climate of Florida.

The woolly mammoth, whose carcasses have been discovered with spearpoints of the American Clovis people, also came to North America from Asia, across a Bering Land Bridge, beginning about 100,000 years ago. This might even have been the species that lured the first Americans here, hunting the mammoths as they traversed the landscape. The first people to establish populations in North America would have followed the migration of their prey, during an Ice Age that exposed dry land where water would have otherwise halted their advance.

The ancestors of the American mastodon had split away from the mammoths sometime around 25 million years ago. They, too, eventually crossed the land bridge, about 15 million years ago, further evolving in their new home some 3.5 million years ago.

The Bering Land Bridge, coming and going depending on sea levels, served as a two-way street. Many animals crossed from Asia to the Americas, but some, such as the horse, originated in America and traveled west to Asia. It was a popular intercontinental highway, albeit the only one, and probably served as a bridge for both Neanderthal and Denisovans, both distant cousins of ours.

This raises the possibility that the American Sasquatch, assuming it was an early, primitive, perhaps ancestral hominin species, migrated along with all the other species in the far distant past. If we want to bestow upon them a higher level of intelligence, which seems perfectly justified, we might even go so far as to call them the first Americans.

True Tales from Across America

This brings us to one of the more interesting archaeological finds of the last few decades—a certain mastodon bone—and it might shed some light on the earliest immigrants to America, including a possible candidate for Bigfoot.

First, some background.

For a hundred years, and up to roughly the year 2008, the consensus theory about who the first Americans were, based first on geological history and archaeological evidence, and then on genetic findings, was that a single population of people, called the Clovis people—because of the discovery of their now-famous stone projectile points near Clovis, New Mexico—migrated from southern Siberia. They traveled across the land mass known as the Bering Land Bridge, crossing over to the Americas some 16,500 years ago.

But discoveries in various places from Pennsylvania all the way to Peru questioned this hypothesis. They all seemed to indicate unmistakable human-crafted stone tools that were much older than a mere 16,500 years. The debate was intense for a few decades until, finally, what was by then called the Clovis-First theory began to fall apart.

When a mastodon bone that seemed to bear the marks of human labor, along with crude stone implements, was discovered in California, it was thought this might help the cause of those who thought Clovis-First didn't take the first people back far enough. Anthropologists hoped dates from this site might push the peopling of the continent back by at least a few thousand years. But when the artifacts were turned over to geochronologist James Paces, who employed a new and improved technology called the uranium-thorium dating technique, he and his team concluded that they were 130,000 years old, give or take 9,400 years. This date corresponded with the accepted age of the layer of rock in which the bones and stone cobbles were found.

These dates far exceeded any established date for settlement of the Americas. Until then, the oldest biological remains from any humans on the continent was a coprolite (fossilized feces) from 14,300 years ago. Some

How Did We End Up Here?

The Clovis culture existed in North America about 13,000 years ago, as judged by artifacts left behind such as these spearpoints.

specialists were willing to concede, based on DNA evidence taken from Native Americans, that humans might have made it over the land bridge that once linked northeast Asia to Alaska some 25,000 years ago, but that was as far back as most genetic specialists wanted to go. So how were they to deal with stones and bones dating back 130,000 years? Could they be evidence of people, or at least the antecedents of people, who came before modern humans? How did they get to this part of the world so long ago? Why hasn't other evidence of their presence ever been found? Did they die out not long after they arrived?

There is no evidence at the California site of hominin remains. Since rock-hammer technology was used by other hominin species, scientists cautioned that any discussion of the identity of these people would be purely speculative. It was possible, in other words, that these findings could be tied back to an early species of ape with only the most ancient connection to modern humans, or no connection at all.

That didn't stop the conversation, of course. People wondered if they had discovered evidence of our ancestral cousins, such as Neanderthals or Denisovans, or even members of the species *Homo erectus*. According to most estimates, anatomically modern humans didn't migrate out of Africa until 100,000 years ago, which would have been 30,000 years after the California artifacts were used.

True Tales from Across America

Could it be possible that a primitive species, who used stone tools, might have been able to cross the land bridge before the last ice age, when the planet warmed and sea levels rose? We know that other species migrated to the Americas during this period, and even well before, and these hominins might have followed them over.

The only other possibility was that they could have used boats to cross the Bering Strait and either sailed or walked down the Pacific coast. This isn't as far-fetched as it seems. Archaeological finds on the Mediterranean island of Crete suggest that hominins were able to cross the sea via boat more than 100,000 years ago.

Conservative archaeologists scoffed at this whole idea. Some called it an example of "grandiose" thinking. One site could easily be misinterpreted, they said. They wanted a bigger sample to study.

Others were only too happy to oblige by pointing to other discoveries. The samples were already there, they said, but they had been ignored because they seemed to contradict conventional thinking, just as this site did.

It's this same reasoning that continues to dismiss evidence presented today as proof of Bigfoot, and that hinders coordinated scientific efforts that would lead to more effective research.

Donald Grayson, a paleoanthropologist at the University of Washington, brought up the uncomfortable, and possibly even embarrassing, fact that academic history is riddled with examples of scientists who misinterpreted strange markings on stone as evidence of human activity. He pointed to a Calico Hills site in the Mojave Desert, which the late archaeologist Louis Leakey believed contained

Archaeologist and paleoanthropologist Louis Leakey's field research in Africa contributed significantly to our understanding of human evolution.

Bigfoot Sightings

How Did We End Up Here?

200,000-year-old stone tools. Subsequent study of these artifacts largely discredited Leakey's claim, saying they were most likely "geofacts," natural stone formations that only look like they were crafted by humans.

The name Leakey remains well-respected in the scientific community. Were we to believe that an otherwise trusted and admired archaeologist had suddenly become "bad at his job," or did academic prejudice seek to discredit his work simply because it didn't seem to fit common, accepted dating techniques? Could the "experts" be drawing conclusions prejudiced by the current, accepted theories about human evolution and migration? There were certainly human ancestors in other parts of the world more than 200,000 years ago. It simply takes a belief that some of them crossed an early land bridge or navigated the seas earlier than we had believed to make Leakey's claim credible.

In short, there were many scholars who sought to shove the California find under the rug, just as they had other renegade claims. While complaining that there wasn't *enough* "evidence," they were quick to dismiss every piece of evidence that arose without granting it even the most cursory review.

> *While complaining that there wasn't enough "evidence," they were quick to dismiss every piece of evidence that arose without granting it even the most cursory review.*

It's not being suggested that the 130,000-year-old California artifacts were, in fact, the work of Bigfoot. But, at the very least, they raise the possibility of an early stone-wielding species of ancestral human cousins who had arrived in the Americas long before modern humans migrated out of Africa to Europe and Asia. Nor is the intent to criticize only traditional academics. It might be that their more radical colleagues are capable of bad science, too. They might, indeed, have had a moment of "being bad at their job." Haven't we all?

Take, for example, the controversy surrounding the claims of Jeremy Hance. Hance claims to have discovered genetic evidence proving the existence of Bigfoot.

True Tales from Across America

A study released in the *DeNovo Scientific Journal* in February 2013 claimed to uncover DNA evidence for Bigfoot.

Enthusiasts had long argued that Bigfoot was an unidentified ape species. This new study suggested that genetic evidence proves that Sasquatch is a hybrid of modern human females who mated with an unidentified primate species some 13,000 years ago.

According to this article, a team of forensic scientists studied 111 specimens of hair, blood, skin, and other tissues that were said to come from Bigfoot. The samples were gathered from 14 states and two Canadian provinces.

> *Enthusiasts had long argued that Bigfoot was an unidentified ape species. This new study suggested that genetic evidence proves that Sasquatch is a hybrid of modern human females who mated with an unidentified primate species some 13,000 years ago.*

We discussed this evidence when talking about DNA, but it's worth revisiting in a bit more detail. The lead author was Melba Ketchum from DNA Diagnostics, who wrote:

> We soon discovered that certain hair samples—which we would later identify as purported Sasquatch samples—had unique morphology distinguishing them from typical human and animal samples. Those hair samples that could not be identified as known animal or human were subsequently screened using DNA testing, beginning with sequencing of mitochondrial DNA followed by sequencing nuclear DNA to determine where these individuals fit in the "tree of life."

She said that the *mtDNA* (mitochondrial DNA) was clearly human, but the *nuDNA* (nuclear DNA) showed a mix of human and primate features.

Mitochondrial DNA comes only from a maternal line. Nuclear DNA is a mix of both maternal and paternal ancestry. So the "AncestryDNA" came back saying that mom was definitely human and dad was at least partially primate. This led the team to theorize that Bigfoot is the offspring of human females with as-yet-unidentified primates. They swore they had eliminated any possibility of contamination of the samples.

Ketchum continued:

> While the three Sasquatch nuclear genomes aligned well with one another, and showed significant homology to human chromosome 11, the Sasquatch genomes were novel and fell well outside of known ancient hominin, as well as ape sequences. Because some of the mtDNA haplogroups found in our Sasquatch samples originated as late as 13,000 years ago, we are hypothesizing that the Sasquatch are human hybrids, the result of males of an unknown hominin species crossing with female Homo sapiens.

Ketchum went on to suggest that Bigfoot be given the name *Homo sapiens cognatus*, or "blood relative" to *Homo sapiens*.

This should have been welcome news to Bigfoot enthusiasts. But as it turns out, the *DeNovo Scientific Journal* was a publication bought by Ketchum and her team shortly before they published the paper. As a matter of fact, it appeared that the journal was acquired just for that purpose. This, obviously, raised some suspicion.

Ketchum admitted that the team acquired the rights to the journal just before publication but insisted that the paper was peer-reviewed. In scientific terms, "peer-reviewed" means that it was reviewed by an independent committee of experts before publication.

On her website, Ketchum wrote that "rather than spend another five years trying to find a journal to publish, and hoping that decent, open-minded reviewers would be chosen, we acquired the rights to this journal and renamed it so we would not lose the passing peer reviews that are expected by the public and the scientific community."

In other words, their paper had not actually been reviewed by anyone either, but they *expected* it to be and

True Tales from Across America

were confident that it would be reviewed positively. Since its publication, the study has come under some intense scrutiny.

Dr. Stuart Pimm, for instance, an ecologist at Duke University who runs the conservation nonprofit Saving Species, said that believing in Bigfoot—a large hominin roaming North America undetected—denies the very basics of biology.

Dr. Stuart Pimm is a theoretical ecologist and Doris Duke Chair of Conservation Ecology at Duke University.

Those who believe in Sasquatch, the Loch Ness Monster, and unicorns have to overcome the inevitable requirements of sex. Any remaining individual needs two parents, four grandparents, eight grandparents, and so on, back to a population large enough to have been viable to persist long enough to remain a genetically distinct species. For large bodied species, such populations must occupy considerable geographical space, making the chance that they would remain "elusive" improbable. Those who imagine the hundreds of Sasquatch needed to persist scattered across 14 States are, in effect, assuming a mode of reproduction alien to this planet.

He went on to say that even indigenous people who live in voluntary isolation, such as the remote Amazon rainforest, still leave behind "abundant evidence of their presence."

The counterargument to his central point, ignoring Pimm's rather immature habit of ridicule, is easily made. Even though the samples tested for the paper were from 14 locations, sightings of Bigfoot point to a population spread across 49 states and seven Canadian provinces. That's an area large enough to easily handle

Bigfoot Sightings

How Did We End Up Here?

the sexual-biological needs of a sustainable breeding population. Notable scientists, including Jane Goodall, have stated they thought it was possible that some unknown, large-bodied primate lived in North America. It is true that most dismiss the idea, citing lack of physical evidence, but it is certainly a plausible theory in terms of geographical area.

Further, there is no accounting for the possible migratory patterns of Bigfoot populations or a consideration of what a Bigfoot clan's, or individual's, territorial range might be. It could well be that Sasquatch are creatures that are always on the move. They might travel alone, as many species are known to do during mating seasons, as they search for breeding partners. They may travel in small family units or larger, but undetectable, clans.

That brings us back to the central negative argument, however—one that is made time and time again. Is it possible that a breeding population of Bigfoot could escape detection, at least in terms of physical evidence, and fly under the radar of twenty-first-century science? Certainly, if sightings, footprints, audio recordings, oral history, and photographs are considered, Bigfoot is doing anything *but* "flying under the radar." That kind of growing evidence makes the species almost conspicuous.

While the argument is that the existence of a community of Bigfoot requires a large breeding population, that's only the case if we apply our current understanding of genetics based on known species—particularly, ourselves.

Small populations tend to die out due to a few reasons. They have low levels of genetic diversity and are more susceptible to changing conditions and a number of detrimental genetic effects. This lack of diversity makes it difficult for them to adapt to environmental changes. Any cataclysmic event is likely to wipe out the entire population due to its small numbers. The more individuals in a population, the more likely the chances that *some* of them survive. It's simple odds.

Small populations lack breeding diversity, and mating occurs among closely related individuals—inbreeding.

True Tales from Across America

We know that inbreeding leads to decreased biological fitness (inbreeding depression) and decreased vigor, size, and fertility in a population. It's why we don't marry our sisters. (Go read up on the 16 generations of inbreeding among the Spanish Hapsburg dynasty that came to an end with the death of Charles II.) Obviously, any fertility issues caused by inbreeding, or other reasons, would be catastrophic to an already small population.

There are, however, examples of species that successfully inbreed. Thus, we are making assumptions about the genetics of a creature we aren't even positive exists.

Perhaps Sasquatch have evolved to breed with close relatives with no ill effects. Perhaps they are genetically immune to infertility. We could imagine that a mating pair of Sasquatch produced twins at each birth and that those twins could be a mating pair. Theoretically, no more than two Sasquatch would have to be living at any given time for the species to have the potential to continue. A population of, say, a few hundred spread over North America would be precariously close to extinction but not at all unimaginable.

That's not an active theory; it's more of a musing to demonstrate that our mainstream conclusions are often based on what we *believe* we know, and our curiosity is stifled due to a lack of creative thinking.

We mentioned previously that caribou travel over 700 miles in their migratory pattern and that a wolf was once discovered to have traversed 4,500 miles. Caribou travel in herds and wolves travel in packs, but North American mountain lions live largely solitary lives, sometimes only interacting with their own species for mating purposes. To support this "lifestyle," mountain lions can have a territorial range of nearly 800 square miles. In this way, they have survived eradication attempts that drove their numbers near extinction.

If Bigfoot was a relatively solitary creature covering wide ranges of territory and interacted with others of its species only rarely, primarily for mating, the rarity of sightings, and the fact that most encounters are with single creatures, would make a lot more sense. If, ad-

How Did We End Up Here?

Dr. Klaus Schmidt is well known for leading two digs at Göbekli Tepe in modern Turkey.

ditionally, Bigfoot possessed some of the genetic traits discussed to allow interbreeding, its overall population could be quite low.

But there are those who will not believe anything but the evidence of a captured, living specimen or, at the very least, a carcass. Does lack of that kind of evidence prove that Bigfoot does not exist?

No. The history of archaeology is full of discoveries that sat in plain sight for years before finally being acknowledged, even though there was ample circumstantial evidence of their existence. As Carl Sagan said, "The absence of evidence is not the evidence of absence."

Take, for example, the now-famous story of Göbekli Tepe and, by extension, the entire lost civilization that gave it birth.

In 1995, the Klaus Schmidt began to dig in Turkey at a place the locals called Potbelly Hill. We know it today as Göbekli Tepe; the entire complex of sophisticated buildings surrounding it is known as Taş Tepeler: The Land of Mysterious Stone Hills.

For more than a hundred years, Egyptologists had been arguing that Egypt and Sumer were the first civilizations to appear on the earth, going back some 6,000 years. Oral history and the occasional ancient discovery suggested sophisticated civilizations had existed prior to Egypt, but no one had ever excavated such a site. As a matter of fact, those who wanted to do so were denied funding because "everyone knew" it would be a waste of money. No one in the world was capable of such a giant undertaking before the Old Kingdom society that existed in the Nile River Valley on the Giza Plateau in 2589 B.C.E. If they had, it would certainly have been found by now. "Show us the proof of an earlier

True Tales from Across America

The ruins of Göbekli Tepe date back some 11,000 years, yet the stone megaliths are extremely sophisticated, comparable to stone work in ancient Egypt some 7,000 years later.

civilization who accomplished such things," they said, "and we'll believe you!"

Then, in 1995, the proof was revealed to the world. Göbekli Tepe was built 11,600 years ago! That's 7,000 years older than the Great Pyramid of Giza and thousands of years before Stonehenge was begun.

The dating is beyond question. The surrounding hillside is littered with flint tools from Neolithic times. Knives, projectile points, choppers, scrapers, and files are found virtually everywhere, and in all stages of use.

Even more intriguing, and troubling to those who believe in the traditional version of our path to civilization, is that there is absolutely no evidence of existing agriculture in the surrounding area. The temple seems to have been built, impossibly, by hunter-gatherers who had no communal support structure except for hunting teams that would fan out, kill what game they could, and bring it back to the workers.

How did a hunter-gatherer culture supply the manpower to carve and move 16-ton boulders? It must have taken hundreds, if not thousands, of laborers. What

Bigfoot Sightings

How Did We End Up Here?

motivated them? Religious temples supposedly weren't built until after the Agricultural Revolution, when settled communities found the time to develop traditions of public worship, yet here was a fully developed religious temple, built thousands of years before religion was thought to have been organized enough to even attempt such a thing. Göbekli Tepe seems to be the largest building project ever attempted by humankind up to that point in history. One day there was nothing. The next, Göbekli Tepe. It defied belief. But there it stood.

If that wasn't enough, just when it began to be expected that Göbekli Tepe was an anomaly, a whole complex of similar structures was discovered surrounding it.

And then came the most puzzling discovery of all. After Göbekli Tepe was completed—the work must have taken an immense amount of labor over an untold number of years—it was deliberately buried.

The whole complex, it would seem, had been hiding in plain sight all along, but archaeologists had ignored all the stories, rumors, and circumstantial evidence because they had refused to believe it possible.

Could the same principle apply to the existence of Bigfoot in North America? "Clovis-First" reigned supreme in the scientific community, and nothing—not the rich oral tradition, mythology, or evidence of ancient peoples going back far more than a mere 16,000 years—could change the academic mindset.

The locals in Turkey knew the truth. There were plenty of references throughout their oral history. But the experts "knew better," so the discovery went unnoticed. Could the many stories of hairy wild men of the woods be another truth that the established scientific community refuses to acknowledge?

Let's begin by examining a little of the tradition held by those who should know the Bigfoot of our continent the best, the indigenous people of North America. According to them, Sasquatch was here when they got here. They interacted with the Sasquatch and have passed down a fully developed oral tradition about them. If we really want to know what we're dealing with, perhaps we should listen to them.

True Tales from Across America

OUR FIRST TEACHER IS OUR OWN HEART

Throughout North America, Bigfoot is known by many names. We've already mentioned how "Sasquatch" comes from the Salish *Sasq'ets*, which means "hairy" or "wild" man. The Algonquin tales of the *Witiko*, or *Windigo*, certainly hint at a similar being. Their legends give him a kind of superpower. Other nations tell of a hairy wild man who warns humans to change their ways.

During the 1800s and into the early 1900s, European settlers found footprints, had occasional encounters, and even took some photographs of a creature that resembles a Sasquatch—if you think current pictures of Bigfoot are blurry and grainy, imagine trying to get the creature to stand still for twenty seconds for the exposure. Early settlers described the creature they encountered as being somewhere between a large, upright ape and a powerfully built, hairy human, standing over eight feet tall.

It's hard to believe that so many accounts, over such a span of time, are attributable simply to hysteria, overactive imaginations, or outright deception. We also must acknowledge the consistency among witness descriptions. So, assuming there is something to all this hype, just what is this thing?

When the first Europeans came to North America—at least those who arrived with and after Columbus—they followed a misguided practice that continues to the present day. They met the people who already lived there, labeled them all "Indians," and thought of them as one

True Tales from Across America

civilization, unified in their way of life and beliefs. In doing so, they minimized or ignored the diverse cultures that they encountered. The Europeans saw these original inhabitants as only savages. Their beliefs were thought to be those of a primitive and ignorant people who had not achieved the "enlightenment" of the Europeans.

The pre-Columbian population of North America was comprised of many nations, languages, beliefs, DNA ancestry, and cultural customs. They had built civilizations and constructed advanced and highly technical cities, many of which easily outclassed anything the Europeans had ever seen. They utilized far-flung trading systems that covered thousands of miles. Learning about the ancient civilizations of the Americas has shown how much more advanced they were than the invaders.

It is unjustifiably ignorant how dismissive early colonizers were of the intelligence, skills, complex cultures, and advanced civilizations of the native peoples they encountered.

> *The existence of Bigfoot was mostly taken for granted among the original North America inhabitants, but opinions vastly differed as to who or what it was.*

Were it not for the superior weaponry the Europeans had and the diseases they brought with them that decimated the native peoples who did not have the immunities the Europeans had developed, things might have been different. They might never have succeeded in wiping out entire populations and taking over what they presumptuously called the "new" world.

This is important because, when it comes to traditions about Bigfoot, a creature found in the oral history of just about every native nation, opinions about this elusive entity are many and varied. The existence of Bigfoot was mostly taken for granted among the original North America inhabitants, but opinions vastly differed as to who or what it was.

In the Northwest, Bigfoot was greatly respected but

generally seen as a physical entity who shared the resources of the planet with his neighbors. He ate, slept, and cared for family members like any other sentient being.

Nevertheless, he was special and set apart. Generally called Sasquatch, the Indian elders seemed to view him as part-animal and part-human. This gave him a special sort of position and special kind of power.

Native Americans had a respect for the Sasquatch, beings they regarded as simply wild humans.

It's not that Bigfoot was superior to the people. The Indians of the Northwest didn't think in those terms. They didn't consider humans as superior to animals, nor did they rank certain animals as better or less than others. Sasquatch was seen as an elder brother, or even teacher, because he was more adept at survival skills and instincts.

Sometimes the tribes of the Northwest referred to Bigfoot as a race of very tall Indians. They were called *tsiatko*, "wild" people, or *steta'l*, "stick" people—*ta'l* means "spear" or "stick." It was understood that they generally wandered free through the forests, living by hunting and fishing. Their homes were hollowed-out sleeping places that resembled nests. It was because these homes differed so greatly from human habitations, and because of the creatures' semi-nomadic nature, that they were characterized as "wild," which just meant wandering freely through the woods.

Bigfoot were generally nocturnal and over six feet tall. Their language consisted of a sort of a whistle, and even though people rarely saw them, their distinctive call was often heard in the distance. They had no canoes and did not travel by water.

Often, these giant wild men liked to prank the village Indians. At night, they would steal supplies and fish from their nets. They were capable of performing a kind of hypnosis, using their close-up whistles to render their victims helpless, at which point they would remove their target's clothes or tie their legs together.

They were rarely considered dangerous, so long as men did not try to hurt them. This was similar to how the native people viewed other creatures they shared habitat with, such as bears and mountain lions. These beings used similar weapons to native people and were not relegated to simply throwing rocks and sticks. Indeed, when threatened with real harm, Bigfoot could turn vicious, tracking down and killing perpetrators with an arrow from their bow.

> *In some tales, the creatures were said to steal children, carrying them off into captivity to become wives or slaves. For this reason, children were taught not to go out alone at night, or tsiatko would get them.*

In some tales, the creatures were said to steal children, carrying them off into captivity to become wives or slaves. For this reason, children were taught not to go out alone at night, or tsiatko would get them. However, these stories could have been "bogeyman"-type legends utilized to keep children from wandering from the safety of their villages.

But was it only to protect the young ones from wild animals like bears and wolves and cougars that, on warm summer nights, when shelters were left open to the breeze, children always slept in the center, surrounded by their parents and elders? Or was it so they could not be grabbed and whisked away by a marauding Sasquatch?

Conflict with the giants was avoided, and women often lived with the fear of being kidnapped—a fear that lasted their whole lives, indicating that the creatures' abductions weren't only for procreation. During the winter of 1934, for instance, a 70-year-old woman reportedly heard the whistle of a giant one morning and refused to leave her home before dawn, as had been her normal habit, to visit the nearby outhouse.

Our First Teacher Is Our Own Heart

Sometimes, according to folklore, a Sasquatch was captured or killed. The Bigfoot Field Researchers Organization (BFRO) tells the story of such a reported capture that took place around 1850:

> *In my grandfather's time, his people captured a tsiatko boy and raised it. The child slept all day, then went out nights when everyone else was asleep. In the morning, they would see where he had piled up wood, or caught fish, or brought in a deer. Finally, they told him he could go back to his people. He was gone many years and then came back once. He brought his tsiatko band with him, and the Indians could hear them whistle all around. He said he came just for a visit to see them. Then he went away for good.*

The story continues:

> *A man from Skykomish who was a little older than I am told me that he and some friends killed a tsiatko once. There were several of them but the others got away. It was in the daytime and maybe they couldn't see so well. The one they killed had a bow and arrow and was dressed in some kind of skin. Cougar, I guess.*

It's clear that the wild giants in these last tales are more like their human cousins than the ape-like creatures we might typically imagine. Their use of bow and arrows, and the wearing of animal skins, suggest they are seen as more like another tribe among the native people rather than another species.

On the western plains, the Hopi, the Sioux, the Iroquois, and the Northern Athabascans considered a being of similar description to be a supernatural spirit, whose appearance always signaled that a life lesson was forthcoming. He was a psychic messenger.

These tribes believed that the creature knew when humans were searching for him and that he chose the circumstances of every meeting. That was why he so easily

True Tales from Across America

avoided contact if he chose to do so. He was seen not as an animal or monster but as a revered relation.

The Lakota people, or western Sioux nation, called him *Chiye-tanka*. *Chiye* means "elder brother," and *tanka* means "great" or "big." When speaking English with the first Europeans, they generally used the term "the big man."

The late Peter Matthiessen was the author of *In the Spirit of Crazy Horse*, written in 1980. It became the basis for the movie *Thunderheart*, starring Val Kilmer, Graham Greene, Ted Thin Elk, and Sam Shepard. During research for his book, Matthiessen was privileged to interview a Hunkpapa Lakota named Joe Flying By, who stated the following:

Naturalist, Zen teacher, author, and two-time National Book Award winner Peter Matthiessen conducted research in which Native Americans told him about their Sasquatch encounters.

> *I think the Big Man is a kind of husband of Unk-ksa, the earth, who is wise in the way of anything with its own natural wisdom. Sometimes we say that this One is a kind of reptile from the ancient times who can take a big hairy form. I also think he can change into a coyote. Some of the people who saw him did not respect what they were seeing, and they are already gone.*

During an interview with Oglala Lakota medicine man Pete Catches, Matthiessen recorded this reverential statement:

> *There is your Big Man standing there, ever waiting, ever present, like the coming of a new day. He is both spirit and real being, but he can also glide through the forest, like a moose with big antlers, as though the trees weren't there.... I know him as my brother*

Our First Teacher Is Our Own Heart

> *... I want him to touch me, just a touch, a blessing, something I could bring home to my sons and grandchildren, that I was there, that I approached him, and he touched me.*

These descriptions may have helped inspire the idea of Bigfoot as a kind of shy, peaceful, gentle giant. This is in stark contrast to the idea that it is a creature who swipes children in the night or eats men or abducts women for sex.

Of course, the native people living in harmony with nature only to have the Europeans come along to abuse and vilify it wouldn't come as much of a shock, would it?

But, again, the native people often considered these creatures to be supernatural, similar to how they viewed the spirits of animals, rivers, or mountains to be both a part of the physical world and to exist, in some manner, beyond it.

Ray Owen is the son of a Dakota spiritual leader from Prairie Island Reservation in Minnesota. He was quoted in the *Red Wing Republican Eagle* in July 1988:

> *They exist in another dimension from us, but can appear in this dimension whenever they have a reason to. See, it's like there are many levels, many dimensions. When our time in this one is finished, we move on to the next, but the Big Man can go between. The Big Man comes from God. He's our big brother, kind of looks out for us. Two years ago, we were going downhill, really self-destructive. We needed a sign to put us back on track, and that's why the Big Man appeared.*

The same article quoted Ralph Gray Wolf, a visiting Athapaskan Indian from Alaska:

> *In our way of beliefs, they make appearances at troubled times, to help troubled Indian communities get more in tune with Mother Earth.*

True Tales from Across America

If these traditions are correct, they might explain why sightings and physical evidence are infrequent. If Bigfoot crosses over into foreign dimensions, for instance, we wouldn't expect to find many carcasses on this side of our perception fence.

There are other descriptions of creatures that we could imagine to be Sasquatch. And, in most cases, you can leave the multiverse theories to Marvel comics.

In 1836, a Comanche raiding party in Texas captured a woman named Rachel Plummer. Two years later, she was freed and published an account of her time as a Comanche prisoner, moving across the Southwest. In her book, she described encounters she had with such animals as prairie dogs, mountain sheep, elk, wolves, and bears, which were considered exotic to most of the white people back East. She also wrote about what she called a Man-Tiger:

> The Indians say they have found several of them in the mountains. They describe them as being of the feature and make of a man. They are said to walk erect, and are 8 or 9 feet high.

The famous Buffalo Bill wrote in his autobiography, *The Life of Honorable William F. Cody, Known as Buffalo Bill,* that he once received as a gift from the Pawnee Indians of the Plains a giant thigh bone from "a race of man whose size was about three times that of an ordinary man." The story told to him was that they had lived at an ancient time in history and were destroyed by a great flood.

The great Daniel Boone boasted of killing a *yahoo* in Kentucky. He described the animal as a 10-foot "hairy giant."

Even President Theodore Roosevelt used to tell his own Bigfoot story. He heard it from a "weather-beaten old mountain hunter" named Bauman and wrote about it in his book *The Wilderness Hunter.*

Two mountain trappers, he said, walked into a wild and lonely mountain drainage area in search of beaver. Their camp was destroyed by a large, bipedal animal

Bigfoot Sightings

Our First Teacher Is Our Own Heart

with "a strong, wild beast odor." Bauman's partner was killed by the "great goblin-beast," but Bauman was able to escape down out of the mountains.

Probably the most well-known supernatural stories that could be based on Sasquatch sightings and encounters are associated with the beliefs of western tribes concerning Skin-walkers. The Navajo tribe especially believed that these Skin-walkers were shape-shifters who could assume the form of any animal, allowing them to travel quickly and giving them the ability to hide in plain sight.

One gains the power to become a Skin-walker when one is initiated into what is called the Witchery Way. This initiation involves murdering a close relative, especially a sibling, or committing necrophilia and grave-robbing. Once initiated, the Skin-walkers become pure evil. Although Bigfoot is not necessarily considered to be a Skin-walker, there are many supernatural crossovers between the two traditions.

The Hopi continue the tradition of Bigfoot being a mystical, rather than just a physical, creature. Their elders believe Bigfoot appears to warn not just individuals, or even communities, but humankind in general. The creature is a messenger who appears in evil times as a warning from the Creator when human disrespect for sacred instructions upsets the harmony and balance of existence. When people lose the will to "walk in beauty," the Creator sends a warning. The "big hairy man" is just one form that the messenger can take. They claim that this is why reports of Bigfoot sightings are ever increasing, particularly over the last several decades; the Creator is upset, as well he should be, according to the Hopi elders.

Skin-walkers are shape-shifting witches from Navajo culture. They can turn into a variety of animal forms.

True Tales from Across America

A statue of a Rugaru is on display at the Audubon Zoo in New Orleans, Louisiana.

The Turtle Mountain Ojibway, in North Dakota, echo this belief. The *Rugaru*, a hairy apparition, appears when danger or psychic disruption affects the community.

Rugaru is not a native Ojibway word. The Turtle Mountain band was forced to move much farther west than most of the tribes who can still be found in the upper Midwest. *Rugaru* (also spelled *Rougarou, Roux-garoux,* and *Rougarou*) sounds as though it might be derived from *loup-garou*, the French word for werewolf. This would make sense, because French-Canadian trappers and missionaries were the first Europeans the Ojibway dealt with. Many Ojibway have French surnames, for instance, so it would make sense that the Turtle Mountain Tribe came to employ the French name for a hairy, human-like creature, while adapting the positive, even reverent attitude of their western neighbors.

The Cree of the western plains, in a similar fashion, took the name *Wendigo or Windigo* ("evil spirit") west with them when they migrated, but the mythology surrounding the mysterious creature morphed as they shared stories with their new western neighbors. This mixing of cultures might have produced an interesting variation of their belief system, which may say more about the human race and our habit of usurping, adapting, and combining legends and tradition than it does about Bigfoot itself.

The *Wendigo* is seen as a fierce, malevolent cannibal. Descriptions of humans turning into these creatures are always the result of suffering through extreme hunger and being threatened with starvation. The *Wendigo* is often associated with winter and cold and famine.

It might be that the *Wendigo* came to be the embodiment of the hidden, terrifying temptation humans sometimes have to eat other humans when no other food is to be had. He may still be an "elder brother" but a brother who represented a deep-seated fear of cannibalism. Elders would often tell stories of this frightful being, and ceremonial dances were meant to reinforce the seriousness of the *Wendigo* increasingly during times of scarcity. Thus, the appearance of *Wendigo* represented a warning to them—a reminder that a community whose members turn to eating each other is doomed much more surely than a community that simply has no food.

In this way, *Wendigo* still retains the identity of a "messenger" who comes to warn humankind of impending disaster, but at the same time he *is* the disaster.

According to one legend, *Wendigo* was once a lost hunter. Facing starvation during a brutally cold winter, his intense hunger drove him to cannibalism. Shortly after feasting on human flesh, the man transformed into a beast-like creature, destined to roam the frozen forests of Canada and Minnesota in search of people to eat, never to be satisfied. The creature was said to be gaunt to the point of emaciation. Its skin was pulled tautly over its bones, which pushed out against its skin. Its ash-gray complexion resembled death, and its eyes pushed back deep into their sockets. In other words, the *Wendigo* looked like a gaunt skeleton recently disinterred from the grave. Its body was filthy, and it gave off a bad odor—a common characteristic among Bigfoot accounts.

It doesn't sound much like the Bigfoot most of us imagine today, roaming the forests of the continent. However, it's not difficult to imagine what stories might arise from the terrified imaginations of a people who had seen a large, hairy, bipedal creature lurking in the trees or even attacking, perhaps killing, one of their tribe members.

The Wendigo is an evil spirit originating from Algonquian folklore.

True Tales from Across America

The Six Nations Confederacy, called Iroquois by Europeans, lived near, and traded extensively with, the Algonkian tribes of New England and the East Coast. Their views about a mystical Bigfoot-like creature were similar to those of the Hopi of the West. Bigfoot, they believed, was a messenger from the Creator, who came to warn humans to either change their ways or face disaster.

While Iroquois and Algonkian tribes have "Bigfoot" legends, they also have a rich history of dealings with the "little people" who are said to inhabit the Adirondack mountains. These tales exemplify how diverse native peoples believed human, or humanlike, inhabitants of the earth to be.

There is a rich folklore there consisting of sightings of little people who inhabited the mountains long before the first Indians arrived. They have strange customs, seemingly able to move into and out of our physical dimension and carefully choose who they wish to reveal themselves to. This resembles their beliefs about Bigfoot.

Washington Irving's fictional Rip Van Winkle met up with some of these little people in the Catskill Mountains, where they put him to sleep for 20 years. When he woke up, his wife and family were gone, and he had missed the entire American Revolution.

Other stories about small, mystical little people are found in many places in the world, especially Europe, with its folklore about fairies, dwarves, and, most notably, the leprechauns of Ireland.

Unlike the magical explanations of the Emerald Isle, stories in the Americas may be more easily tied to nature. Take, for instance, a story of the Kiowa of the American West.

They describe a group of young men who travel south from their Texas home into Mexico until they come to a strange jungle, where the trees are home to small, furry human-like creatures with tails. Unable to wrap their heads around such a sight, they quickly return home.

It is easy to see how monkeys could inspire legends

Bigfoot Sightings

and influence oral history, but stories about little people are told throughout North America, even in the Northeast, which is far from southern climes and monkeys.

Take, for example, the mysterious *Pukwudgie* found in Wampanoag folklore. The term means "little wild man of the woods that vanishes," and it is used to describe a human-like creature, about two to three feet tall, found from Delaware in the south, north through New England, and all the way to Prince Edward Island in Canada. They can appear or disappear at will, shape-shift, and, most frighteningly, lure people to their deaths. They use magic freely, have been known to shoot poison arrows, and create fireballs in swamps.

Most Native Americans believe that *Pukwudgies* were once friendly to humans but turned against them following countless acts of betrayal. Now they are best left alone, because to encourage them is to be subject to all sorts of cruel tricks, some that lead to disappearance and death.

One of the most frequently mentioned areas of *Pukwudgie* activity is the notorious Bridgewater Triangle, only 30 miles south of Boston. It covers about 200 square miles and is bounded by the towns of Abington, Freetown, and Rehoboth. In the middle of this area is the town of Bridgewater, home of the historic Hockomock Swamp, which was a battlefield during King Philip's War in 1675.

The first reported sightings of *Pukwudgies* in this area date back to 1760. A "sphere of fire" was reported to hover over New England at 10 A.M. on May 10,

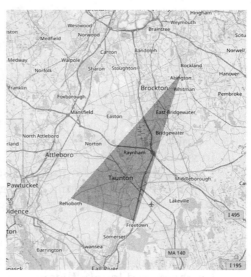

The Bridgewater Triangle is an area in southeastern Massachusetts in which reports of paranormal activities are frequent.

True Tales from Across America

1760. The light was so bright that it was reported from Bridgewater to Roxbury.

Since then, according to author and podcaster Jeff Belanger, the area has become the center for more paranormal events per square mile than any other spot in the United States: "I think per square foot we've got more weirdness here than the Bermuda Triangle could hold a candle to."

It is, undeniably, a place of great tragedy and death. King Philip's War was, per capita, the bloodiest battle in U.S. history. Between 75 and 85 percent of the natives were wiped out, and 25 percent of the colonists. That kind of history, for those who believe in the metaphysical, leaves a huge stain on the landscape, and people continue to report paranormal experiences in the triangle.

Glowing balls of colored lights move across the Hockomock Swamp and then just disappear. People report seeing what they believe to be *Pukwudgies* beckoning to them, urging them to move into the forest, presumably attempting to lure them to their death.

According to Belanger:

> *I believe there's paranormal activity that goes on here. Whether it's a vortex or not, I don't know. But I do know the reports come up again and again, and they are from credible sources. It's the past coming to the present, and that happens here, it happens everywhere.*

Not surprisingly, the area is a hotbed of Bigfoot sightings in modern times. Is this because Bigfoot is a supernatural, dimension-hopping creature? The kind that you might expect to be coming and going regularly around some sort of metaphysical vortex?

The *Pukwudgies* even have a direct link to a giant being of the area. According to native legends, Maushop was a good giant who liked people, did much of their work for them, and taught them all the things they needed in this world. He created Nantucket when he emptied the sand from his giant moccasin.

Our First Teacher Is Our Own Heart

The *Pukwudgies*, according to the tales, were envious of the relationship humans had with Maushop. They began tormenting the people, craving their devotion. Eventually, the people were exiled to different parts of North America. Since then, *Pukwudgies* have been hostile to humans. They even took their revenge by killing Maushop's five sons. Some stories say they destroyed Maushop himself.

It's not being suggested that Maushop has a direct lineage forward to Sasquatch, but the story is another that may have lent to the "idea" of Bigfoot. Conversely, glimpses of a Sasquatch among the eastern forests, or even living in some semblance of harmony with these creatures, could have led to the creations of such legends.

> *It's not being suggested that Maushop has a direct lineage forward to Sasquatch, but the story is another that may have lent to the "idea" of Bigfoot.*

Europeans entered the American Southeast in 1540. At that time, one of the most prominent tribes inhabiting the region were the Cherokee. An agricultural people, they numbered some 50,000 people and controlled almost 40,000 square miles (103,600 square kilometers) of land in the Appalachian Mountains, spilling out onto the lowlands below. The name for their Bigfoot candidate was *Tsul 'Kalu*, the "slant-eyed giants," who, they said, had inhabited the land long before the Cherokee arrived.

The history of the Cherokee people is both glorious and tragic, spanning the glory days of their dominance to the loss of many of their people to wars and diseases brought by the settlers—from their attempts to live in peace by learning the ways of the white invaders to the infamous Trail of Tears. Many Cherokees believe their ancestors were descended from the Ten Lost Tribes of Israel who, some seven centuries before the Common Era, migrated to what would become America. Although DNA samples have not confirmed this, some tribal elders maintain the tradition, confident that someday their claims will be proven. There are similarities between their traditional language and ancient Hebrew, and a few interesting customs and artifacts indicate a distinct possibility of a connection.

True Tales from Across America

In *The Appalachian Bigfoot*, Dr. Russell Jones noted that Tsul 'Kalu was thought to be able to control and read minds.

James Mooney, a self-trained anthropologist, dedicated his life to researching Native American culture, and during his many trips to the Eastern Band of the Cherokee in the late nineteenth and early twentieth centuries, he seemed to confirm the belief in this power. In 1900, for instance, he recorded a story about a widow who lived with her daughter in the old town of Känuga on Pigeon River. When the young girl became old enough to marry, the widow insisted that she should consider no man who wasn't an excellent hunter and who could care for her.

One night, a stranger appeared, wanting to court the girl. He assured the widow he was just such a man. Taking him at her word, the widow allowed the man to enter their dwelling and stay the night. Before dawn, the man said he must go back to his own place but promised to leave the carcass of a deer outside. The mother was pleased after he did this, and she and her daughter feasted on venison steaks that morning.

The act was repeated the next day, but this time the man left two deer outside. Although the widow was pleased with the offering, she mentioned to her daughter that she wished the stranger would leave some wood for their cooking fires.

At this point in the story, we begin to suspect that the stranger was a mind-reading *Tsul 'Kalu*, because the next morning, knowing their thoughts, he told the girl, "Tell your mother I have brought the wood." Sure enough, when dawn broke over the eastern skies, there were several trees lying in front of the door—roots, branches, and all.

The old woman was angry, and said, "He might have brought us some wood that we could use instead of whole trees that we can't split, to litter up the road with brush." The stranger, again knowing the thoughts of the widow, left nothing the next day.

This back-and-forth went on for some time. The

stranger visited almost every day and always left venison for the larder. Finally, the widow began to get impatient. "Your husband always leaves before daylight. Why doesn't he wait so I can see what kind of a son-in-law I have?"

When the girl told this to her husband, he said he could not let the old woman see him, because the sight would frighten her. "She wants to see you anyhow," said the girl. She began to cry, until at last he had to consent, but he warned her that her mother must not say that he looked frightful.

The next morning, he waited until daylight before preparing to leave. When the old woman saw him in full light, she saw a great giant, with long slanting eyes, lying doubled up on the floor. His head was against the rafters in the left-hand corner at the back of their house, and his toes scraped the roof in the right-hand corner by the door. She gave only one look and ran crying, *Tsul 'Kalu!*

The girl's husband was angry. He told his young wife that her mother could never see him again and that he would go back to his own country to live. With that, he left.

When the Cherokee were forced to migrate to Oklahoma along what would become known as the Trail of Tears, they apparently took some of their Bigfoot stories with them.

> *When the Cherokee were forced to migrate to Oklahoma along what would become known as the Trail of Tears, they apparently took some of their Bigfoot stories with them.*

In a July 10, 2023, blog entry entitled "Was the Tshul'gul' of Cherokee Legend a Sasquatch?" on *Texas Cryptid Hunter*, Michael Mayes posted the following story.

> *The Cherokee Nation of Oklahoma is the largest of three Cherokee branches/tribes recognized by the U.S. government. The members of the Oklahoma-based tribe are descendants of the Old Cherokee Nation who "voluntarily" relocated or who were forced to march west to Indian Territory on the Trail of*

Tears, due to increased pressure from American settlers in the East. The Oklahoma Cherokees now reside on a vast reservation that spans all (or parts of) fourteen counties. The tribe's territory includes much of the mountainous eastern border of Oklahoma, a region rich in historical Bigfoot sightings and lore. If the sasquatch is, or was, a real animal, then the Cherokee Tribe of Oklahoma should have known about it. The following excerpts from a Cherokee folktale support the idea that these Native Americans were, indeed, familiar with these creatures in the distant past.

Tsunihl'gul' (or Tsul 'Kalu) was the subject of many Cherokee tales. Cherokee elders described Tsunihl'gul' in various ways and related many stories of encounters with this being to folklorists Jack and Anna Kilpatrick. A tribesman named Asudi shared, "He was very wicked.... People didn't want to live near where he was. The older people used to say he would lean on something and that he was very tall. He used to fall over upon people and mash them. Tsul 'Kalu did a great many things and was always to be feared."

Asudi went on to share a story told to him by his father, who had learned it from his mother:

It was in the Old Cherokee country where these Tshul'gul' lived. They were very tall men.

There was a couple there who had daughters of marriageable age. These daughters had heard many times about these tall, huge Tshul'gul'. These daughters were very desirous of seeing for themselves because they had heard fantastic tales of these tall, huge men. They had heard that these men could pull up large trees with their bare hands alone. That's what they had heard, and that's what these young women desired to see.

Bigfoot Sightings

At sunset they would hear a whooping in the west. In the Old Cherokee country there is a great mountain that begins in the east and does not end until it gets to the west. When he (Tshul'gul') whooped in the west, he whooped four times in traversing that mountain. His whooping ceased when he reached the end of the mountain in the east. At sunset the next evening he began whooping at the east end of the mountain. He whooped as he traversed the mountain and ceased as he reached the west end.

When they got to the top of the mountain, everything was quiet. Then they heard him whoop right behind them, just out of sight, and they heard another noise, sounding "Daaast!" The noise was as if he was breaking sticks. Then they saw the limbs of trees shaking.

Then they saw the tall man—swaying. While he was swaying, he was knocking over the smaller trees, and that's what they were hearing. There was a large area where Tshul'gul' had flattened the trees.... The man that they saw there was whooping.

Then the young women came up and took a look at his face. They saw that he had slanting eyes, and they fled and said, "He has slanting eyes!"

In those days, Tshun'gul' were fond of women and would visit them. But when he went to a neighbor's house, if it were still light, he always turned his back away from the people who lived there. The young women would circle him and try to see his face but he would always turn in another direction.... Early in the evening the Tshun'gul' arrived. When they gave him a chair by the fire, he sat down and turned away from the fire.

... God permitted them all to live among people like us (of normal size); but they were always taking all the women and wives away from ordinary-sized men until smaller men were without women.... So God declared that this was not the place for Tshun'gul'. God decided to send them all to the west, to the end of the world, and that's where they live now. Someday they may return, and we will see them, they say.

A tribe of giants banished to the wilderness of the Pacific Northwest, perhaps—where, beyond question, the most sightings of Bigfoot occur?

The Cherokee were not the only southeastern tribe to remember Bigfoot in their oral mythology. The Creek tribe, in Georgia, who covered an even larger territory than the Cherokee, had similar legends. In 1997, a giant footprint was found along Elkins Creek in Pike County. It recalled tales of the *Altamaha-ha*, who is said to live along the many small streams and long-abandoned rice fields near the mouth of the Altamaha River. This river is where the creature gets its name. Jeffery Wells's book *Bigfoot in Georgia* records some of these stories.

There is a popular joke in America's Southeast that pokes fun at the southern accent that pervades the area. Because bluegrass and country music are so popular, people often ask if there is a difference between a violin and a fiddle. The true southerner will always reply in the affirmative. With a perfectly straight face, he will say, "A violin has strings. A fiddle's got *strangs*!"

Perhaps that is the derivation of Alabama's most famous mythical creature, known as the White Thang. Although legends go back to pre-European contact, sightings of the White Thang have been reported in a triangle marked by Morgan, Etowah, and Jefferson counties since the 1940s. He is described as white in color and very furry. He stands about 8 feet tall and glares out of the darkness with glowing red eyes. Supposedly, he can move extremely quickly, and his eerie screech sounds like the scream of a woman.

In the Bigfoot capital of Alabama—Evergreen—you

Our First Teacher Is Our Own Heart

Georgia's Altamaha River flows for 220 miles through the center of the state until it reaches the Atlantic Ocean. Surrounding it are 14,000 square miles of drainage basin, including forests, swamps, and grasslands that are perfect hideouts for the local Bigfoot.

can learn more about the creature At the annual town fair, you can even listen to Bigfoot-calling contests.

Although tales of Bigfoot and similar creatures go back deep into history, it's still easy to think of it as a modern phenomenon. But the original inhabitants of the continent have been sharing sightings for thousands of years. When attempting to settle on what kind of creature they were observing and on what our understanding of Sasquatch might be today, it's important to consider a couple things.

First, we humans have quite a penchant for exaggeration. Second, when we come across things we don't understand, we tend to imbue them with supernatural origins and powers.

For instance, by taking a clinical look at world religions, and especially their early beliefs that were later explained by science, we can see how easily our species can create, share, and accept (often en masse) some of the most outlandish stories. Even within the modern community of paranormal and unexplained mysteries, we come across people who are willing to hold fast to easily disprovable theories.

To be taken seriously, Bigfoot researchers need to strip away the folklore, magic, alien, and religious aspects of the centuries of accounts and apply critical thinking, relying on available facts and evidence. To that end, where can we see the common threads?

We can't know the origin of Sasquatch at this point, but our knowledge of animal and human migrations, our understanding of evolution, and recent advances in fields such as DNA analysis would all suggest that the creature branched off our own family tree about the

True Tales from Across America

same time as the Great Apes. This suggests that it is a primate, a cousin of ours with a mental capacity somewhere between monkeys and people.

Physically, Bigfoot falls within the bounds of that same scale. It's larger than modern man, dense like a gorilla, and covered from head to toe with a hairy coat.

Understanding if it's a creature that has survived largely undetected, or if current belief is more folklore, legend, and superstition—which that will eventually be proven as foolish as belief in the sun's sentience—is the crux of the thing. For the most part, we all have the same basic idea of what Bigfoot is, driven largely by the Patterson-Gimlin footage and subsequent blurry photos and witness accounts. Stripping supernatural connotations from the Yeti/Sasquatch/Bigfoot lore is probably sensible—at least until such extraordinary claims have extraordinary evidence to support them.

The North American Wood Ape Conservancy, whose mission is to research the existence of the unlisted primate species known as the wood ape, has an excellent section on its website regarding Bigfoot's description. The conservancy has adapted this from the writings of the late British Columbia wildlife biologist John A. Bindernagel.

Among its many other names, Bigfoot is also known as the "wood ape," an appelation given to it by biologist John A. Bindernagel.

The wood ape (a name that is interchangeable with Sasquatch and Bigfoot) resembles a human in shape but is a much larger specimen. It is massively broad chested with wide shoulders and a short, nearly nonexistent neck. Descriptions suggest a musculature difference in the trapezius (those muscles that make a cross from your upper, middle back to your neck, and across the shoulders—where they are most visible).

As opposed to the snout

Bigfoot Sightings

of a bear, the wood ape has a flat face. Its nose is wide and flat, and its chin protrudes. In comparison to a human, the wood ape has disproportionately long arms, reaching nearly to its knees.

The hair of the wood ape has been described as various shades of brown, black, red, and even white. Hair distribution is what one would expect from a great ape with a bare face and chest. Gender is often visibly discernable as the female of the species has breasts like a human woman.

The wood ape moves with graceful large strides, its arms swinging in much larger, more exaggerated arcs than those of the average person. It appears stooped, mainly due to its bent-knee gait, in which the leg never fully straightens during its stride. On occasion, the wood ape will drop to all fours and move like a chimpanzee. This behavior is most often seen in juveniles.

The description is what the bulk of the population conjures in their mind when thinking of Sasquatch. We mostly agree on what Bigfoot *should* look like. It's the proof and the intimate details that elude us.

If the continued growing interest in Bigfoot is any indication, these things may not evade us much longer.

Access to information and the speed at which we can share that information (and misinformation) certainly account for much of the growing fascination with the legend, but it would be borderline sacrilegious to write a book about Bigfoot without a nod to the four men who, for better or worse, are most directly responsible for the surge of Bigfoot interest among the few serious academics and the many amateur researchers and hunters.

Before we move further toward the current state of Bigfoot beliefs and research, let's visit these colorful, influential characters.

True Tales from Across America

THE FOUR HORSEMEN OF SASQUATCHERY

"The Four Horsemen of Sasquatchery" are René Dahinden, John Green, Grover Krantz, and Peter Byrne. All have died since they rose to fame. Dahinden, Green, and Byrne worked together on the 1960 Pacific Northwest Bigfoot expedition, led by Texas millionaire Tom Slick.

This was the beginning of the field of Bigfoot research projects, and the four men were a mixed bag of skepticism, science, and enthusiasm. They paved the way for the many organizations, television shows, books, and research papers to follow. No study of the field of Bigfoot research can be complete without an examination of their work and influence.

Four men with the common goal of proving (or disproving) the existence of Bigfoot. Four men willing to endure a lifetime of ridicule in pursuit of this quest. Four men who pretty much seemed to hate each other.

The colorful name attached to them as a group came from Peter von Puttkamer's classic 1999 documentary, *Sasquatch Odyssey: The Hunt for Bigfoot*. In recent years, they have shared the screen only once, in the television special *A Flash of Beauty: Paranormal Bigfoot*. The show is very well done, featuring beautiful music, some spectacular photography, and interviews that contrast the four men. There's the cantankerous René Dahinden, the reserved and official-looking John Green, the clinical Dr. Grover Krantz with his scientific approach, and the impeccable outdoorsman Peter Byrne.

True Tales from Across America

Of course, the show also covers some fringe characters. One woman, representing the paranormal contingent, claims that Bigfoot is "from the planet Hercules Mercury," but she is easily ignored. There's a little more of this kind of thing, but overall the documentary is well worth the time.

Let's look at the principal characters.

It's difficult to find the right word to describe Swiss-born Bigfoot researcher René Dahinden. He has been described as irascible, cantankerous, feisty, grouchy, and passionate.

He was, for all practical purposes, a full-time Sasquatch hunter and a major advocate for the controversial 1967 Patterson-Gimlin film. Many think the film is a hoax, but one wouldn't have wanted to make the mistake of saying that in front of Dahinden. He would interrupt a symposium, no matter who was presenting, if the speaker implied anything but complete acceptance of the film.

He worked only to make enough money to get by. For a while, Dahinden acted as spokesman for Kokanee beer and appeared in some hilarious commercials in Canada. In one of the most famous, he talks to the camera while a Bigfoot sneaks in behind him to steal a six pack from Dahinden's refrigerator.

For many years, his main occupation was as "mining lead" at the Vancouver Gun Club. Shotgun shells contain many small, lead pellets that fall to the ground after even a successful shot at a target. The lead shot tends to stay where it lands, polluting the ground or, in the case of waterfowl hunters, the lakes and rivers. Dahinden would move into action, scraping up flat shovelfuls of lead-pellet-laced dirt from backstops at the club. He would then sluice the dirt

René Dahinden discusses Bigfoot searches in Tracking the Sasquatch: With René Dahinden.

The Four Horsement of Sasquatchery

through a trough, just like sluicing for gold dust, thereby separating the spent pellets from the dirt. Gathering up the pellets, René could then sell them back to the club for recycling. The club produced "reloads" by filling empty shotgun shells with the old pellets that it could sell back to club members.

Dahinden only worked a few days a week, earning just enough to get by and leaving as much time free as possible to continue his quest. He could sometimes wax eloquent about folks who wasted their lives on "foolishness, like toiling for thirty years to pay a mortgage."

Dahinden was born in Switzerland in 1930 but immigrated to Canada in 1953, where he lived for the rest of his life. He became interested in the Bigfoot phenomenon shortly after arriving in Canada, and during the next few decades he conducted many field investigations and interviews throughout the Pacific Northwest.

With Don Hunter, he wrote the book *Sasquatch* in 1975. This was followed in 1993 by *Sasquatch/Bigfoot: The Search for North America's Incredible Creature*.

In the 1987 movie *Harry and the Hendersons*, David Suchet's French-Canadian Bigfoot-hunting character is based on Dahinden.

Dahinden famously talked about being employed by an Alberta farmer after he immigrated to Canada. While working, he heard a radio report about an expedition in the Himalayas, in search of the Yeti. He turned to the farmer.

"Now wouldn't that be something," he said, "to go on a hunt for that thing?"

"Hell, you don't have to go that far," answered the farmer. "They got them things in British Columbia."

So off to British Columbia he went.

Dahinden was hooked. He spent years in the bush. After more than 50 years, he still had not witnessed Bigfoot. To his credit, he never claimed he had. Certainly, it must have been tempting to justify his life's work. It speaks volumes to his credibility, in my opinion.

True Tales from Across America

One of the things he was most known for was his collection of plaster footprints casts, acquired over his lifetime. Most pictures of him show him holding at least one of these casts. "Something is making those goddamn footprints," he used to say, "and I'm going to find out what."

He finally narrowed down his expectations, resigned to never glimpse the object of his quest and intent on simply getting science to take the Sasquatch seriously. In the end, despite his dogged determination (or more properly, because of it), even his own lifelong faith seemed to waver.

While traveling the country to investigate and then encourage others to do the same, it was no surprise that he met many people who claimed to have witnessed Bigfoot, but his own experience made him skeptical about most of their encounters.

Dahinden would never admit defeat. He wouldn't have dreamed of giving his detractors the satisfaction. An author researching for a book about the Paterson-Gimlin film claimed that Dahinden once said to him, "I've spent over 40 years, and I didn't find it. I guess that's got to say something."

René Dahinden died on April 18, 2001, after a two-year cancer battle, still believing in Bigfoot's existence, even if that belief had become slightly shaken.

"If you see a Bigfoot, write down every detail you can think of. If you have a camera, get a picture. If you are carrying a gun, shoot it."

With these words, John Green very clearly comes down on one side of a hot debate among Sasquatch researchers today. There are those who, like Green, believe Bigfoot to be a bipedal primate. Grainy pictures just aren't going to convince anyone. Plaster casts of tracks won't do it either. We're going to need a body to satisfy the skeptics, and that's all there is to it. If we have a body to study, we can find out exactly what we're dealing with.

The irony of this argument is the belief that shooting Bigfoot is the only thing that will get him on the endangered species list. We have to kill it to save its life.

Others are adamantly opposed. They insist that since Bigfoot sightings are so rare, they must have very small populations, and killing even one might have devastating effects. Earlier, we floated the theory that these beings may be able to interbreed without suffering ill genetic consequences, allowing them to maintain a very small population.

Think of it in terms of the giant panda, a solitary creature living in only a handful of regions in China, which only gather to mate. Due to human expansion, the giant panda has lost about 99 percent of its range. Pandas have a very low birth rate in the wild and are notoriously difficult to breed in captivity.

In 2020, two pandas that had been housed together in a Hong Kong zoo for 10 years mated for the first time. Zoo officials stated that the couple had taken that long to figure out exactly *how* to do the deed, but others point out that pandas in the wild don't demonstrate such a lengthy learning curve. That this happened during a global pandemic, when the zoo was closed to the public, seems to support the idea that pandas are shy about doing their business in front of prying eyes. Understandable enough.

Giant pandas do not reproduce very quickly, and because of this and loss of habitat, they quickly became rare and would have gone extinct without captive breeding programs in China.

The point remains: in the wild or otherwise, pandas do not procreate very prolifically. That birthrate suffers more as the bears continue to lose habitat due to human encroachment. The loss of even one panda from the breeding pool is substantial.

And doesn't that whole description of pandas remind you of our own protagonist?

Some would agree on shooting a suspected Bigfoot with tranquilizer darts as an option, but they say it's foolish to kill something when we don't even know what it is. Besides, what if it turned out to be a guy in a gorilla suit?

John Green is seen here in an interview posted by Squatch Mafia on YouTube.

John Green, the second of the "Four Horsemen of Sasquatchery," was a well-spoken, highly respected elder of the Bigfoot research community. He was willing to talk for hours about the most mundane details. He compiled a database of more than 3,000 sightings and track reports even before the advent of the computer.

It was Green, along with Ray Wallace, who first suggested to Roger Patterson that Bluff Creek, California, might be of interest in his search for Bigfoot. When Patterson and Bob Gimlin filmed their famous encounter there on October 20, 1967, Green was one of the initial researchers to understand the footage's importance and get a screening of it to scientists at the University of British Columbia (UBC).

Green was born in Vancouver, British Columbia, Canada, in 1927. He graduated from UBC and earned his master's degree in journalism at age 20 from New York's Columbia University. He and his wife, June, bounced around Canada for a bit—Toronto, Vancouver, and Victoria—before settling in Agassiz, British Columbia, where Green became the owner and editor of the local newspaper, the *Agassiz-Harrison Advance*.

Bigfoot Sightings

The Four Horsemen of Sasquatchery

It was while operating the newspaper that John met René Dahinden in 1957. The meeting forever changed the direction of Green's life and, eventually, earned him the affectionate moniker of "Mr. Sasquatch."

Dahinden showed up in Green's office, inquiring about reports of Abominable Snowmen in the area. As Green himself learned of some of these reports—many coming from people he had known for years and who he believed to be trustworthy—his inquisitive nature and desire for answers that led him to be an investigative journalist in the first place took over. Initially a skeptic, Green became a firm believer in the existence of Bigfoot, and his skills as a writer helped bring the phenomenon to the public consciousness.

Green became particularly interested in an alleged sighting that had occurred some 13 years prior, in Ruby Creek, not far from his home. He interviewed several people with close ties to the case and found the accounts to be plausible. This was when Green started to shift from skeptic to believer. His visit to Bluff Creek cemented his belief in the Sasquatch when he saw footprints as long as his arm.

"The impact is with me to this day," Green said in 2011, recalling the experience. "Yeah, this is real."

He would go on to collaborate with the cantankerous Dahinden, interviewing witnesses together and sharing information of alleged sightings. They were both brought on to the Tom Slick expedition, though Dahinden would leave the group early. Many of the reports of his behavior in camp suggest he may have been encouraged to do so.

In 1967, the two men visited Bluff Creek and took plaster casts of suspected Bigfoot tracks. As mentioned, Green would go on to suggest that Robertson conduct some investigating at Bluff Creek which led to the famous film.

One could imagine how this might have impacted René Dahinden, who had given up or lost everything, including divorcing his wife only a couple of months prior, to follow his life's quest. It would have been dif-

True Tales from Across America

ficult for him to have been that close to seeing Bigfoot, only to have someone else—someone he no doubt considered an amateur—not only see it but capture it on film. It's been suggested that this was the beginning of the end of relationship between Green and Dahinden.

There were other issues between the two men, such as Green's statements about shooting the creature. Unlike Green, Dahinden thought the Sasquatch was more human than ape, and he found the idea of killing one appalling. Dahinden also seemed to take exception to Green's willingness to work with other researchers, many of whom Dahinden disliked. Dahinden seemed to want to keep his research close to his chest, in large part hoping it would eventually pay off in fame and fortune, while Green thought sharing and collaborating served the greater good.

Green would go on to write several books on the subject of the mysterious bipeds. His *Sasquatch: The Apes Among Us* (1978) is widely regarded as the best-written book on the subject.

John Green also authored *On the Track of the Sasquatch* (1968), which has sold more than 250,000 copies since its publication; *Year of the Sasquatch* (1970); *The Sasquatch File* (1973); *Encounters with Bigfoot* (1980); and *The Best of Sasquatch Bigfoot* (2004). Income from his books enabled Green to sell the newspaper in 1972 and dedicate more time to his research, writing, and civic interests.

For those of you who might know how much most authors make on even decent-selling books, it should be noted that Green also received an inheritance from his father—who was a longtime member of the Canadian Parliament and a Cabinet minister—and he was a successful investor and philanthropist. This may or may not have had bearing on his difference of opinion with Dahinden about "cashing in" on his work.

Green isn't a "tin-foil-hat-wearing kook." He had a passion for history, founded the Kilby Historical Society, and was a 40-year board member of the Fraser Heritage Society. His efforts led to the designation of the 1906 Kilby Historic Site, in Harrison Hills, as a designated heritage location. He was involved in local search

The Four Horsement of Sasquatchery

and rescue, the Boy Scouts, and the Lions Club. Green spent several years on the Harrison Hot Springs municipal council and, in 1963, was elected mayor of the village, serving two years.

Green was a dedicated and dogged advocate for Bigfoot research. A display at the Kilby Historic Site displays his desk and file cabinets. The drawers are opened to show his massive amount of research, index cards meticulously documenting sightings, and letters to government agencies and private donors in search of funding for Sasquatch searches. The latter is reminiscent of Andy Dufresne sending letters for funds to expand the prison library in *The Shawshank Redemption*.

Of the four "horsemen," Green may have done more to influence and encourage others to take up the mantel than any of them. He was prolific and open in his research. John Green died on May 28, 2016, at the age of 89.

Grover Krantz is featured on a Squatch Mafia video called "Dr Grover Krantz — Greatest Hits COMPLETE Bigfoot, Sasquatch, John Green, Rene Dahinden," which is available on YouTube.

As the son of devout Mormons, Grover Sanders Krantz may have been an unlikely candidate to go on to become a well-liked and respected professor of evolutionary anthropology and primatology at Washington State University, having earned his doctorate in 1971 with his dissertation titled "The Origins of Man." Even more unlikely was Krantz's fascination with cryptozoology, and particularly with Bigfoot, which fueled a lifetime of research despite heavy criticism from colleagues.

In his time, Krantz was considered the only scientist or professional to seriously consider Bigfoot. If Dahinden was the passion and Green was the mouthpiece that drove interest in the mystery of North America's hairy hominid, Krantz was the brains. And, though

True Tales from Across America

often mocked by "serious" academics, his credentials couldn't help but lend some small bit of legitimacy to the whole affair.

Krantz authored an influential paper on the emergence of humans in prehistoric Europe and the development of Indo-European languages. His professional work was diverse. He helped prove that *Ramapithecus* – an extinct genus of primate – was not ancestral to humans, as many anthropologists believed. He was the first to identify the function of the mastoid process. He was known as a specialist in all aspects of human evolution.

Beginning in 1963, Krantz began dedicating serious time and effort to Bigfoot research. He chose the "Sasquatch" moniker when discussing or writing about the creature, probably because it sounds more sophisticated and scientific than "Bigfoot." Krantz was an original skeptic of the Patterson-Gimlin film, coming to believe in Sasquatch's existence through his own studies and the "Cripplefoot" plaster casts gathered in Bossburg, Washington, in 1969 that he believed were authentic. He would later study the Patterson film more fully and, basing his opinion on the creature's gait and purported anatomy, become an advocate for the film's validity.

Krantz put great effort into having others examine the "Cripplefoot" evidence. He created biomechanical models that established that the tracks were made by an animal 8 feet tall and weighing around 800 pounds. He had primatologist John Napier and Dutch professor A. G. de Wilde examine the prints and attempted to have the FBI and Scotland Yard do the same.

Krantz never wavered in his belief. He wrote ten books in his lifetime, five of which were on Sasquatch. Like the three other "horsemen," Krantz never claimed to see a Sasquatch with his own eyes, but whenever he heard of someone encountering Bigfoot, he would jump in his 1966 Cadillac and go see what they had to say and try to make casts of footprints.

At a meeting of the International Society of Cryptozoology, Krantz attempted to formally name the creature *Gigantopithecus blacki* by referring to it as such in the paper he was presenting. As *G. blacki* was already an existing taxon, the International Commission on Zoological Nomenclature disallowed it. Further, the organization said, the creature was lacking a holotype (basically a physical sample of an organism presented when naming, as a sort of master example).

Krantz argued that his plaster casts were suitable holotypes and suggested alternative names. He attempted to publish his paper, "A Species Named from Footprints," in an academic journal, but reviewers rejected it.

In a 1990s TV interview, Krantz said the creature "is a large, massive, hairy, bipedal, higher primate. You could describe it as a gigantic man covered with hair and being rather stupid, or an oversized, upright walking gorilla." He believed the creature was descended from an ancient Asian ape called *Gigantopithecus*, which lived millions of years ago, and that the migration to North America occurred over the Bering Land Bridge when sea levels were very low.

Krantz was also, it seems, an actual genius, having been accepted into the high IQ societies of Intertel and Mensa.

Diagnosed with pancreatic cancer, Krantz arranged to have his skeleton, and that of his beloved dog, Clyde, articulated for display. His intent was to have the display serve as a testament to man's fondness for his pet and his own lifelong commitment to anthropology. According to David Hunt, a forensic and physical anthropologist who carried out the request, when discussing his wish to donate his body to science, Krantz said, "Well, I've been a teacher all my life so I might as well be one when I'm dead."

Grover Sanders Krantz died on Valentine's Day, 2002. His body was shipped to the University of Tennes-

Peter Byrne discusses his experiences in the documentary A Flash of Beauty: Bigfoot Revealed, *available on YouTube.*

see, where it was studied by scientists studying human decay rates to aid in forensic investigations. His skeleton was then shipped to the Smithsonian's National Museum of Natural History, joining the bones of his four favorite Irish Wolfhounds—Clyde, Icky, Yahoo, and Leica. In 2009, the bones of Krantz and Clylde were articulated and displayed in the museum's "Written in Bone: Forensic Files of the 17th-Century Chesapeake" exhibition.

The museum does not mention Krantz's cryptozoological research or how he was both ridiculed and revered for his efforts to apply the scientific method and his knowledge of human origin to prove the existence of Sasquatch. The description next to the display case of Krantz and his dog identifies him as an anthropologist who loved his dogs.

Maybe that's enough.

We've had the passionate researcher, the journalist spreading the story, and the academic to lend a splash of legitimacy. Who rides atop the fourth horse?

Peter Byrne was born in Dublin, Ireland, in 1925. Byrne was a Royal Air Force veteran who served with distinction in World War II. His life story reads like a mashup of 1980s action movies. If any of the four horsemen seemed both willing *and* capable of taking down a Sasquatch, it would have been Byrne. (For the record, he opposed killing the creature.)

The skeletons of Grover Krantz and his dog Clyde are on display at the Smithsonian Institute in Washington, D.C.

After the war ended, while Byrne waited for a ship home, he and a friend decided to set off on a private search for the Yeti they had heard so much about while serving in India. This would be the first scratch at what would become a lifetime itch for Peter Byrne.

The Four Horsement of Sasquatchery

Instead of returning to Ireland, Byrne got a job with a British tea company near Darjeeling. He would take two, one-month-long Yeti expeditions during his four years with the company. He would also have a fortuitous encounter that led to him becoming friends with the king of Nepal's brother and subsequently to being gifted property in the nation, on which he led big game hunts.

On the second Nepalese expedition, a friend told him of a Yeti expedition being financed by a Texan named Tom Slick. Byrne and his brother Bryan would serve as Slick's guides and continue the quest after Slick was hurt on the hunt.

During this time, Byrne was involved in the infamous case of the Yeti hand of the Pangboche Monastery. Byrne had come across the monastery and, when he told the monks that he was searching for the Yeti, was informed that they had a mummified hand of one of the creatures. According to Byrne, he asked the monk if he could buy the hand or take a sample. The monk refused.

Byrne met Slick in London and then returned to the temple, a human hand in tow and offering a large donation. During this visit, Byrne said, he was able to convince the monks to exchange one finger from the Yeti hand with a human finger from the hand Peter had brought from London. There is speculation that Byrne stole the finger and covered his deed by replacing it with the human one.

Byrne then enlisted film actor Jimmy Stewart and his wife, whom he met in Calcutta, to smuggle the finger back to the United Kingdom for analysis. It's unclear why the beloved star of such cinematic classics as *It's a Wonderful Life* and *Rear Window* got involved in all of this, but he managed to get the relic to London, hidden among his wife's more "sensitive" garments.

While Byrne would later claim the testing as inconclusive, primatologist William Charles Osman Hill of the Zoological Society of London—an associate of Slick's who had long searched for the Yeti—declared it to be of human origin upon inspection. He bequeathed the sample to the Royal College of Surgeons.

True Tales from Across America

In 1991, the television series *Unsolved Mysteries* obtained samples from the finger and determined that it was "similar" to human tissue but it could only be verified as "near human." After the broadcast, the entire hand disappeared from the monastery and supposedly was sold on the black market to a private collector.

In 2011, further analysis on samples from the hand concluded that they contained human DNA.

Slick would go on to sponsor Byrne's Bigfoot research in the Northern California town of Willow Creek. For two and a half years, Byrne used four-wheel-drive vehicles, all-terrain motorcycles, photo and video equipment, and all-weather camping gear in the heavily forested terrain. He set up headquarters and enlisted a team experienced in the rugged landscape. He called it the Great Search.

> *Byrne suggested that the Yeti was gone, as there had been no sightings or footprint finds in several years. But he said the Bigfoot mystery offered the real possibility of an extraordinary discovery, particularly with the introduction of new, high-tech equipment.*

Unfortunately, Slick died in a small plane crash in October 1962. His family no longer sponsored the project, and Byrne return to his big game hunting career in Nepal.

Another serendipitous meeting brought Byrne back to the United States, and the Great Search, over 30 years later. In 1994, Byrne led an eco-safari in the jungles of southwest Nepal for an Illinois man named David Ransburg and his family. Around the campfire, talk turned to the Yeti and, eventually, to America's version, Bigfoot.

Byrne suggested that the Yeti was gone, as there had been no sightings or footprint finds in several years. But he said the Bigfoot mystery offered the real possibility of an extraordinary discovery, particularly with the introduction of new, high-tech equipment. Not long after, Ransburg contacted Byrne and offered to sponsor a new search.

During the five years of Bigfoot Research Project 111, Byrne became convinced of the high probability of a small group of Sasquatch living in the Pacific Northwest. As with the other horsemen, Byrne would never witness Bigfoot with his own eyes. He documented hundreds of witness accounts and located several sets of footprints.

Byrne had sent hair samples to the FBI but thought he was ignored until, 40 years later, he discovered that the reply had been "lost in the mail." Those samples turned out to be deer hair, but that didn't deter Byrne.

Peter founded the nonprofit International Wildlife Conservation Society. Along with guiding big game hunts, he established a whitewater rafting business in Nepal and was an avid paddler for eight years. Of the 20 books he wrote, *The Search for Bigfoot*—an account of his research work—is widely regarded as one of the best in the field.

Peter Cyril Byrne passed peacefully on July 28, 2023, at age 97, in Tillamook, Oregon. He was the last surviving member of the Four Horsemen of Sasquatchery.

These four men, who dedicated their lives to the search for Bigfoot, brought the mystery to a wider public and inspired thousands of others to take up the hunt. They remain revered in the field.

In August 2021, Saba Aziz published an article in the *Global News* about Bigfoot sightings across Canada. The article visited the two questions at the heart of Bigfoot research: Does Bigfoot really exist? And if it does, why can't anyone get a good-quality photo or video of it?

When the article was published, it had been 54 years since the legendary California Bigfoot video. Since that time, the mysterious primate has been notoriously camera-shy. More on that later.

Research and the hunt for Bigfoot are now centered firmly in North America. Maybe people in other areas of the world are busy with more pressing matters to be bothered with the search for Bigfoot. Or maybe, as Peter Byrne thought, the creatures have died out or migrated away from those areas.

While nearly every region from the humid, southern tip of Florida, through the Midwest, and up to the northern tundra of Alaska has claims of Bigfoot or Bigfoot-like creatures roaming the woods and wilderness, the primary focus remains the Pacific Northwest.

In Canada, reported sightings have continued to grow. They have been mapped out and illustrated as Canadian Bigfoot hunters have surged, with some people devoting their whole lives to researching the phenomenon. They continue to search for physical proof, such as hair, bones, or a body. But after more than five decades, the search has yielded little more than a few blurry photos,

True Tales from Across America

a bunch of incredible stories, and the certainty, at least among believers, that proof is right around the corner.

Map projections reveal a few curious facts:

At first glance, the sightings seem to correlate with migration patterns of early humans into North America, across the proposed Bering Land Bridge. If, as most propose, Bigfoot migrated from Asia to North America during periods of low sea levels, they appear to have followed similar terrain corridors, perhaps because they depended on hunting similar migrating species of megafauna (large mammals and birds). This might explain the very early archaeological dates attached to primitive stone tools found on the West Coast and Mexico, discovered in sites with megafauna. These simple stone tools might indicate Bigfoot kills, not those of early humans or even human cousins, such as Neanderthal or Denisovan.

> *The maps indicate that Bigfoot sightings correspond with heavy human populations, concentrated on the coasts.... This might be because "more people" corresponds to "more sightings," or it might be because humans and Bigfoot prefer the same kind of environment, and humans are continuously encroaching on that environment.*

The maps indicate that Bigfoot sightings correspond with heavy human populations, concentrated on the coasts. This is somewhat surprising, due to the creatures' assumed desire to remain hidden. This might be because "more people" corresponds to "more sightings," or it might be because humans and Bigfoot prefer the same kind of environment, and humans are continuously encroaching on that environment. Of course, the coasts are typically where the mountains are. That might also explain the distribution, if Bigfoot prefers that type of terrain, as evidence suggests Yeti do in the Himalayas. One could even imagine that Bigfoot is drawn to human population centers for the same reason that common wildlife like deer, bear, and coyote are. People provide a lot of food sources through the crops and animals they raise, as well as in the amount of waste they produce.

Sighting densities might also mean that people show

O, Canada

Bigfoot sightings in Canada are more prevalent near urban areas, which makes sense if you simply consider that more people equals a likelihood of more reports.

a marked tendency to see what they want to see. Since most Bigfoot sightings take place at night, or under low-light conditions, people could have easily mistaken the evidence that seems so real to them. Under these conditions, bears, or even other humans, can look bigger, hairier, and more frightening than they really are. This is not even accounting for potential hoaxers.

Speaking of hoaxers, they would more likely perform their prank where someone would be around to observe it, rather than hoping someone would show up. That means population centers with adjacent woods and mountains, rather than places where few people ever go.

All that being said, there are differences in density between Canadian Bigfoot sightings and those in the United States. Maybe that indicates population differences or more wide-open spaces in the Canadian wilderness for Bigfoot to seek shelter from prying eyes, but here is a summation of sightings across Canada. While this is by no means exhaustive, you'll see there is no shortage.

In 1929, a Canadian government agent named J. W. Burns published an article in *Maclean's* magazine titled "Introducing B.C.'s Hairy Giants: A Collection of Strange Tales about British Columbia's Wild Men as Told by Those Who Say They Have Seen Them." It was based on various legends told by his friends in the indigenous Sts'ailes community of British Columbia. This article presented Sasquatch to the rest of Canada, and once interest was piqued, it did not wane.

Command central for Bigfoot interest is undoubtedly the town of Harrison Hot Springs. Robert Reyerse, the retired executive director of Tourism Harrison River Valley, says, "People literally come here on a pilgrimage, and more than you might think."

Harrison Hot Springs in British Columbia is near the U.S. border and close to Sasquatch Provincial Park in Kent. The town is a hot spot of Bigfoot activity.

Harrison Hot Springs is the home of the famous Sasquatch Museum, where visitors can take a Sasquatch tour with the Harrison Lake Nature Adventures or walk the Sasquatch Trail while taking selfies next to Sasquatch statues. Every June, visitors attend Sasquatch Days, which were first held in 1938 and attended by over 2,000 First Nations people from across Canada and the United States. The event features canoe races, salmon barbeque, and Sts'ailes Sasquatch dances.

"Your first thought is, these [visitors] are going to be crazy, but they're not," said Reyerse. "They're like ordinary people and some of their stories are pretty compelling."

Bonnie Kent became the manager of the Sasquatch museum after serving for 15 years as a volunteer with British Columbia Search and Rescue, where she helped locate and extract lost hikers from the surrounding mountains and forests. She was, at first, skeptical that such a creature existed. But the stories told by visitors from as far away as New Zealand changed her opinion. "My first response was that people around here used to smoke too much weed and see big hairy guys! Out

O, Canada

Todd Standing, shown here in his 2017 documentary, Discovering Bigfoot, *has said he has seen Bigfoot many times and has taken people into the wilderness to see the creature, too.*

in the bush there are a number of times when your hair stands up; there are areas that you just feel you're not supposed to be there." Now she remains open-minded.

Todd Standing, from Edmonton, Alberta, claims he encountered his first Sasquatch, a nine-foot-tall bipedal specimen with a human-like face, while hiking high in the Rocky Mountains of British Columbia. His video of the sighting, which he posted on YouTube, received more than 300,000 views and changed his life. He has been interviewed and featured on TV shows on the Discovery Channel, Netflix, and Amazon Prime and in news outlets such as CNN, BBC, and the *New York Times*.

Since then, he claims to have shown dozens of people that Bigfoot exists by guiding them to actual encounters. The Canadian TV show *Survivorman* and his own 2017 documentary, *Discovering Bigfoot*, recorded some of these encounters. As he reported to the *Global News*: "Over 80 per cent of people I take out are either having a live interaction or a sighting with the Sasquatch. The species is clearly out here and they're trying to communicate with us with the tree breaks and the signs that they leave behind."

There are, of course, those who swear *by* Todd Standing and those who swear *at* him. Some believe him to be the most credible and successful of all the Bigfoot researchers operating today. Others believe him to be an outright fraud and the ultimate hoaxer.

In 2018, Standing filed two lawsuits, one in British Columbia and the other in California, against the appropriate fish and wildlife government agencies for not recognizing Bigfoot as an indigenous species and listing them as endangered. Both times he was unsuccessful. The courts simply filed the lawsuits away as being frivolous. Standing's position was that without official recognition, anyone with a gun could start blasting away when encountering the species. He even offered to take a representative into the wild and show them a real, live Bigfoot, but he wouldn't reveal the specific locations of sightings for fear of the species being killed, as no safeguards against such violence were in place.

As of this writing, neither government has acknowledged the existence of a Sasquatch species. Standing remains insistent.

"There's just so much evidence out there. When you review the evidence, including with the DNA, it's preposterous to think they don't exist."

Belief is always "obvious" to the believer, and the evidence they present is always clear, in their eyes. We have a word for it: faith.

Having watched quite a bit of footage of Standing's recordings and listened to the arguments of both his admirers and detractors, the best that can be said is that it's all "inconclusive." For now, the jury is still out except in the minds of those who fervently believe in Standing or adamantly do not.

This still from Discovering Bigfoot *clearly shows the face of the creature, which Standing maintains is a real species in need of government protection. You can learn more about his work on the ToddStanding.com website and watch his films on YouTube at https://www.youtube.com/user/toddster45.*

Bigfoot Sightings

In his mind, there is no doubt about the species' existence, and he claims to have a hair sample to prove it. He found the sample when filming an alleged Sasquatch head during an episode of *Survivorman*. Standing claims that geneticists he has approached have either refused to acknowledge it or haven't agreed to sequence a full genome. A Thunder Bay, Ontario, lab concluded the sample was human, but Standing rejects that conclusion.

"They don't want to be the ones that have acknowledged the existence of Bigfoot," said Standing, implying a cover-up or conspiracy, but he continues to move forward. "This discovery is coming," he says.

Stories about Bigfoot are among the most popular of the Canadian First Nation mythology. The Sts'ailes Nation, also known as the Chehalis, who live in the Lower Mainland region of British Columbia, consider the creatures to be protectors of their land and thus an entity to be left alone.

The Haida, whose traditional homeland consists of the Haida Gwaii, an archipelago just off the coast of British Columbia, view them as supernatural beings to be respected. They believe the beings have lived in this territory for at least 12,500 years and are respected for their seamanship, craftsmanship, and trading skills.

Another British Columbia resident worth listening to is Leon Thompson, from the Okanagan Valley. He claims to have seen a young Bigfoot with a moose when he was only nine years old. Publicity was apparently the last thing he was thinking about. He kept his story quiet for more than 30 years because he was afraid of what people might say about him. He came forward because he saw YouTube videos of other animals interacting with each other, even though they weren't of the same species, in just the same way that "his" Bigfoot had interacted with the moose.

In his account to the *Global News*, he said, "All I can say is, it set a precedent that maybe that is what I was observing." By 2016, he was curious enough about the reactions and accounts of others to found the Bigfoot Okanagan, a group dedicated to archiving and verifying evidence of Bigfoot or Sasquatch experiences.

Since then, the closest the group has come to such verification is through finding tracks. It has no final proof such as photos or DNA samples, but it's very thorough in its investigations. The group follows a simple procedure. When it receives a report, the team reviews the observation and records on a map where the sighting took place. If it stands up to rigorous questioning, it investigates the site. It's careful to avoid any possibility of contamination. The group seems to hold a certain level of skepticism, which is necessary to have any future claims taken seriously.

Take this story, for example. Bonus: it starts with a poem!

A January 14, 2021, *Toronto Star* article by reporter John Boivin began with a holiday theme:

> 'Twas the night of Christmas
> And through the West Koot
> Not a creature was sighted
> Except maybe Bigfoot

The holiday poetry was inspired by a group of travelers who reported a Bigfoot sighting near Silverton, British Columbia, on Christmas night.

Assuming they weren't suffering from holiday excess, their encounter occurred as they were heading home on Highway 6. The people in the front of the vehicle saw what looked like a "huge, man-like figure" on the side of the road.

"I didn't see the creature myself, I saw the prints," said Erica Spink-D'Souza, who was in the back seat and missed the actual sighting. She reported that "the person on the front seat cried out 'Oh my gosh look at that!' They said it looked like a huge grizzly, or it was a large man standing up."

The figure quickly disappeared into the forest.

"We tried to turn around and look again, but it was gone," she reported.

The group drove on to their house, put their kids to bed, and returned to the scene to look for signs of the mysterious creature.

"We saw all these different tracks, and then we saw these tracks that were really alarming," recalled Spink-D'Souza. "They were bipedal tracks in a straight line into the woods … I got a little spooked, it was alarming to see such big prints. But there were no bear tracks."

They photographed the tracks and filed a report with the Bigfoot Field Research Group. Matt Moneymaker, who for a few years hosted *Finding Bigfoot* on Animal Planet, described the tracks as "un-hoax-able."

"The surrounding pristine snow proves the tracks were not fabricated by humans," he said. "The stride length is beyond the ability of a human trying to leap through knee-deep snow. The drag marks and depth of the tracks prove they are not from a leaping rabbit. The linear pattern shows that it was not a bear."

He also pointed out the improbability of someone trying to hoax random travelers on an empty stretch of road on Christmas night.

Spink-D'Souza was new to the area and wasn't sure how her story would be received, but she needn't have worried. The locals generally accepted her claim. To them, it wasn't anything new.

"Well, it's the Kootenays," she says. "I tell them what happened, and they start telling me their Bigfoot stories. People were saying, 'Oh, that's The Wanderer.' There's a Sasquatch who wanders around here. It sounds like around here people are pretty open to the possibility there is one."

The Kootenay Region of southeastern British Columbia encompasses four major

Matt Moneymaker expresses excitement for his work in Animal Planet's Finding Bigfoot.

True Tales from Across America

mountain ranges and is considered prime Sasquatch habitat. This prompted some members of an Okanagan Bigfoot group to return to the location about 10 days after the sighting. Unfortunately, after investigating the scene and examining the tracks carefully, the team put a damper on the excitement.

"They suspect the tracks are from a very large moose," said Moneymaker. "The witnesses may have seen a large female moose facing forward and mistook it for a man-like figure." Nevertheless, he didn't discount the witnesses report. "It's up in the air. In most cases I can usually say it's looking more one way than the other, but in this case I can't. I think there are moose tracks in the area, yes, but there are witnesses who said they did not see a moose." He said he'd love if someone with a drone would fly it along the trail of the purported tracks to see where they lead.

For Spink-D'Souza, the whole incident left her with a larger sense of the magic of the world. She has learned that Sasquatches are accepted by her new neighbors in West Kootenay. No convincing physical evidence has ever been found to support any claims, but true believers often do not need physical evidence. Tradition and oral history are enough proof for them.

The Bigfoot Okanagan group may not be so accepting, since it has experienced a lot of hoaxes and misinformation over the years, and many of their investigations lead to dead ends.

A camper, for instance, who was hiking in Westbank, near Kelowna, British Columbia, claimed he was chased by a Sasquatch. He abandoned all his camping gear, got into his van, and drove home to Vancouver.

Thompson and his team examined the area. At first, they were encouraged. It seemed to consist of a natural wildlife corridor that ran through a mountain range to the shore of Okanagan Lake, which they surmised would be a likely route for a Sasquatch to follow. Their investigation turned up nothing of value, and they lost contact with the witness, so they couldn't follow up further on the report.

O, Canada

Soon after that incident, a woman, along with her husband and kids, reported a sighting while visiting her parents at their old homestead. According to Thompson's report:

> *That night, the daughter and her husband said that there was all sorts of aggression shown to them as they were in the old house. Rocks and logs thrown at the house, wall-banging, loud vocalizations. When they asked the parents about it, [the parents] claimed that they believed they had a Sasquatch on the property. It appears that the aggression was due to the subjects not recognizing the husband, who had showed up for the first time on the property.*

The incident was not repeated, and nothing further could be done. According to Thompson, "I follow the evidence. If the evidence shows there is no factual basis proving that Sasquatch exists, so be it."

Thomas Steenburg, from Mission, British Columbia, studied Sasquatch sightings for almost 50 years. He said he may have had a quick glimpse of Sasquatch in March 2004.

"I saw a figure. It appeared to be walking upright, and it was jet black in color," he recalls. But that's as far as he could honestly go. He believes the only thing that will ever prove the existence of the Sasquatch is a body, a piece of the body, or sufficient skeletal remains.

Thomas Steenburg, seen here in The Sasquatch Files *available on YouTube, has been researching Bigfoot for 50 years.*

Steenburg has written four books on the subject, including *In Search of Giants: Bigfoot Sasquatch Encounters*, and has appeared as a guest speaker on the subject at events such as Alberta Culture Days, but he insists he is still a skeptic: "I accept the

True Tales from Across America

possibility that the Sasquatch may turn out to be nothing more than mythology and folklore, and that alone makes it worth looking into."

If Sasquatch is real, Steenburg subscribes to the theory that it is an unclassified primate, possibly *Gigantopithecus blacki*—the supposedly extinct ape from southern China—that could have crossed the Bering Land Bridge and remained concealed in North America's vast boreal forest. But the fact that no one has produced credible documentation of Sasquatch bothers him.

Ultimately, he believes, the burden of proof lies with DNA studies: "Science needs what science has always demanded: a body or piece of body."

Mainstream scientists will only be turned around in their skepticism if solid, irrefutable evidence can be presented.

Another key figure in Bigfoot news from British Columbia is John Zada, who traveled to small indigenous communities on the central and north coast between 2012 and 2015 to conduct in-person research with the community who knows most about it. He wrote a book in 2019 about his experience called *In the Valleys of the Noble Beyond: In Search of the Sasquatch*.

Although he didn't personally encounter a Sasquatch during his adventures, he says he remains cautiously hopeful. "I don't think it's entirely out of the question. Fields like quantum physics put forward a lot stranger and more illogical ideas than the idea that there may be a surviving primate living on the planet." He recounts numerous stories and shares his meetings with many people who claim to have encountered or glimpsed Sasquatch.

Zada shares Steenburg's opinion that the only way "mainstream science" will officially accept and categorize the Sasquatch is if a body is discovered.

If sufficient proof emerges to convince science of the animal's existence, we'll have to account for why society was so stubbornly dismissive of the reports for so long. If, however, Bigfoot turns out to be a creature of our own mental making, then we have a conundrum of perception that's just as mysterious as the Sasquatch itself. In either case, we might learn much about ourselves.

Steenberg no longer cares about proving the existence of Bigfoot to anyone else. He only does the research because "I want to know. If there is no such thing, and there never was, then I have done my part recording a great piece of western Canadian mythology and folklore."

Sewid has posted a wealth of information about the importance of the Dzoonakwa to the tribe, and the high regard with which it is held, on his Facebook group page, Sasquatch Island.

Thomas Sewid and his wife, Peggy Seaview, live in Seattle, Washington, and have undertaken numerous expeditions across British Columbia. Seaview ardently believes that proving the creature's existence would be "a pivotal moment for humanity." Although she has never had a real encounter herself, she describes her interest as pivotal in her life and feels an "ache in her stomach" when people emphatically say Bigfoot is just a legend and not real. "I know so many people who would be disrespected by their own true experience."

Sewid is a member of the Kwakwaka'wakw First Nations tribe, who call the creature Dzoonakwa. Sewid has posted a wealth of information about the importance of the Dzoonakwa to the tribe, and the high regard with which it is held, on his Facebook group page, Sasquatch Island. His goal is less to prove the creature's existence than to teach about its close connection to his people.

Has science reached into the Bigfoot legend so much that it has uprooted the magic? Has it made us all into automatic skeptics—"No body, no reality"?

The natives who know the old stories say, "If you're able to see him, hear him or see his footprints, there's some type of good fortune that's going to come your way because he's making sure that you know that he's there and that you still have to live by the rules. They live off the land, they live on the land, they are the land."

This hints to another reason that may drive belief in Bigfoot. As Thomas Steenburg writes in his books, "Sasquatch, if it exists, is a symbol that there's still wilderness out there. We haven't tamed everything."

British Columbia is Canada's "ground zero" for Sasquatch sightings, research, and belief. This is not surprising as it would, per the Bering Strait migration theory, be one of the first places that the first ancestors of the creatures reached in North America, and it provides a large expanse of remote wilderness that would serve to keep the creatures isolated from humans. Still, Canada is a vast country with a *lot* of remote wildernesses.

The Alberta Sasquatch Organization consists of Bigfoot enthusiasts who have made it their mission to chronicle the existence of Sasquatch in the province of Alberta. You can read more about them at sasquatchalberta.com. They have compiled a wealth of eyewitness sightings and reports about encounters in locations such as Banff, Jasper, Nordegg, Waterton, and Kananaskis.

Most Alberta sightings have been in the western mountains, but during a visit to Fort McMurry in 1969, near the eastern border of the province, the whole town was abuzz about a possible sighting.

About 23% of Canada's land area (7 million square kilometers or 2.7 million square miles) is considered wilderness. That's a lot of room for even a Bigfoot to hide in!

Alberta sightings go back in history to at least 1811, when a surveyor and trader for the Northwest Company named David Thompson attempted to cross the Rocky Mountains near the present-day town of Jasper. Thompson kept a journal, which was transcribed by T. C. Elliott in 1914 and

Bigfoot Sightings

published in the *Oregon Historical Quarterly*. The journal also became the basis for a book called *Narrative*, which Thompson published himself.

His entry dated January 7, 1811, records:

> *I saw the track of a large Animal. It had 4 large Toes abt 3 or 4 In long & a small nail at the end of each. The Bal of his foot sank abt 3 In deeper than his Toes—the hinder part of his foot did not mark well. The whole is about 14 In long by 8 In wide & very much resembles a large Bear's Track. It was in the Rivulet in about 6 In snow.*

Forty years later, when he published *Narrative*, he enlarged his initial entry:

> *January 7th. continuing our journey in the afternoon we came on the track of a large animal, the snow about six inches deep on the ice; I measured it; four large toes each of four inches in length, to each a short claw; the ball of the foot sunk three inches lower than the toes. the hinder part of the foot did not mark well, the length fourteen inches, by eight inches in breadth, walking from north to south, and having passed about six hours. We were in no humor to follow him; the Men and Indians would have it to be a young mammoth and I held it to be the track of a large old grizzly bear; yet the shortness of the nails, the ball of the foot, and its great size was not that of a Bear, otherwise that of a very large old Bear, his claws worn away, the Indians would not allow.*

The experience so moved him that he later commented on it again:

> *I now recur to what I have already noticed in the early part of last winter, when proceeding up the Athabasca River to cross the mountains, in company with ... Men and*

four hunters, on one of the channels of the River we came to the track of a large animal, which measured fourteen inches in length by eight inches in breadth by a tape line. As snow was about six inches in depth the track was well defined, and we could see it for a full hundred yards from us, this animal was proceeding from north to south. We did not attempt to follow it, we had not time for it, and the Hunters, eager as they are to follow and shoot every animal, made no attempt to follow this beast, for what could the balls of our fowling guns do against such an animal? Report from old times had made the head branches of this River, and the Mountains in the vicinity the abode of one, or more, very large animals, to which I never appeared to give credence; for these reports appeared to arise from that fondness for the marvelous so common to mankind: but the sight of the track of that large a beast staggered me, and I often thought of it, yet never could bring myself to believe such an animal existed, but thought it might be the track of some Monster Bear.

In these three expanded entries we discover a common occurrence among witnesses, both those who claim to have seen the physical creature and those who have seen only evidence of the creature's presence. Many people find that they cannot forget what they saw. They continue to gnaw on the bone of their experience, remembering, filling in gaps, and expanding on their initial thoughts. Are these kinds of memories reliable, or do they suggest a fertile mind seeking to make sense out of something quite remarkable but not initially understood?

Bragg Creek in southern Alberta is in an area of Canada where quite a few Bigfoot have been reported.

Bigfoot Sightings

O, Canada

Two hundred years later, Alberta is still providing reports of possible encounters. In June 2018, a man identified only as Chuck B. reported an occurrence on Highway 66 near Bragg Creek, Alberta. This account is of a less common occurrence of what seems to be an attempt by Sasquatch to communicate with humans.

> *I had decided to go out into Kananaskis country to take pictures of the setting sun behind the mountains. I had found a spot on Highway 66 where there was a pull out, so I could set up my tripod on firm [pavement]. I had gotten there earlier than I needed to so that I could prepare my equipment.*
>
> *As I was sitting in my car, waiting for the right amount of sunlight, I heard a wood knock but didn't think anything of it. (The car was turned off.) I also heard a lot of birds.*
>
> *When I heard the second knock I thought, "Ok—what is that."*
>
> *I then went to the back of my car and got out a baseball bat that I had in my vehicle. I went and did a wood knock myself, thinking "Yeah, like I'm going to get a reply."*
>
> *About 2 minutes later I got a knock, but it seemed to be a little closer. The first one was like 2 kilometers away and this one was about 1 kilometer away. I then went and hit a different tree to make it sound like I was a different one. This one was answered from even closer to me like maybe 800 meters. I thought, "Great, I will try again, but delay on doing it right away."*
>
> *I did a knock and went back to my car to get my camera just in case. Nothing happened, so I grabbed my camera and was walking across the road to see if I could see anything*

True Tales from Across America

to take a picture of whatever was there when a knock came from about 300 meters away. This was all happening on the north side of the road. I went back to my vehicle, got the bat again, and struck another tree. This time, I heard a scream-howl from the south side of the highway (the side I was on) about 2 KM's west, followed almost right away by another tree knock on the north side again about 300 meters away.

All of this happened between about 9:45 and 10:45 at night.

The Alberta Sasquatch Organization has many more such stories in its records, but these two, separated by more than 200 years, illustrate the long, rich history of Sasquatch sightings in the province. Applying our Asia-to-North-America migration theory, Alberta makes perfect sense as an area the creatures would have settled in, while others continued the expansion south and east. Indeed, a map of human migration patterns from 16,000 years ago, superimposed over a map of Bigfoot sightings in Canada and the United States, lines up amazingly well.

Believing that Bigfoot shares many traits with apes and *Homo sapiens*, and that their migration presented both humans and Sasquatch ancestors with the same geographical choices, it only makes sense that the two species would overlap territories, even if those choices were separated by thousands of years. Some individuals would continue south, while others would have been content to stay where they were, becoming the resident population discovered later by both ancient and modern peoples.

Continuing southeast through Canada brings us to the province of Saskatchewan.

I spent a week in the wilderness of northern Saskatchewan in 2022 on a whitetail hunt. Although I wasn't there to search for Sasquatch, I kept my eyes open, knowing that there had been reports in the area.

Bigfoot Sightings

O, Canada

I lost count of the number of deer I saw. I watched and listened to a red-headed woodpecker in search of a meal. A couple of ruff grouse practically sat next to me in my blind, and I was surprised at the size of the ravens that bullied some deer over a pile of grain. More than once, I caught a lynx in the headlights of the ATV.

But I didn't see a Sasquatch.

One afternoon, while deer movement was slow, I decided to do a little exploring around my hunting spot. I came across some wolf prints in the snow, which was both exciting and a little disconcerting. I would get to hear them howling later that evening. Not far beyond the wolf prints, I came across some considerably larger prints.

The snow on the ground was reasonably deep but compact. My own footprints were about four to five inches deep. The other prints were at least that deep, maybe a bit more. For the record, I weigh about 180 pounds. The prints were elongated, and at first glance, they appeared larger than my own and were spaced wider apart than I could stride. It was ... interesting.

Later, trying to sound only vaguely curious, I asked my guide about the prints, describing them as best I could. I told him of the wolf prints and where I'd come across this other set.

"Ah!" he exclaimed, as recognition hit. "The cougar."

Turns out there was a large cougar in the area that had been caught on some of their game cameras. Ryan, my guide, later went with me to investigate the tracks. As he explained what the tracks told his trained eye, it became more obvious to me that these were, indeed, just evidence of the local wildlife. Granted, the cou-

Sometimes, a footprint is just a print from a wild animal. In this case, Jim Willis found evidence of a cougar. An impressive animal, but certainly not a Bigfoot.

True Tales from Across America

gar is elusive in its own right, but it's no Bigfoot.

It became clear that the cat had moved quickly through the area where I had observed the tracks. It wasn't moving at a full run but was quick enough that the strides were significantly exaggerated. That movement also caused more severe entry and exit angles at the track, making the "foot" seem longer than it actually was. It just goes to show how easily someone can let their imagination (and hope) run away with them and introduce the potential to misidentify evidence.

Saskatchewan is the Cree word for "swift-flowing river." But don't tell Fox sports announcer Jeff Wade that.

On February 11, 2016, the Utah Jazz were playing the Dallas Mavericks. Play-by-play broadcaster Mark Followill commented that Jazz forward Trey Lyles was the first person from Saskatchewan to play in the NBA. Lyles was a 6-foot-10 rookie from the University of Kentucky. He's a tall man, as tall as many descriptions of Bigfoot. Wade wasn't likely thinking about that comparison, but it did turn his thoughts toward the legendary being. "Of course, that region's known for being home to a lot of Sasquatches. That's what it's named for," Wade said.

It was an outlandish statement, so of course it quickly made its way to Saskatchewan, where Canadians besieged Twitter, mocking Wade. Saskatchewan premier Brad Wall said that the province was as well-known for Sasquatches as Utah was for jazz. Stephano Barberis, a Canadian music video director, suggested that America must have been named after somebody named Erica. Science

Canadian athlete Trey Lyles (with ball) is a Saskatchewanian who was once compared to a Bigfoot for his height. And no, the province doesn't get its name from Sasquatch.

writer Chris Rutkowski told CTV news that Sasquatch sightings aren't common in Saskatchewan. "Sasquatch or Bigfoot are mostly associated with the Pacific Northwest," he said.

Wade loved the whole incident. "It was the greatest moment of my life ... ever."

Even though it's not *Sasquatch*-ewan, and despite Premier Wall's comment, sightings in the region seem to be increasing. On December 14, 2006, CBC News reported on sightings of a large hairy creature walking upright in both Saskatchewan and Manitoba. This appears to have sparked interest in the legendary creature. CBC radio host Tom Roberts interviewed people from the northern community of Deschambault Lake, Saskatchewan, some of whom described a recent sighting.

A woman was driving to Prince Albert when she saw what she thought must be a Bigfoot near the side of the highway, near Torch River. The afternoon skies were clear, so she got a good view. According to Roberts, "She slowed down, thinking it was maybe a bear, but she stopped and watched [it for a while] and saw it going alongside the hill and knew it was not a bear."

The woman continued driving until she was in cell phone range, then stopped to call home. She described seeing a large, "very hairy" creature that walked upright.

When men from the village drove down to the area, they found footprints, which they tracked through the snow. Along the trail they found a tuft of brown hair and took photographs of the tracks.

According to the Bigfoot Field Researchers Association, there had been only seven Bigfoot sightings in Saskatchewan up until then, mostly in the northern part of the province. Was Bigfoot on the move for some reason? Perhaps climate change was driving the creatures there from another region, in the way it is affecting many migratory animals. Or maybe continued encroachment into their habitat was pushing them to new areas. It could also have been the result of more people starting to look for Bigfoot, or that people's perceptions were being influenced by other reports they heard.

True Tales from Across America

Whatever the case, the next week, Greg East of Flin Flon, Manitoba, reported something similar. He was on a fishing trip with a friend when they encountered a creature on the Manitoba side of the Manitoba–Saskatchewan border.

"I looked over to the fellow driving the truck, a friend of mine, and said, 'What did you just see?' His response, as he looked at me with a quizzical look on his face, was 'Sasquatch?'"

East said he was afraid his friend was going to say that. "I was sort of hoping he was going to say bear. I knew it didn't look like a bear, but I wanted some verification that I hadn't actually seen what I thought I saw."

John Bindernagel (shown here in the documentary Discovering Bigfoot) *was a wildlife biologist who was definitely in the Bigfoot-is-real camp.*

They described the creature as dark in color, with dirty yellow patches over its face, chest, and abdomen. As they got closer, it ran out of sight.

When the late John Bindernagel, a wildlife biologist who believed Bigfoot exists and wrote extensively on the subject, heard about the sighting, he was intrigued and said he would like to look at photographs of the tracks because "the trail [of a Sasquatch] is different from a human, and very different from a bear."

Meanwhile, in Craven, Saskatchewan, *Global News* reporter Shawn Knox wrote in January 2014 about a video that soon became viral on YouTube. It was taken by a family who were out for a drive when they were shocked to see a "hair-covered biped" walking on a hill beside the road. They pulled over to film the creature just as it was disappearing out of sight.

The 15-second footage shows what looks like a large, hairy biped from the shoulders up. The suspected Sasquatch is walking only about 20 feet from the roadway, down the slope of a hill. The dark figure stands out starkly against the golden autumn foliage and dying yellow grass. The creature turns abruptly to its left and disappears into the brush.

We can only see the creature from the back. The film is not particularly clear—once again, Bigfoot seems to be able to affect the quality of photos and video—and we can't make out any features or see the subject's arms or legs to analyze its gait. If ever a video could be easily re-created with a halfway decent gorilla costume ...

What seems certain is that the frequency of claimed sightings in Saskatchewan is increasing.

Meanwhile, southern Manitoba is no stranger to sightings of the notoriously secretive Bigfoot. It is usually described as a large, muscular, bipedal creature, covered in black, brown, or dark red fur, standing sometimes 15 feet (4.6 meters) tall.

There's little variation to descriptions these days, regardless of where in North America the sightings take place. Usually, the only variation tends to be in the size of the Bigfoot. Does this speak to less variation in the species? Does it suggest dwindling populations and portend of eventually extinction? Is this why, according to Peter Byrne, sightings of the Yeti in the Himalayas had virtually stopped? Or does it say something about our collective consciousness and preconceptions?

Manitoba is the ancestral home to the Norway House Cree Nation, hundreds of whom believe the Bigfoot legend is real, especially after one of their own filmed one on videotape. The short clip even made in onto the entertainment news program *A Current Affair*.

Whether Bigfoot is an ape-like creature according to old legends, a real phenomenon that science has yet to explain, or simply the subject of stories told around a campfire but not to be taken seriously remains the debate. But when Bobby Clarke, a Nelson River ferry operator who operates a vehicle barge at the northern end of Lake Winnipeg, used his camcorder on April 16, 2005, to shoot a two-minute, 49-second clip of a tall, dark humanoid-like figure moving on the riverbank, many doubters quickly became believers.

Clarke's father-in-law, John Henry, was one of those. "It's not a bear or human walking around," he said. "You can tell by the features."

The video shows a figure that stands about 9 feet tall and resembles the many descriptions of the legendary Bigfoot. The video is taken with a home video camera and is subpar quality. Still, it remains compelling.

Joey Robertson was one of the many local people who descended upon Clarke's house to see the video. "A couple of my friends and cousins have seen it, and some of them first didn't believe in anything like that," he said. "When they seen the video, it convinced them."

The Clarke family quickly recognized they might have a gold mine on their hands, so they started to look for an expert who could enhance the video while seeking the best cash offer from a media agency. They were not disappointed. Offers came in from places as far away as Florida and Toronto.

Some may see the search for the highest bidder as vulgar, since they think all such evidence should be made available to help the cause and allow more collaboration. They view it as a cash grab and, without evidence, accuse the Clarke family of faking the whole thing.

Michelle Baril, a Sasquatch researcher based near Fisher Branch, Manitoba, hadn't seen the video herself but seemed confident that it was authentic. "I find that these people aren't looking for fame or fortune," she said. "They're just looking to unload this. You look at this person, and you see the sincerity in their eyes and in some cases, they're almost embarrassed to tell you. I have a general idea of who's telling the truth and who's not. For the most part, if anybody's going to open themselves up to being heckled and ridiculed, I really don't think they're going to come up with some kind of tale."

Linda Queskekapow, a neighbor of the Clarkes, assured folks that if Norway House is home to the legendary Bigfoot, there's nothing to be worried about. "Sasquatch is not harmful," she said after she saw the video.

O, Canada

"I think it's scared of people."

Meanwhile, the Bigfoot Field Researchers Organization has issued other reports from western Manitoba. Bigfoot sightings have been reported near Brandon, Kenton, Rivers, and Rossburn.

On July 29, 2010, an unnamed Brandon man went to check his mailbox and decided to take a back road home. Noticing strange tracks on the road, he got out of his truck and was surprised to find footprints that measured larger than any human foot, displaying a seven-foot stride. They appeared to emerge from a field, walk along the edge of the road for nearly a mile, and then return to the same field.

The Kenton sighting took place in 2000, about 40 miles (72 kilometers) northwest of Brandon, near Highway 21. A farmer was checking to see why his cattle were acting strange. As he rode his tractor near his uncle's farm, he thought he saw his uncle walking on the road away from him. As he got closer, the figure turned toward him and walked across the road. Moments later, the farmer's uncle appeared. It was only then that he realized he was looking at a creature that was at least eight feet tall, walking with a gait that wasn't at all human.

> *On July 29, 2010, an unnamed Brandon man went to check his mailbox and decided to take a back road home. Noticing strange tracks on the road, he got out of his truck and was surprised to find footprints that measured larger than any human foot, displaying a seven-foot stride.*

Rivers is about 25 miles (41 kilometers) northwest of Brandon. Yet another unnamed witness saw a Bigfoot-like creature walking across a grain field in August 1996. He was returning home one evening after dusk when he saw a shape in the ditch on the west side of the highway. He stopped to check if it was a horse from a nearby farm, but instead he saw an upright creature that was covered in dark brown hair quickly walking away.

To round out this quartet of sightings, moving northwest again, this time about 90 miles, we come to Ross-

True Tales from Across America

burn. A suspected Sasquatch was seen in the mid-1960s by a group of people picking saskatoon berries behind their garden. The witnesses claimed the creature made a second appearance shortly after the initial sighting.

On social media, sightings have also been reported anonymously in the Manitoba communities of McCreary and Killarney. Does that discredit them, or add to their credibility? On the one hand, why would a person claim a sighting and not want anyone to know about it, if they were only interested in gaining a few minutes of attention? On the other, why would they report it at all unless they genuinely wanted the public to know about their experience?

Peterborough, Ontario, is the home of Trent University, a public liberal arts university with a reputation for small class sizes and excellent educational opportunities. It is also the home of the Trent University Sasquatch Society (TUSS), whose president is Ryan Willis.

Willis is the host of *Sasquatch University*, a television show that premiered on the Wild TV network in 2023. Now in its second season, the show aims to prove the existence of Bigfoot in Ontario, though they look for witnesses and evidence all over Canada.

According to Willis, "Our goal is to educate the public about Sasquatch/Bigfoot and to spread discussion about Sasquatch in the academic setting. It is a very under-researched field, considering the number of sightings and evidence. We want to inspire University students to create their own organizations, as well as prove the existence of the creature known as Bigfoot."

TUSS believes Bigfoot is more than mythology. Like Grover Krantz before them, they believe it is an elusive creature that deserves academic study.

Willis's interest in all things Sasquatch began when he was about 11 years old. It was television that captured his attention, so it is only natural that he now uses television to continue his passion. "I was watching Animal Planet one night and I stumbled across the show *Finding Bigfoot*, which aired for a while. Then, as I got older, I would just research the subject all the time and go into the woods when I could."

Bigfoot Sightings

O, Canada

About 200 members strong, TUSS is the biggest Bigfoot research group in Canada. It was also the first. As such, Bigfoot researchers from all over the world are in constant contact with them. Its primary goal is to educate students about Sasquatch. Although the group is used to facing ridicule, it hasn't dampened its enthusiasm.

"We take it very seriously," Willis said. "We speak with a lot of academics and a lot of scientists. I think a lot of people don't know how many scientists and PhDs are doing work on this and are very involved in the subject."

Trent University in Peterborough, Ontario, is home base for the Trent University Sasquatch Society.

A television show can command more resources and reach more people than your average Bigfoot researcher. It has the best available equipment for filming and should, if a team encounters a Sasquatch, be able to produce high-quality video as opposed to the shaky, grainy films we normally see. The popularity of *Sasquatch University* gives the team the opportunity to travel extensively throughout Canada in pursuit of the legendary creature.

Their long-term plan is to employ state-of-the-art technology and more traditional techniques involving tree knocking and howling. "We want to try using drones and certain game cameras and different things like that," Willis says.

He is the first to admit that even though the research can be fun, it can also get a little frightening from time to time. Not only must they constantly think about encountering a Bigfoot, but they also face wild Ontario's mix of everything from bears to porcupines.

"We just try to focus on the task at hand and not get too freaked out, but there are some times where it does get pretty freaky out there. It's cold and dark, and that does kind of get to you a bit ... but it's all worth it, to us, for sure."

On my first and only trip into real Québec wilderness, I first flew into Schefferville. The only way to get there is by railroad or plane. There are no roads that go there. One would think that would imply wilderness, but it's not even close. From the small airport, five of us loaded our gear into a small float plane and headed another 500 miles north, landing on the beach of one of the thousands of unnamed lakes that dot the wilderness of northern Québec.

> *What if Sasquatch hibernated in the winter, like bears? That would make things easier for it. If a species needed solitude, here was a great place for it.*

I had flirted with wilderness before, but nothing like this. At the time, I wasn't thinking about Sasquatch. My mind was centered on caribou. But on my first solo excursion into real wilderness, I couldn't help but think that if a previously undiscovered primate were to exist anywhere on earth, this would be the perfect habitat for it. The snow piled up to great heights. There was evidence of 10- or 12-foot levels in the trees, but it was no worse than the kind of environment the Yeti faces in the Himalayas, and the altitude wasn't nearly as much of an issue.

What if Sasquatch hibernated in the winter, like bears? That would make things easier for it. If a species needed solitude, here was a great place for it. There was plenty of wildlife available for food, including the twice-a-year caribou migration. Fish and berries were plentiful, as well as various birds and small game animals.

All in all, I decided as I clutched my rifle a little closer, this was really *good* Sasquatch territory. From the number of sightings in similar areas, Bigfoot might agree with me.

Take, for example, Nunavik, which is a large Arctic area administered by the Kativik Regional Government, lying in the Nord-du-Québec region. That's a vast ex-

O, Canada

panse of land in northern Québec, bordering Hudson Bay, due west of Greenland. It is the traditional homeland of the Inuit of Québec.

Nunavik is served by the *Nunatsiaq News*, a weekly newspaper in operation since 1973. In 2014, it reported the findings of British scientist Bryan Sykes. He published some interesting work about the possibility of Bigfoot being an actual reclusive primate who might exist in northern Québec and other places with a similar habitat. Sykes's work probably should have discouraged Sasquatch enthusiasts. Instead, it had quite the opposite effect.

Dr. Bryan Clifford Sykes, who died in 2020, might be a strange choice of candidate to examine Bigfoot sightings. He was a British geneticist and science writer who was a fellow of Wolfson College and emeritus professor of human genetics at the University of Oxford.

He made his reputation studying the DNA of an alpine iceman. He then chose to publicly take on the popular Thor Heyerdahl, whose theory about the peopling of Polynesia captured public attention after he published his book *Kon Tiki*. The book detailed his 1947 voyage of some 4,300 miles across the Pacific on a balsa wood raft, proving that it was possible that the Polynesian islands were populated from South America. Sykes argued against this theory, based on DNA evidence. Most scientists today dismiss Heyerdahl's theory.

If that wasn't enough, Sykes then went on to analyze hair samples said to come from Yetis and Sasquatches, but which he instead proved came from bears, pigs, and people. To Bigfoot researchers, this was a big disappointment, but it didn't keep Sykes from being named cryptozoologist of the year in 2013.

Patterns of Cuticle

Imbricate (Human)
• Flattened-like

Spinous (Animal)
• Petal-like

Analysis of the cuticles of hair samples can quickly reveal whether the hair is human or animal in origin.

Coronal (Animal)
• Crown-like

True Tales from Across America

His public reputation was enhanced after the success of his book *The Seven Daughters of Eve*. In it, he provided a popular, captivating story of human ancestry, tracing all of us now living back to seven ancestral women. He even gave them all names. It sold so well that his newfound wealth provided funds for a second home in Edinburgh and a blue Mercedes convertible with the license plate D7 EVE. For a geneticist, this was heady fame indeed!

Although Sykes disproved that certain hair samples were Sasquatch in origin, he took people seriously about their interest in proving Bigfoot was real.

He was so inspired after tapping into a new niche that he left academia behind and became a TV personality and author of general-interest science books. Remember, at this time, most people had never even heard the term "DNA sequencing." He was such a good writer that he was able to distill complex scientific principles into everyday language. That led to the British TV show *Bigfoot Files*, a three-part series that captivated audiences in 2013. During this show, he assessed claims about hair and skin samples sent to him by cryptozoologists who were looking for everything from the Loch Ness Monster to the Abominable Snowman.

What gave Bigfoot researchers hope, even while he was debunking hair samples, was his attitude. Instead of ridiculing those who sent him samples, he remained objective.

"Rather than persisting in the view that they have been 'rejected by science,' advocates in the cryptozoology community have more work to do," he said.

It was an encouraging statement that won him hundreds of new fans among a section of the public that is often at odds with the scientific establishment. He even gave them a new avenue of research.

"I have always been interested to know what happened to the Neanderthals.... Whether they just disappeared or whether, as some people who believe in yetis and Bigfoot think, reports of these strange creatures are actually surviving pockets of Neanderthals or other early humans. In other words, I haven't proved that these animals don't exist. All I have done is shown that of the historically famous samples given to me, none turned out to be from another type of human."

Thus it was that while closing the door on one branch of research, he opened another. The people of Nunavik were encouraged. One of them was Maggie Cruikshank Qingalik, who is from Akulivik. She produced pictures of a footprint left by a creature she saw while picking berries with a friend. At first, she thought it was someone else picking in the same area she was, but then she noticed the being was covered in long, dark hair. The footprints measured 15 inches (40 centimeters) in length. The women watched as it walked upright along the side of a hill, taking long strides. Sometimes it would stoop over and crawl.

"We weren't sure what it was first," she reported. "It is not a human being, it was really tall, and kept coming towards our direction and we could tell it was not a human."

It didn't appear to be vicious or threatening in any way. As a matter of fact, it wasn't interested in them at all. Nevertheless, the women were frightened, mounted their ATV, and headed back to the community to warn people about what they saw.

The sighting was exciting at first but began to draw skeptical replies later, because she claimed to have caught the whole incident on video, but refused to show it to anyone.

"Many people want to see the video and are starting to make negative comments," Qingalik said. "We want to post it, but we don't want to scare the children."

Meanwhile, other sightings were reported in the area. A young boy from the village saw an animal moving far away that he thought was a Sasquatch. Campers heard an animal hollering and assumed it to be Bigfoot.

True Tales from Across America

"They are used to hearing wolves," said Qingalik, "so they know what they are hearing. Some people were trying to convince me it was a grizzly bear, because those grizzlies stand up, but they don't have long arms like Bigfoot. You can tell if an animal is like human or animal. Bigfoot has two legs and arms and a head like a person, and a bear has four legs and a big bum and a very little head."

She says other people from the village have reported sightings to friends, but no one else. She claims others have seen the creature but just keep quiet. "They don't report because of the nonbelievers," says Qingalik. "I mean those skeptics. We live in a small town."

Loren Coleman is the director of the International Cryptozoology Museum in Portland, Maine. He has studied Sasquatch and Bigfoot sightings in North America for more than 50 years. When Qingalik's experience was related to him, he said, "It sounds like a traditional kind of sighting. I think the only thing I would wonder about would be the height of 10 feet with a footprint as large as you said. But that happens. People exaggerate."

According to Coleman, Bigfoot tend to be six and a half to eight feet tall, though reports have varied. He said they have been spotted throughout the United States and Canada since the 1800s. Since the region has become more populated, the sightings have been relegated to the wilderness. He hopes more people will take accurate measurements and good photographs. "If someone could go back there and take some plaster casts, that might be quite helpful in terms of comparing it to the database of other footprints in Canada," he said.

He believes Bigfoot may hole up in caves to protect themselves from the elements. They may sustain themselves on a diet like that of caribou. However, he said, omnivores are opportunistic and could eat a range of food, including salmon or roadkill. He admits to being skeptical when he first investigates a sighting, wanting to make sure it is not just a common animal, or people trying to make a buck.

In August 2013, CBC News reported that a hunter from the Cree village of Wemindji in northern Québec, located on the eastern shore of James Bay, sighted a Bigfoot and has photographs to prove it.

Melvin Georgekish said he saw two Bigfoot while driving his pickup truck along a road in a wooded area near his town. He first saw two sets of red eyes staring at him from the forest. After a restless night, he set out to investigate the next day and found footprints in the moss.

According to Cree legends, Bigfoot are protectors of their people.

"I was thinking and thinking, and there's no animal that has red eyes over here," Georgekish said. "I am a hunter, and I've never seen something like that. In the footprint, you can see the toes. It's like a human foot, but way bigger than a human foot. Wider, too."

According to legends, Bigfoot are protectors of the Crees. There have been many stories of sightings, but not much proof to date.

Georgekish's photographs caused quite a stir. "There's definitely a buzz in town," he said at the time. "There are people of the opinion who say that if I don't see it, I don't believe it."

Other reports have come into the Sasquatch Canada organization, including a detailed one from a resident raking his lawn in February 2013.

> *It all began when early one spring I was out raking the grass in my yard. My lot is over an acre, and I save myself the grueling task of cleaning it up after a winter by raking the grass that is exposed as it melts. This makes things easy for me as I only have to do a few feet a day as the snow recedes.*
>
> *For the most part, most of my yard is inaccessible throughout the winter because the snow*

> is very deep. So ... I'm raking and I get to a large pine tree and as I get under it I notice that the snow has been disturbed and then I see just one big clear handprint under the canopy of the tree ... like someone had been hiding under the branches when they were all weighted down by the snow. It makes kind of a shelter. I was completely freaked out, measured the handprint, which was overall about 13 inches by 13 inches. I took photos but not being a professional and using my crappy little camera, the detail was not as clear in the photo as it was in person. The detail in the print was quite something. It was not just a flat print. You could see the texture in the palm like where the thumb muscle came down and what looked like calluses at the point where the fingers connect to the hand. You can see in the photo my size eleven boot print to the left of it for scale.

The report continues, revealing exacting details that sound authentic, providing much more detail than necessary if the witness was simply making up a story. He went so far as to talk about "unidentified piles of poop often near the apple tree."

The witness continued:

> I was out in the front of my house around 10 or 11 pm, having a cigar and enjoying the quiet before heading up to bed when I heard something that drew my attention to my neighbor's yard across the street. There was a sound like someone quietly muttering to themselves and the tone, for lack of better comparison, sounded a little like Marge Simpson. I know that sounds funny but I'm serious. After all this time, that's the closest comparison I can give you. It was gruff but feminine sounding in pitch and quiet ... then I saw it.

He went on to describe a creature with long and glossy hair, comparing it to the Cousin Itt character from *The*

Addams Family TV show. It was about 7 to 8 feet tall, with no distinguishable neck, a shoulder the size of a human hip, and overall very muscular looking.

He ran inside for a camera and began shooting flash photos blindly into the adjacent woods. He wasn't able to catch the creature on film, and he never saw it again.

As of this writing, the whole northern part of Québec still seems to be a hotbed of Bigfoot activity, but until more definitive information flows in, all we can do is wait and see.

The story of Sasquatch sightings in Newfoundland and Labrador is a complicated one. On the one hand, sightings are few and far between. On the other, the very first North American sighting might have taken place right here.

> *As of this writing, the whole northern part of Québec still seems to be a hotbed of Bigfoot activity, but until more definitive information flows in, all we can do is wait and see.*

Human habitation in the area goes back at least 9,000 years, beginning with what is now called the Maritime Archaic people. Over the years, they were gradually replaced by the Dorset culture, and then by the Inuit in Labrador and the Beothuk in Newfoundland.

A little more than a thousand years ago, the Vikings settled in Newfoundland, on the tip of the Great Northern Peninsula. They built a village called L'Anse aux Meadows, which has been excavated and is now an official UNESCO World Heritage Site. The area was inhabited first by the Beothuk, which the Norsemen called *Skrælings*, and later by the Mi'kmaq.

When the Vikings first landed in North America, they were led by Leif Erikson, or Leif the Lucky. He was the son of Erik the Red. Many of Leif's records are still intact, and they tell of him and his crew seeing "huge hairy men" who lived in the woods and had both a "rank odor" and a "deafening shriek."

When Leif says they were "huge," keep in mind that the Vikings were called Berserkers by those unfortunate

Recreation of a Viking settlement in Newfoundland similar to what L'Anse aux Meadows would have looked like. The early Vikings had stories of "huge hairy men" they encountered in this new land.

enough to be on the receiving end of some of their European "business trips." They were big, powerful men. If they sighted "huge hairy men," those "men" must have been very big, indeed. They had several run-ins with them before leaving the island. These reports contain the first European sightings of what might have been Sasquatch.

The indigenous North Americans, of course, had been familiar with Bigfoot for thousands of years, just as the locals who inhabited the Himalayas were familiar with Yeti before European contact. But in keeping with what is now called the Eurocentric historical perspective, these were the first sightings to reach Europe.

If the first Europeans to reach the shores of North America encountered Sasquatch, it's strange that sightings since then have been relatively rare. Author David J. Puglia made it his business to investigate why.

In *North American Monsters: A Contemporary Legend Casebook*, Puglia wrote the entry "Sasquatch-Like Creatures in Newfoundland: A Study in the Problems of Belief, Perception, and Reportage." He examined the work of Michael Taft, later the head of the Archive of Folk Culture at the American Folklife Center, who "set out to investigate the dearth of Sasquatch findings in Newfoundland. While this essay would mark the beginning and end of his career as a monster researcher, his Sasquatch studies would follow him to the day of his retirement, when colleagues filled his vacant seat with a Sasquatch yard ornament."

As it turns out, Taft was a bit of a maverick. "Why would a folklorist, in a region renowned for its fabled supernatural and cryptozoological beings and peopled with talented raconteurs eager to spin wondrous yarns, choose to study a monster not reported to exist in Newfoundland?"

Academics can be a strange lot, driven to pursue things that, for whatever reason, strike their fancy. Taft had been working in the Memorial University of Newfoundland Folklore and Language Archive, so he was familiar with strange sightings submitted to the archive. He noticed that many accounts were not reported as Sasquatch, despite presenting all the necessary criteria that, in other areas, would constitute Bigfoot sightings.

As a result of further research, he concluded that he could neither confirm nor deny the existence of Sasquatch in Newfoundland or that Newfoundlanders had sighted Sasquatch. But he did respect the typical Newfoundlanders' ability to report what they saw in accordance with their traditional cultural experience. In doing so, he raised an issue that resonated across North America. Simply stated, it was this: When a person reports a Bigfoot, is it because he or she is culturally trained to see one? In other words, do they see what they expect to see?

Taft concluded that because Newfoundlanders had no cultural tradition of Sasquatch, they tended to describe the creature as something more familiar to them. As a result, the 77 known sightings of Sasquatch-like creatures in Newfoundland were reported as being "wild Indians"; ghostly "treasure guards"; the bogeyman; local fauna, such as bears; or even exotic wildlife, such as gorillas.

Taft believed that people see what they have been culturally attuned to see. If they live with bears, they are more likely to mistake a hairy monster for a bear than to mistake a bear for a hairy monster. That would reduce the number of reported Sasquatch sightings. This also speaks to the earlier assertion that the commonality in recent Bigfoot sightings is largely due to the expectation of what Bigfoot would look like.

Since Europeans started to explore Newfoundland, Sasquatch sightings have increased. Europeans have a rich history of exotic, monster-like folklore creatures. It would be no surprise for them to be open to tales of unusual, even supernatural, beings that they had no previous knowledge of. After all, why wouldn't this new land harbor monsters as different from those of their native lands, as the landscape and habitat in this "New World" were different from what they were used to?

Among the many myths coming from the Newfoundland area during the time of Norse settlers is that of the sciapod, a dwarf-size humanoid with one leg and one foot.

Consider the following examples:

- Somewhere around the year 1000, a Norse sailor was supposedly killed by an arrow from a sciapod, which is described as a hopping one-footed humanoid.
- In 1610, sailors and dock workers in the Newfoundland port of St. John's reported a malevolent, frightening-looking mermaid.
- The traditional culture of Newfoundland somewhat crosses over to European folklore. Fairies, devils, ghosts, jack-o'-lanterns, spirits, mermaids, witches, magicians, wraiths, and other human, part-human, or human-like creatures abound. For example, fairies are described as "little people" or "the good people" to distinguish them from other perceived phenomena.

Folklorists love this kind of stuff. It tends to discourage Bigfoot researchers, however, who consider it be-

O, Canada

side the point and academic double-speak. It means that when confronted with a fairy, ghost, or devil, the Newfoundlander recognizes it as such, because that's what they are culturally trained to do. Others from outside that tradition, however, might see something different. Like a Bigfoot.

Periodically, we've mentioned the Bigfoot Field Research Organization (BFRO). It offers perhaps the most compressive database of Bigfoot sightings in North America. If you go to its website, you will discover a wealth of information, which assigns a classification to every reputable, reported sighting, depending on such factors as reliability of the witness, weather conditions, and the potential for misinterpretation.

Class A reports, for instance, involve clear sightings in circumstances where misinterpretation or misidentification of other animals can be ruled out with greater confidence.

Class B incidents indicate where a possible Sasquatch was observed at a great distance or in poor lighting conditions and otherwise obstructed views. They also include "sound-only" cases.

Class C reports represent second-hand or third-hand reports. These are the most difficult to judge. (See page 214 for more details on these classifications.)

Since 1983, there have been only eight sightings listed with the BFRO that occurred in New Brunswick:

- August 2021 (Class B): Likely road crossing sighting of a Sasquatch 20 miles southeast of Moncton, New Brunswick, Canada
- June 2006 (Class A): Motorists observe creature along the Trans-Canada Highway

Such evidence as well-documented footprints are considered to fall under Class A Bigfoot reports.

True Tales from Across America

- July 2002 (Class A): Daytime sighting by a motorist close to the Maine/New Brunswick border
- Summer 1997 (Class A): Extended daylight sighting from a tower at Kelly's Bog in Kouchibouguac National Park
- April 1997 (Class A): Ape-like figure seen running through the woods
- October 1994 (Class B): Hunters notice tracks resembling those of a barefoot child in the mud of a remote logging road
- August 1990 (Class A): A loud, screaming, brush-crashing creature frightens a group of U.S. and Canadian soldiers
- 1983 (Class A): Sighting by campers

A typical report looks something like this:

> *NEAREST TOWN: Sackville*
> *NEAREST ROAD: Walker Road*
> *TIME AND CONDITIONS: Apprx 8:45 am*
> *Sunny, around 20C (68F), 7.6 kph (4.7 mph) SW, 98% humidity*
>
> *OBSERVED: I was driving our truck and following Scott (my husband) driving his tractor out of what has become known as the "tower road." We turned onto Walker Road heading NE towards Highway #2.*
>
> *It was a nice sunny morning and we were both wearing short-sleeved t-shirts. As we approached the first of two crests, I watched a "man" casually walk across the dirt road in the distance heading in a southerly direction. Both sides of the road are forested. It took "him" about 4 or 5 steps to get across the road, which is about 10 meters (35 feet) wide.*
>
> *I thought to myself: "This guy is huge." My first thought was that it was a Bigfoot, but I*

never heard of any Bigfoot sightings in New Brunswick, so I dismissed the thought.

This "guy" was at least 2 meters (7 feet) tall and appeared to be wearing heavy winter clothing. The only thing I could see was "his" silhouette; no colors. "He" looked like he was wearing a toque with ear flaps that went to "his" shoulders; somewhat similar to an aviator or trapper hat where the forehead portion was flat. "He" also appeared to be wearing a heavy winter jacket that went to "his" knees. The sleeves or "his" arms were long and almost reached "his" knees.

About 3 steps in, "he" turned around and faced the road to watch Scott drive by. "He" didn't seem to twist at the waist but instead moved "his" legs to turn "his" body. After Scott drove by, "he" again used his legs to turn around and 2 steps later, "he" was gone. By the time I got to "his" location, I looked in and couldn't see anything. There is a steep downhill bank, and I didn't stop; I kept driving.

After we got home, I asked Scott if he saw that huge guy that walked across the road in front of him. He said no, he was looking in the woods to his right. I said, "How could you miss him; he was huge!"

Scanning through the TV a few nights later, I came across an episode of Expedition Bigfoot and watched it. I learned that Bigfoot has next to nothing for a neck. I then decided to search for Bigfoot sightings in New Brunswick and was surprised to find several sightings.

Sightings in Canada tend to thin out on the East Coast. But they are there, even though their numbers are small. This may be due to climate, human population density, or the overall direction of the migration pattern of the species if it did move from the Bering Land Bridge in a generally southeastern direction.

These are the kinds of things that the BFRO is attempting to analyze in a data-driven, scientifically sanctioned manner. It will be interesting to follow their progress in years to come. If Bigfoot research ever becomes mainstream and accepted, it will be because of organizations such as this who are putting in the effort now.

The provinces of Prince Edward Island and Nova Scotia are lumped together mainly due to the lack of credible sightings. They are so few that I was tempted to simply write, "nothing to report." But then I came across a video from Prince Edward Island that purported to capture the creature on film.

The books of eloquent Canadian author Farley Mowat helped open the hearts, minds, and wallets of people around the world who caught his vision of the natural world of Nova Scotia and sought to protect it. Eclipsing his work in popularizing the area is the success of the show *The Curse of Oak Island*, which enhances the coffers of local residents due to the influx of tourists who want to see firsthand what is going on in the fabled "Money Pit" of Oak Island. Beyond money, however, the work of the brothers Marty and Rick Lagina and their teammates is, quite literally, rewriting the history of North America.

The late, award-winning Canadian author Farley Mowat championed environmental causes and the beauty of Nova Scotia.

As for Prince Edward Island, it is probably best known as being the locale where the novel *Anne of Green Gables* takes place. When it was published in 1908, many readers were not even aware that Prince Edward Island was a real place.

It is the smallest Canadian province in terms of land area and population, but it is the most densely populated. It is considered the traditional home to the Mi'kmaq Indians, who, to this day, continue a rich oral history, including stories about Sasquatch. The Mi'kmaq spread throughout the Canadian Maritimes and Northeastern Woodlands down into Maine, where there is also an old tradition of Bigfoot sightings.

These traditions caution folks to be careful when it comes to Sasquatch. They describe Bigfoot as a gigantic humanoid with an unending appetite for human flesh. Its heart is made of ice in the shape of a human figure, and it is a creature feared with a deep, primal dread.

Its Mi'kmaq name is *Chenoo*. The females are stronger and more dangerous than the males. This means the males can sometimes be reasoned with by those who are clever enough to befriend one. But they are cannibalistic and associated with witchcraft.

Chenoo are said to have a loud and horrible shriek, a common trait associated with Bigfoot or Sasquatch. According to the Mi'kmaq, those who hear it die instantly. The species creates its own camouflage by rubbing its body with pine resin before rolling around on the ground to cover itself with leaves and fallen forest branches. This makes it easy to be mistaken for a tree at first glance.

In some versions of the story, the *Chenoo* was once a human being, but as a punishment for cannibalism it became demon possessed. Its heart was turned to solid ice, and it became stronger as it consumed the hearts of its own kind.

This heart of ice became the creature's greatest weakness. A *Chenoo* can be killed if you make it eat salt because salt will de-ice a frozen heart.

The previously mentioned video from Prince Edward Island claims to capture a Sasquatch running through an opening in a wooded area. The film was shot in 2001 as a scene for a home movie in which a man is being chased by "bad guys." The film begins with the cameraman clearly directing an unseen person to begin. A man then runs from the forest at great speed, seemingly being chased by something, glancing back over his shoulder. From the trees opposite from where the man emerged, what appears to be a Sasquatch or a gorilla crosses the opening to where the man came from. Bigfoot researchers who studied the film estimate the ape-like creature to be running at 25 to 30 mph.

As is the case with so many Bigfoot photos and videos, many think it is a hoax. It's certainly not definitive.

There are ten provinces and three territories in Canada. Ninety-seven percent of Canada's population live in the provinces, which function like states in the United States, in that they exercise their own constitutional powers. The territories, which are organized by statute and are under federal governance, cover more than 1.5 million square miles—a vast area containing only 3 percent of Canada's population. This leaves the potential Sasquatch a lot of land in which to roam and hide! It is no wonder that the entire area boasts a rich oral history of Bigfoot activity. It also explains why bona fide sightings, pictures, and evidence are somewhat paltry in the territories compared to parts of Canada that are more densely populated. Few people who live and operate there carry cell phones or cameras at the ready, and they are there precisely because they want to live apart from other people, not share every intriguing story they come along.

Let's examine the territories one at a time.

The Yukon is wild, mountainous, and sparsely populated. It's estimated that there are only 0.1 people per square kilometer, and most of them live in the capital of Whitehorse. The Yukon boasts Canada's highest peak, Mount Logan, and both the Kluane National Park and Reserve and Ivvavik National Park. This means that what population *is* there is concentrated in a relatively small area.

Many Americans received their introduction to the Yukon by watching the exploits of the old television series *Sergeant Preston of the Yukon*, which ran from 1955 to 1958. Created by George W. Trendle and Fran Striker, the show featured Sergeant William Preston of the Roy-

O, Canada

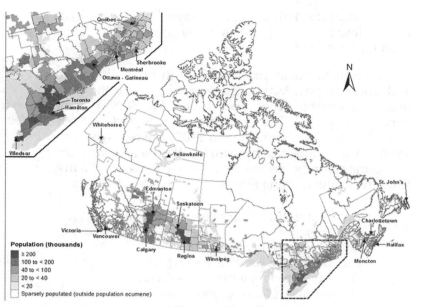

Canada's population is concentrated in the south and in urban areas, leaving broad swaths of the country open to Bigfoot habitat.

al Canadian Mounted Police, his famous horse Rex, and faithful dog, King. A whole generation of Baby Boomers grew up shouting, "On King! Mush, you huskies!" whenever they took off en masse to go somewhere on their bikes.

If you are too young to remember this one, you might have gained your first Yukon exposure through the 1964 Rankin/Bass television show *Rudolph the Red-Nosed Reindeer*. A key character in the perennial holiday special is Yukon Cornelius, a prospector who befriends Rudolph and Hermey, the elf with dentistry ambitions, while they are trying to avoid the Abominable Snow Monster of the North (or Abominable Bumble), a Bigfoot knockoff. From this classic film came the catchphrase cry of an entire generation when they stumbled and fell—"Bumbles bounce!"

If you missed these shows, you perhaps read about the Klondike Gold Rush, which took place between 1896 and 1899. When news of the first strike reached Seattle and San Francisco, it triggered a stampede of some 100,000 prospectors who descended upon the Klond-

True Tales from Across America

ike region of the Yukon. As is always the case in a gold rush, a few lucky early birds made some money. Most didn't. Many died.

The event has been immortalized in films, literature, and photographs. Maybe the one who made the most money from the event was Robert W. Service, who penned the poem "The Cremation of Sam McGee," featured in *Songs of a Sourdough* in 1907. Anyone who ever attended a summer camp, during the heyday of summer camps, surely has memories of sitting around a fire, listening to the famous words:

> *There are strange things done in the midnight sun*
> *By the men who moil for gold;*
> *The Arctic trails have their secret tales*
> *That would make your blood run cold;*
> *The Northern Lights have seen queer sights,*
> *But the queerest they ever did see*
> *Was that night on the marge of Lake Lebarge*
> *I cremated Sam McGee.*

Prospectors navigate Chilkoot Pass on their way to the Klondike Gold Rush in this 1898 photograph.

Bigfoot Sightings

Red Grossinger, of Whitehorse, is a Métis resident of the area whose ancestry is Algonquin-Huron. His 1997 book, *Nahganne: Tales of the Northern Sasquatch*, was sparked by an encounter he had while fishing on the Takhini River. He saw a big, tall, hairy, two-legged creature along the river, and his life was changed forever.

"It looked strange to me," Grossinger later recalled. "I mentioned it to one of my friends from the Teslin Tlingit Council, and the lady mentioned quite clearly, 'Well, that's a Sasquatch, a wild man.'"

Nahganne is the Dene word for Sasquatch. Grossinger says there are many names for the creature. He's not a fan of its most popular moniker.

"A lot of people call it Bigfoot, which I despise. It's the same as calling someone big ears, big nose."

After his own experience, Grossinger went on to investigate other encounters and eventually felt the need to write a book after collecting 70 reports, 34 of which are sightings. When interviewed in 2022 by Sara Connors of the APTN National News, he recalled one encounter that especially got his attention.

In 2011, a witness saw a tall, Sasquatch-like figure walking along Crestview, on Azure Road, in the Whitehorse neighborhood. He made a right toward the Alaska Highway when something most unusual took place: "The Sasquatch became somewhat translucent and gradually became transparent." The witness went on to say that at one time, he could see the outline; he could see right through it and see a bush behind it. Then there was nothing left.

Grossinger thinks this could explain the lack of physical evidence, including bodies, that plagues Sasquatch researchers. He points out that there have been reports of Sasquatch tracks ending abruptly, with the creature leaving the prints appearing to vanish into thin air in British Columbia and the Northwest Territories. "What happened to the track maker?" he asks. "Who the hell was walking there?"

Another of Grossinger's anecdotes involves Grant Pauls, a member of the Tahltan Nation. In the fall of

1995, while moose hunting near his home in Ross River, Yukon, Pauls fell asleep in the bush and awoke to strange noises that he said seemed to emanate from heavy creatures. Two days later, he returned to the area and saw two figures on the side of the road. Unable to see them clearly, Pauls assumed they were other people camping in the bush.

"I was kind of embarrassed, because I had been calling using a moose call and decided that I'd go see them and ask how my call was and have a good laugh." But when he got closer, he saw no sign of a camp.

"My mind started racing, 'What did I actually see?'" Because in the moment of initially seeing them, he thought the people seemed quite large. "There was no sign of them, so, in my mind, I was like, 'I got to get out of here.'"

Pauls estimated the size of the figures to be around eight to nine feet tall, with shoulders four to five feet wide. The incident scared him enough that he gave up hunting for a few years, but he decided to share his story as a warning to others to be respectful and have good intentions when going into the bush.

> *Pauls estimated the size of the figures to be around eight to nine feet tall, with shoulders four to five feet wide. The incident scared him enough that he gave up hunting for a few years.*

"I don't know if they would harm you or not, but it's very disturbing," he says.

One might question why, if Grossinger noted their great size to begin with, it was only on returning to the scene that it appeared to have struck him.

According to Grossinger, most First Nations people in the territory have been reluctant to speak about their encounters. "That has to be respected," he says. "They know a lot more than we do."

Of course, even Grossinger admits that only bones or a body will eventually solve the mystery. He's not adamant about the issue. "I'm not trying to convince anybody at all to believe in *Nahganne*. I'm presenting what it is and that's it. If you want to believe it, OK. If not, too bad."

O, Canada

It seems we always come back to not only a lack of evidence but also a stark divide between those who believe Sasquatch is a real creature and those who write it off as myth, folklore, and madness. If you ask Grossinger, it's partly because Sasquatches don't want to be seen and partly because humans don't want to admit they've seen them.

"Sasquatches are very smart. They know when they are being watched. The human mind plays tricks on us. If there's something that we don't immediately recognize, then our mind will try to cover that with something we know. Very few people will have an open mind to double check things that they see, never mind report it."

Yukon Sasquatch sightings offer another possibility as to what species Bigfoot might be. Because oral history is so strong in this area and goes back such a long way, native First Nation people from different tribes, some of whom called Bigfoot "Beaver Eater," were shown a series of pictures and asked to see if they corresponded with what they considered to be a "Beaver Eater." Examples included an unusually large grizzly bear, a surviving short-faced bear called *Arctodus Simus*, and an extinct species of beaver called *Castoroides*.

According to Red Grossinger, a Métis, Sasquatches are actually very smart, which helps them to avoid unwanted human contact.

Surprisingly, though, the picture that most often prompted a reply was that of an extinct ground sloth. Ground sloths were herbivores, however, and all five genera that are currently known to have lived in North America went extinct 11,000 years ago.

One sloth species, called *Megalonyx jeffersonii*, was native to the Yukon area. Could such a species have avoided extinction by becoming a beaver eater? If we can propose that an ancient primate or humanoid has survived

True Tales from Across America

undetected, couldn't the same claim be made about a ground sloth thought to have died out?

In 1996, a paper published by the Universidad de la República in Montevideo, Uruguay, suggested that at least some giant ground sloths may have been omnivores. Dr. Richard Fariña and Dr. Ernesto Blanco put forth the proposal that the sloth could have scavenged meat, taken kills made by large carnivores, or even been an active hunter, using its long front claws and great strength to overturn *glyptodonts*, which were giant armadillos.

Megalonyx jeffersonii *was a giant sloth that lived in North America from five million years ago to about 13,000 years ago. Or might there still be some surviving today?*

This theory has not gained much traction in the wider scientific community. It may be worth noting, though, that a meat-eating ground sloth would not be the first instance of a member of an herbivorous family evolving to exploit resources or fill an ecological niche, and they may have simply gone extinct (or not) before evolving to the point of developing specialized meat-eating features that would be obvious from fossils. Modern herbivores, such as hippos and deer, have been known to sometimes eat carrion or bones to obtain necessary nutrients, and under the right circumstances this occasional behavior may become necessary or beneficial enough to encourage the evolution of a more omnivorous species.

Modern tree sloths are known to sometimes feed on carrion and small animals, and isotopic analysis of a specimen of *Megalonyx* from Virginia showed that, although it was primarily a herbivore, it might have consumed a small amount of meat. On the other hand, some cryptozoologists think the "Beaver Eaters" feed on beaver lodges, which are composed of branches, bark, and other vegetation, not on the beavers themselves.

Then there are the beavers themselves. Some of these species, such as the giant beaver (*Castoroides*), were native to North America. They could grow to more than seven feet long and weigh nearly 300 pounds. If they were around as recently as 10,000 years ago, they likely coexisted with early humans. Could it be that modern sightings are echoes of ancient stories that preserve the memory of a creature that, long ago, humans once interacted with?

*The North American giant beaver (*Castoroides*) is another candidate for a possible species that survived presumed extinction.*

The Northwest Territories are home to more than 43,000 people, but half of them live in the capital city of Yellowknife. The remainder occupy smaller settlements. Half of the population is of indigenous First Nation descent, and many of them report encounters with the being they call *Nàh-gą*, or bushman.

Stories of this creature, told in the Tlicho region and language, go back thousands of years. They tell of terrifying human-like creatures, known for stealing people from bush camps.

John B. Zoe, a Tlicho columnist for the *Northwest Territories News/North*, described them in an article written in July of 2010:

> *Generally, they are silent, and for the unfortunate few who have seen them, these symptoms can be experienced: the back of the neck will tingle, skin will break into goose bumps, unstoppable shivers, the heart beats faster, accompanied by shortness of breath.*

It sounds like Zoe is describing a heart attack. Such a reaction might not be so unexpected if you were to come face to face with such a creature. According to Zoe, the creature is still present and active. He interviewed a man named Tony Williah, who was marooned for two days alone on an island after capsizing his canoe.

Near the northern tip of Lac La Martre, Williah saw a plastic bag bobbing in the waves and slowly maneuvered his boat up beside it to remove it from the water. Just then, a wave rocked the boat, causing him to fall over the side and into the frigid water. He struggled to pull himself back up into the boat, but his clothes, heavy with the weight of the water, kept pulling him down. He grabbed a plastic bag of supplies and began the long, tiring swim to shore.

"I managed to swim to an island at the end of the point," Williah reported after he had eventually been rescued and brought to a hospital in Yellowknife. That's when he says he encountered the Nàhgą.

"All of a sudden, there was a big man standing beside me. He must have walked away because I heard some branches break throughout the bushes. I packed up my clothes in a white bag and readied myself to leave."

Williah swam to a different location and spent another 48 hours alone in the wilderness before he was rescued by the Royal Canadian Mounted Police.

Michel Louis Rabesca is a Tlicho elder who learned about Nàhgą as a young boy living in the bush with his parents.

Williah swam away from the island and spent another 48 hours alone in the wilderness before he was rescued by the Royal Canadian Mounted Police.

"I got the story from my grandma, because my grandma lived in the bush all the time," he remembers. "The Tlicho people and Nàhgą have lived in the same region since time immemorial. They look just like human beings and even wear modern clothes. But," he says, "Nàhgą have powerful magic. They lure people toward them and steal them, never to be seen again. There are even stories of Nàhgą stealing moose and caribou carcasses."

Rabesca remembered a story about one of his relatives who encountered a Nàhgą and was never seen again. He was a child when he heard it, but he never forgot it:

> *The Nàhgą appeared suddenly on an island. They used medicine power to push him into the shore. They did it. They took him. So we never seen him. Never heard him again. Some people heard him talking, screaming "Help," but nobody can do nothing.*

It must have appeared to be déjà vu almost a century later when Rabesca had his own encounter with *Nàhgą* while driving toward the Frank Channel Bridge, between Rae and Edzo, one morning. He saw a man standing in the middle of the narrow bridge, so he slowed down as he approached. Suddenly the man jumped over the side of the bridge. Rabesca hurried out of his vehicle to look over the side to see if the man was OK, but there was no one there.

"I didn't see him. I don't know what happened to him."

Rabesca has since collected similar stories to pass along to the younger generation, believing that as people push further into the bush, interactions with bushmen will only increase.

Stories such as these now make up a dedicated Facebook page called Northwest Territories Bigfoot Stories. You can find some fascinating reading there.

Nunavut means "our land" in Inuktitut. Nunavut formed as a territory on April 1, 1999, when it was officially separated from the Northwest Territories and began to stand as its own political entity. Its capital is now called Iqaluit, located on the south coast of Baffin Island, but until 1987 it was called Frobisher Bay.

Even though its official designation as a territory is relatively new, there has been a continuous indigenous population there for some 4,000 years. Many historians identify the coast of Baffin Island with Helluland, which is described in Norse sagas, so it is possible that the inhabitants of the region had occasional contact with those Norse sailors, who wrote about their experiences with what they described as big, hairy, fierce warriors.

It's a sparsely populated, massive territory, formed mostly by the Canadian Arctic Archipelago. Its islands consist of expanses of tundra, craggy mountains, and remote villages, accessible only by plane or boat.

One of the unique features it boasts is the artwork, carvings, and handmade clothing of its indigenous Inuit population. Inuit art is displayed at the Nunatta Sunakkutaangit Museum in Iqaluit, which brings us to a particular piece of art carved from a woolly mammoth bone. It illustrates that stories about Sasquatch and First Nations contact go back at least 600 years.

The carving consists of a female Sasquatch that seems paralyzed on one side of its body. One side is carved in detail, while the other side seems to indicate an atrophied figure. Anatomically it is female, with the face and hair carved in fine detail.

A strap was once wrapped around it, indicating it was worn as an amulet of some kind, and it is indented from a thumb repeatedly rubbing it. Obviously, it had religious symbolism of some kind, but its unique purpose is unknown. Why the body is apparently paralyzed is a mystery. Perhaps the figurine was based on a real creature.

The many islands, harsh climate, and sparse population of Nunavut provide an ideal habitat for a cold-weather creature that wants to stay aloof and separate from humans, and the sea provides ample food. Along with so much of the Canada's vast, mostly uninhabited landscape, it seems ideally suited to Bigfoot.

While Canada would seem to be the ideal environment to support a population of unknown primates capable of living in harsh climates and eager to remain hidden from their human cousins, it's the neighbor to the south that boasts the most modern Bigfoot encounters, the most intense researchers, and the most fervent believers. The United States has large, uninhabited spaces that would be suitable to Sasquatch. And if any population were going to take the Bigfoot phenomenon to the extreme, it would be no surprise for it to be the Americans.

THE UNITED STATES OF BIGFOOT

We've spent a lot of time stepping way back into the past to discuss the potential origin of Bigfoot, to look at the legends and folklore associated with such creatures around the world, and to review some of the most influential evidence and sightings that have helped to make Bigfoot/Sasquatch a cultural icon. Although there have been reports of the creatures in countries all over the world, there may be no citizenry more enamored with the hairy hominid that that of the good ol' U.S.A.

A 2020 poll noted that 1 in 10 American adults believe Bigfoot to be "a real, living creature." Of the more than 660,000 internet searches for the terms "Bigfoot" and "Sasquatch," roughly one-third of them are from the United States. As the U.S. government continues to release previously classified information on UFO sightings and evidence of alien lifeforms, the public interest in paranormal phenomena grows even more.

When it comes paranormal experiences, conspiracy theories, and government cover-ups, Americans have shown, especially over the last decade or so, that they are an eager and enthusiastic audience.

Popularized by the Animal Planet series *Finding Bigfoot*, the act of searching for the creature has become known as Squatching. Those engaging in such activity are commonly referred to as Bigfooters. It's quite a subculture, and the 2024 book *The Secret History of Bigfoot: Field Notes on a North American Monster*, by journalist John O'Connor, does an excellent job exploring this community.

True Tales from Across America

Throughout this book, we've turned to information from the Bigfoot Field Researchers Organization (BFRO), and we do so again. The BFRO maintains an excellent database of reports from across North America that it launched in 1995. All reports receive some level of examination by the BFRO, from complex investigations involving field research, surveillance, and lab analysis to simpler cases that involving phone interviews and other relevant verification steps.

Once evaluated, reports are assigned a classification prior to public release. We touched on how these ratings are determined in the last chapter, but it bears revisiting. The BFRO explains the system like so:

> *All reports posted into the BFRO's online database are assigned a classification: Class A, Class B, or Class C. The difference between the classifications relates to the potential for misinterpretation of what was observed or heard. A given witness might be very credible, but could have honestly misinterpreted something that was seen, found, or heard. Thus, for the most part, the circumstances of the incident determine the potential for misinterpretation, and therefore the classification of the report.*

Class A

> *Class A reports involve clear sightings in circumstances where misinterpretation or misidentification of other animals can be ruled out with greater confidence. For example, there are several footprint cases that are very well documented. These are considered Class A reports, because misidentification of common animals can be confidently ruled out, thus the potential for misinterpretation is very low.*

The United States of Bigfoot

A Class B incident is when a Bigfoot is observed at a great distance.

Class B

Incidents where a possible sasquatch was observed at a great distance or in poor lighting conditions and incidents in any other circumstance that did not afford a clear view of the subject are considered Class B reports.

For example, credible reports where nothing was seen but distinct and characteristic sounds of sasquatches were heard are always considered Class B reports and never Class A, even in the most compelling "sound-only" cases. This is because the lack of a visual element raises a much greater potential for a misidentification of the sounds.

Class B reports are not considered less credible or less important than Class A reports — both types are deemed credible enough by the BFRO to show to the public. For example, one of the best documented reports ever received by the BFRO is a Class B report from Trinity County, California. It involved a very credible witness who backpacked into a remote area that has a history of sasquatch-related incidents. He described various occurrences around his camp at night that are strongly suspected to be sasquatch-related. The report is still considered Class B though because there was no clear visual observation to confirm what was heard outside the tent.

Almost all reports included in the database are first-hand reports. Occasionally a sec-

True Tales from Across America

ond-hand report is considered reliable enough to add to the database, but those reports are never Class A, because of the higher potential for inaccuracy when the story does not come straight from the eyewitness.

Class C

Most second-hand reports, and any third-hand reports, or stories with an untraceable source, are considered Class C, because of the high potential for inaccuracy. Those reports are kept in BFRO archives but are very rarely listed publicly in this database. The exceptions are for published or locally documented incidents from before 1958 (before the word "Bigfoot" entered the American vocabulary) and sightings mentioned in non-tabloid newspapers or magazines.

The BFRO's report classification system rates the circumstantial potential for misinterpretation, not the credibility of the witness or how interesting the report is. If you are checking the Recent Additions page periodically for new reports, or to steadily gain a better understanding of behavior and geographic range, you should pay attention to both Class A and Class B reports.

In the United States, the BFRO database lists more than 5,600 reports. The only state not represented is Hawaii. Not surprisingly, Washington (724) and California (463) top the list. And while the more than 300 reports from Florida—with its well-documented history of outlandish stories (search "Florida Man" if you have any questions)—is not surprising, the Midwest states of Michigan, Ohio, and Illinois high up the list might raise an eyebrow. The northeast of the country, consisting mainly of the New England states, accounts for relatively few sightings, though many would consider even one or two credible sightings of Bigfoot to be a lot.

Bigfoot Sightings

The United States of Bigfoot

Another well-known research organization, the North American Wood Ape Conservancy (NAWAC), maintains a similar database. Previously known as the Texas Bigfoot Research Conservancy, NAWAC has a list of 316 reports (at the time of this writing), from 1917 to October 2024.

There is no shortage of sightings. While Texas has a good share, largely due to shear landmass, and the Midwest is no slouch, the significant concentration of sightings tends to be in the Pacific Northwest and the Southeast Appalachia area, particularly in northeastern Kentucky and Tennessee. There has even emerged a bit of a West vs. East rivalry between the two regions.

Most of the time, the creature is identified as Sasquatch (probably more common in the West) or Bigfoot (popular in the East). In some cases, locals refer to their particular Bigfoot-like creature by a name unique to the region.

The large number of sightings in Florida often reference the "Skunk Ape." This southern biped is sometimes called a "cousin" of Bigfoot, though many consider it to be the same creature and not a different species or variant. It's generally described as being smaller than its western relative, standing from five to seven feet tall, with a range that stretches into Alabama and Georgia. The creature is named for its foul smell, reminiscent of a skunk's spray, and presumed to be largely due to its swampy habitat.

A statue of the "Skunk Ape" can be seen near the Everglades Big Cypress National Preserve on US Route 41.

Reports in the region of a "man-sized monkey" go back as far as 1818. There was a rash of sightings in the 1960s. In the 1970s, two sheriff's deputies reported shooting at an ape-like creature. Following the trail,

True Tales from Across America

they claimed to have recovered hair from a barbed wire fence.

Multiple sightings in Broward County from 1971 to 1975 represent some of the earliest popularizations of the "Skunk Ape" name. Newspaper reports alleged that the creature had invaded homes, killed livestock, and even stalked people. A police officer reported hitting one with his car.

In Arkansas, the local legend is called the Fouke Monster. This regional moniker has a derivative associated with an even more specific region. Stories of the Boggy Creek Monster—a "large, bipedal creature covered in long dark hair"—inspired the 1972 docudrama horror film *The Legend of Boggy Creek*.

The skunk ape is found in the forests and swamps of Florida.

The Fouke Monster reportedly attacked the home of Bobby and Elizabeth Ford on May 2, 1971. The Fords claimed to have heard something moving around outside several nights prior to their encounter. Elizabeth initially thought the creature was a bear when it reached through a screen window while she was asleep on the couch.

Bobby and his brother, Don, chased the creature off, firing several shots that they believed found their mark, but no blood was located. During the search, however, three-toed footprints were found close to the house and there were scratch marks on the home's porch.

Three weeks later, three individuals saw the ape-like creature crossing Highway 71. Additional sightings led to more footprints being found, the best being in a soybean field. Confirmed authentic by game warden Carl Galyon, these prints indicated, like those found at the Ford home, that the creature had three toes.

The United States of Bigfoot

Arkansas's neighbor to the north, Missouri, has a "massive, dark haired, man-like" creature of its own know as Momo the Monster. Despite its Muppet-like moniker, Momo is a frightening creature.

The most well-known sighting of Momo was by a young woman named Doris in July 1972. When she heard the screams of her two young brothers, who were out in the yard playing, she looked out the window to see the beast holding what appeared to be the carcass of a dog. Doris described the beast as having large, glowing orange eyes and a pumpkin-shaped head.

Other sightings occurred that same year, with a fire department chief who was also a city council member reporting catching the giant upright creature in his car headlights. A 20-person posse was formed to investigate, but nothing was found.

A slight variation of the typical Bigfoot description occurred in Michigan with its legendary cryptid, the Dogman. The Dogman is said to be seven feet tall and bipedal, but more canine than ape-like.

The first report of the Dogman occurred in Wexford County. Two lumberjacks claimed they saw the creature in 1887. In 1937, a man in Paris, Michigan, was attacked by five wild dogs, one of which he claimed walked on two legs.

Michigan sightings would continue: in Manistee in the 1950s, in Cross Village in 1967, and in Ottawa County in the mid-1990s.

In 2017, a Michigan truck driver claimed he encountered the Dogman in the Manistee National Forest, an apparent favored stomping ground of the Dogman. The timing of this sighting coincides with a piece of folklore that has surrounded this version of the fur-covered half-man/half-beast.

Dogman is a creature that has been reported by witnesses in Michigan.

True Tales from Across America

It's said the Dogman appears every ten years, with new sightings occurring in years ending in 7.

The Dogman inspired a song, "The Legend," by DJ Steve Cook, which helped to spread the story and led to an increase in sightings. A 2007 film purported to catch footage of the Dogman attacking and killing the cameraman. While there are many who still want to claim the film is authentic, it was debunked some time ago and the filmmaker shared his methods.

For the record, as a lifelong Michigan resident who has spent a lot of time in the woods, I have encountered neither the Dogman nor any sign of his presence. To be fair, I wasn't really looking until recently. And who knows? 2027 is just around the corner.

Michigan's hairy hominids are not only of the canine variety, however. Others have claimed to see an actual Sasquatch and forged a relationship with it.

In October 2022, *Midland Daily News* staff reporter Angela Mulkawrote about Casey Dostert, from Michigan's Upper Peninsula, who claimed he had been trading handmade gifts with Bigfoot for nearly two years. He said he had become friends with the creature. His TikTok posts, detailing how he leaves food items on what he calls his "gifting rock" and then finds "simple handicrafts" left by Bigfoot in return, have garnered millions of views.

Is he taken seriously by all his viewers? Of course not! One went so far as to say, "You all know this is a big joke?"

But Dostert (*@fowl_mitten_outdoors*), who created his page to share his love of the outdoors, is not alone. So many people have responded with similar stories that Richard Meyer was inspired to create the Upper Peninsula Bigfoot/Sasquatch Research Organization (UPBSRO) and an annual Upper Peninsula Bigfoot Convention. "We wanted to spread the news, basically, that Bigfoot is real, a real thing, and in Michigan—specifically the Upper Peninsula," he told the newspaper. Since its foundation, the group has reported footprints and multiple sightings, some of which include family groups of anywhere from two to ten Bigfoot at once.

The United States of Bigfoot

The Bigfoot Field Researchers Organization has recorded 225 Bigfoot sightings in Michigan.

"There's a breeding population of Bigfoot, for them to have been around as long as they are, so it's more than one creature," he reports. "There [are] males and females, old ones and young ones."

The *Detroit Free Press* reported that most sightings describe a large creature, covered in fur, standing eight feet tall or more, walking upright, and making only fleeting appearances in eyewitness sightings, blurry photos, and a lot of shaky videos. Some believe it's a close relative of humans, somewhere between man and ape. Others, many of whom attend the convention and believe they have traded gifts with Bigfoot, have quite a different opinion.

Sticking to the Midwest, we can turn to the Grassman of Ohio. Unique among the Bigfoot variants across the nation, the Grassman is as likely to be seen strolling through the rolling fields of Ohio as it is to be spotted in the state's woodlands. The orange-eyed being seems to be at home on any of the Ohio landscapes—farmland, forests, or the lower hills of the Appalachian Mountains. The frequency with which it is spotted near rivers or lakes leads some researchers to speculate that the Grassman is more fond of water than its relatives in other areas.

As in other locations, stories of Ohio's large, bipedal, hair-covered creature can be traced back to the Native American tribes that inhabited the area, like the Shawnee and Delaware. Sightings persisted as Europeans colonized the area, and today, reports are common especially in state parks like Salt Fork State Park—nearly 40 sightings since the mid-1980s—and Cuyahoga Valley National Park.

Anyone who has driven through Ohio knows that, excluding the foothills in the southern part of the state, it's pretty flat. Often, there is nothing but farmland as far as the eye can see. It hardly seems like prime Bigfoot country, but Ohio ranks fourth in the country for Bigfoot reports.

Evidence for the Grassman's existence is much the same as in other parts of the country. Plaster casts of footprints have been made, inconclusive but intriguing photographs have been taken, and a 2015 low-budget documentary explores a series of sightings that occurred around Minerva, Ohio, in 1978.

Minerva Monster was written and directed by Seth Breedlove. It was the first in a series of cryptid-related documentaries produced by the filmmaker, premiering at the Ohio Bigfoot Conference on May 16, 2015.

The film features interviews with eyewitnesses, including a county sheriff's deputy, and film reviewer Robert McCune of *The Independent* wrote that it was "thoughtfully produced" and "tells an interesting story well." McCune points out that the filmmakers offer no commentary of their own but that the film shows a bias in that it heavily features "naysayers and critics."

While the Grassman is a popular legend, the bulk of recent Bigfoot reports come from the state's Hocking Hills area. This area of southeastern Ohio was sculpted by ancient glaciers and rivers and stands in stark contrast to most of the state's flat farmland.

The shaping of the area's sandstone layers has left a stunning landscape of waterfalls, deep gorges, and tunnels. Hocking Hills has a long history of human habitation, with Shawnee, Wyandotte, and Delaware tribes known to have frequented the area. Today it is a popular tourist destination for hiking and camping.

Recognizing the significance and fragility of the remarkable landscape, the state of Ohio purchased land to create Hocking Hills State Park. This has enabled the area to remain mostly unchanged by humans and would seem to benefit any native creatures' survival and their ability to remain in the area largely undetected.

Unknown bipedal creature in Hocking Hills, Ohio (photo: Christen Ballew).

The annual Hocking Hills Bigfoot Festival takes place every August and its growth necessitated a move to the Vinton County Fairgrounds in McArthur beginning in 2025.

On my own visit to the area, I was awed by the beautiful rock formations, caves, and water features. Even on well-worn trails, I felt as if I had stepped back into a time before the arrival of Europeans and the steel and concrete scars across the land that would follow.

Unfortunately, the closest I came to a Bigfoot sighting was the image above, captured by my fiancée. It's certainly a frightening, and probably foul-smelling, beast, but I don't think it's the elusive Bigfoot.

Traveling across the plains and arid desert of the central United States, we come to Arizona and another alliterative giant, the Mogollon Monster. Unlike the orange-eyed Grassman, Arizona's Bigfoot is said to have eyes of red. It stands over 7 feet tall and is covered in long black or reddish-brown hair.

Like the Skunk Ape of Florida and Ohio's Grassman, the Mogollon Monster is said to have a pungent odor, a common Bigfoot trait. It also shares the whistling and screeching vocalizations associated with Bigfoot, as well as a rock-throwing penchant.

Arizona's giant is said to be nocturnal, omnivorous, territorial, and sometimes violent. It has been said to decapitate deer and other wildlife prior to consuming them.

Most sightings occur along Arizona's Mogollon Rim, giving the creature its name, but the oldest known report occurred near the Grand Canyon in 1903. At the time, the creature was described in the *Arizona Republic* as having "talon-like fingers" and "long white hair and matted beard that reached to his knees." So, like a scary member of ZZ Top. The witness claimed the creature was covered in a coat of gray hair and was discovered drinking the blood of two cougars.

A Whiteriver resident claimed to have seen a tall, black thing walking in big strides several times between 1982 and 2004. Several reports have come from the Fort Apache Indian Reservation.

The folklore of the Mogollon Monster often cites curses and transmogrification to explain the origin of the crea-

The Mogollon Rim is a geological feature extending 200 miles through northern Arizona, land ideal for the Mogollon Monster's habitat.

Bigfoot Sightings

ture. One such story describes it as the "phantom of a white man who, as punishment for murdering a Native American woman, was hung from a tree by his hands, stretched to a height of eight feet, then skinned alive and left to die." Damned by the spirits for his evil actions, the man's ghost roams the woods as a Skin-walker.

Kentucky and the greater Appalachia area have begun to give the Pacific Northwest a run for their money when it comes to Bigfoot activity. Charlie Raymond, the founder of the Kentucky Bigfoot Research Organization, says he has investigated more than 500 sightings that he believes are credible. Among the sightings in Kentucky, there even seem to be types of sub-species of Bigfoot being identified. One example is the Midnight Whistler that is said to live in the Mammoth Caves of central Kentucky.

The Midnight Whistler is a fully nocturnal Bigfoot, seven to eight feet tall. For unknown reasons, it seems its only vocalization is whistling. There is said to be a pack of these creatures in the area, peering from the darkness with glowing green eyes that some have attributed to a night vision ability.

The Midnight Whistler is said to be a fully nocturnal Bigfoot, seven to eight feet tall. For unknown reasons, it seems its only vocalization is whistling.

Mammoth Cave National Park and Red River Gorge are the two most active locations for Kentucky Bigfoot sightings, but there was also a recent sighting along the Western Kentucky Parkway, according to a December 27, 2024, posting on the *Sasquatch Chronicles Blog:*

> In November 2024 a motorist observed a large, hairy, bipedal creature walk off the Western Kentucky Parkway and into the forest near Central City, KY. Two more witnesses came forward and shared their encounters very close to this same location.

The eyewitness reported being several miles north of Newcastle when the high beams of his car caught something tall moving near the road. He claimed the creature had black or brown shaggy hair, was at least seven feet tall, and had a large back. As it walked toward the woods, the suspected Bigfoot "froze" when captured in the man's lights but did not turn toward him. He passed within about 20 feet of the creature.

A few days later, on the man's return trip through the area, he said that he counted 14 dead deer in a span of five minutes, some of which appeared to have been fed upon. The interviewer noted that he had seen a similar occurrence in the same area of what appeared to be a deer massacre—or at least an unusually high number of dead deer.

Two other witnesses came forward with their own accounts of sightings in the same area. Both reported seeing similar creatures in 2018.

As we can see, while there may be some variations in reports of a Bigfoot-like creature across America, the general description tracks with that of Sasquatch sightings in the rest of North America and around the world. Could these small differences simply be a product of environment, in much the same way that humans from certain regions have telling physical characteristics in their skin color, the shape of their faces, or their dialect?

Again, it seems with so many Bigfoot roaming the country, we'd have more conclusive evidence. Yet even the best video evidence to be produced is subjective at best. In addition to the much-discussed Patterson-Gimlin film, there are other videos.

A video of an alleged Bigfoot sighting was taken by youth group leader Jim Mills in California's Marble Mountain Wilderness in 2001. The video begins with Mills showing a "shelter" that fits the description of a Bigfoot nest. Discussing broken branches and small trees around the site, the narrator notes that there are no marks of tools and that they appear to have been snapped by "mighty, mighty, strength." About two and a half minutes in, Mills is alerted to a Bigfoot moving down a ridge toward them. He claims the "Bigfoot" is angry and yelling at them, presumably for being in its "camp."

The being is never out of silhouette. Mills continued to film while discussing getting photos or even shooting the creature. At nearly seven minutes, the video is the longest of a supposed Bigfoot sighting.

Commonly referred to as the Independence Day Footage because it is said to have been captured by a group of campers near Independence, California, celebrating Independence Day, a two-minute film clip from the early 1990s is, if nothing else, unique in what it appears to capture.

The camera zooms in on a boulder, and shortly after, a dark figure emerges, walking quickly across an opening before disappearing behind another boulder. The cameraman scurries for a better filming location, attempting to get ahead of the creature.

Screenshots from the "Independence Day Footage" (available at https://www.youtube.com/watch?v=mQ2kU6e8Huo) first shows what looks like a male Bigfoot (top) and is later followed by what appears to be a female holding an infant.

True Tales from Across America

The cameraperson seems close to the creature. In magnified footage, the creature looks like it is aware of the filmmaker's presence.

There are a few moments of inactivity, and then a head pops up from behind yet another boulder. We can then see that it is a larger figure holding a smaller one. The creatures seem to be covered completely in black hair and shaped like an ape. The camera follows what researchers suspected to be a Bigfoot mother and its child as they quickly leave the area.

While researchers claim this is some of the best video of a Sasquatch to have emerged, skeptics say they are clearly costumed individuals. They point out the very human-like gait of the mother Bigfoot.

Hinting at what might be in store for Bigfoot researchers using more modern technology, hunter Rick Jacobs captured some of the most famous Bigfoot images to date. In 2007, Jacobs attempted to capture pictures of deer in the Allegheny National Forest, about 115 miles northeast of Pittsburgh.

Jacobs's tree-mounted camera captured various wildlife and, unexpectedly, what could be a bipedal, hairy creature moving past. The image provided to news outlets suggests a creature moving on all fours, but it has an anatomy that BFRO investigator Paul Majeta called juvenile and "primate-like."

The Pennsylvania Game Commision offered a more conventional answer. Spokesman Jerry Feaser said, "There is no question it is a bear with a severe case of mange."

In 2023, video resurfaced that had been posted to YouTube by Mississippi resident Josh Highcliff. Many consider it to be the best Bigfoot footage ever recorded. It is a two-minute clip that Highcliff filmed in 2015.

Highcliff says he was hog hunting in a Mississippi swamp when he "heard a noise behind a tree." Upon investigation, Highcliff came across a "huge black thing" ripping bark from a cypress tree and throwing it on the ground.

Bigfoot Sightings

The video shows a creature that appears to have shoulders and arms that are primate-like, crouching near a tree about 50 yards away, ripping bark away from it. Highcliff said he thought it might have been trying to dig out the tree stump.

Near the end of the video, the creature appears to stand up. Highcliff estimated that it was seven feet tall and definitely not a bear. At that point, a frightened Highcliff runs away.

Sightings like these helped to keep the embers of Bigfoot interest burning across the "Squatching" community, but cable television and the advent of reality TV poured fuel on the flames like never before.

On May 29, 2011, *Finding Bigfoot* premiered on the Animal Planet cable channel. The show featured four Bigfoot researchers investigating potential evidence of the creature. The show is credited with coining the term "Squatching."

The research team consisted of BFRO founder and president Matt Moneymaker, enthusiasts and researchers James "Bobo" Fay and Cliff Barackman, and biologist and "skeptical scientist" Ranae Holland. Collectively, the team has over 100 years of investigative time dedicated to Sasquatch. Fay and Barackman are close friends who searched for Bigfoot together well before the series began. Moneymaker founded BFRO in 1995. Despite being a skeptic and professed nonbeliever, Holland was exposed to the Bigfoot legend as a child, spending time "Squatching" and watching Bigfoot movies with her dad, who was fascinated by the creature.

Finding Bigfoot *was a television show that ran on the Animal Planet network from 2011 to 2018.*

True Tales from Across America

Over the course of nine seasons, the *Finding Bigfoot* team traversed the country investigating locations where potential proof of Bigfoot's existence awaited them. The show often opened with the team en route and discussing the photographic, video, audio, or eyewitness evidence they were expecting.

The team would interview the person who gathered the evidence, re-create photographs, and invite locals to a "town hall" event where they could share their own stories of Bigfoot encounters. Typically, one team member would stay at the location where the original evidence had been gathered and perform a solo investigation over the course of several nights.

The remaining three team members would go on to investigate additional sites that offered the most promise of an encounter or evidence, based on the information gathered at the "town hall" meeting. Finally, the team would attempt to lure a Sasquatch within sight of their night-vision technology or infrared cameras.

By the third season, the team was investigating sightings and evidence in other parts of the world (some of which we'll discuss in the next chapter). The series-ending 100th episode featured footage of the group returning to the hallowed ground of Sasquatchery—the site of the Patterson-Gimlin film—to attend a 50th anniversary festival celebrating the famous video.

Despite some early issues and criticism from the team itself—regarding Animal Planet's editing choices, which led to the team threatening to quit the show—the series was well received by audiences. It consistently ranked among AP's top shows during its run. It even spawned a couple of spin-offs.

The team's consistent lack of success in proving the existence of Bigfoot led to ridicule even from some Bigfoot enthusiasts. Surely, they felt the failure—despite a large budget and state-of-the-art equipment—only weakened the claim of the creature's existence. Others praised the show's earnest and honest approach to the investigations—reality TV drama editing aside—and the focus on asking questions and attempting to find real and verifiable evidence.

Bigfoot Sightings

That integrity can be largely attributed to the efforts of team skeptic Ranae Holland. She remained impartial and scientific in her analysis and challenged the team to a higher standard of proof than many other Bigfoot researchers bring to the table. In a 2017 TED talk, Holland praised the show for inspiring kids—who were a large part of the viewing audience—to be curious and to go outside and investigate nature. She also suggested that *Finding Bigfoot* could help people by demonstrating ways to have conversations about beliefs "without belittling and making the other side feel ridiculous."

The *Finding Bigfoot* team did not prove the existence of Sasquatch. They did, however, inspire others to search and paved the way for another series dedicated to the cause.

Expedition Bigfoot airs on the Discovery Channel. It premiered in 2019, operating in much the same manner as its Animal Planet predecessor.

Though an actor by trade, *Expedition Bigfoot* host Bryce Johnson says his passion lies in researching the strange and unexplained. He has a special place in his heart for cryptids and has been obsessed with Bigfoot since he was a kid.

> *The* Finding Bigfoot *team did not prove the existence of Sasquatch. They did, however, inspire others to search and paved the way for another series dedicated to the cause.*

In 2013, Johnson starred in Bobcat Goldthwait's found-footage horror film *Willow Creek*, in which he plays a Bigfoot enthusiast hoping to shoot his own Bigfoot footage at the same site as the Patterson-Gimlin film. No spoilers here, but the indie film was well received and has received generally positive reviews.

For Johnson, the experience only amplified his interest in Bigfoot. While researching the role, he met Bob Gimlin, and they struck up a friendship. That friendship led to Johnson's commitment to proving—or disproving—the existence of Bigfoot.

In 2017, Johnson created the podcast *Bigfoot Collector's Club*, where he and fellow actor Michael McMillian chat

Bryce Johnson (pictured) and Alexie Gilmore starred in the 2013 horror film Willow Creek *about a young couple who go Bigfoot hunting in California.*

with "amazing guests about their personal paranormal history and share stories of High Strangeness." He went on to gather the research team and produce *Expedition Bigfoot*, in which he is host and investigator.

The research team for most of the show's run consisted of Russell Acord, Ronny LeBlanc, and Dr. Mireya Mayor.

Acord is a retired Army sergeant, survivalist, author, and part-time filmmaker. He also serves as event coordinator for the International Bigfoot Conference. Raised in Montana, he has been actively searching for Bigfoot since the 1970s when, like so many others, he was inspired by the Patterson-Gimlin film (its influence on the subculture really can't be overstated).

Acord has written two of three planned books in his Bitterroot Series, *Footprints of a Legend* and *Bigfoot and the Tripwire*. The books are about interactions with the giant cryptid.

Ronny LeBlanc is a well-known figure in the world of the paranormal, Bigfoot, and UFOs. Author of the best-selling book *Monsterland: Encounters with UFOs, Bigfoot and Orange Orbs*, LeBlanc cast a Bigfoot track in

2010, the first in Massachusetts to do so. His book details the history and connection of various phenomena and focuses on an area in central Massachusetts known as Monsterland.

LeBlanc is a regular speaker on the paranormal and unexplained conference circuit, was featured in a *Boston Herald* cover story, and appears on national radio programs like *Coast to Coast AM* (as have the humble authors of this book). Along with speaking engagements, LeBlanc has parlayed his popularity as a humorous, fun-loving, but passionate researcher into a regular segment on Boston radio, a popular podcast, and even a Monsterland branded hard cider and IPA. His second Monsterland book is coming soon.

LeBlanc cited controversy within the Bigfoot community regarding the harassment of a teenage cryptozoologist as his reason for leaving *Expedition Bigfoot* following season 5.

The brains of the operation is Dr. Mireya Mayor. The world-renowned primatologist spent two decades as a wildlife correspondent, and two of the episodes she hosted of *Ultimate Explorer* for the National Geographic Channel earned Emmy Award nominations for Outstanding Science, Technology, and Nature Programming.

Dr. Mireya Mayor searches for proof in the TV series Expedition Bigfoot.

Mayor was part of a research group to Madagascar that discovered a new species of mouse lemur that is considered the world's smallest primate. In 2019 she began to direct the Exploration and Science Communication Initiative at Florida International University.

A Miami native of Cuban heritage, Mayor earned her bachelor's degree in anthropology and English at the University of Miami and her Ph.D. from Stony Brook University. For four years she was an NFL cheerleader for the Miami Dolphins and is considered a role model for young women interested in the sciences. She tells her own story in her book *Pink Boots and a Machete: My Journey from NFL Cheerleader to National Geographic Explorer*.

The *Expedition Bigfoot* team is more immersed in the wilderness and in pursuit of Bigfoot than the *Finding Bigfoot* team would typically be. Where *Finding Bigfoot* was more of an investigative series going to various locations, *Expedition Bigfoot* is more of an ongoing research expedition.

> *The* Expedition Bigfoot *team is more immersed in the wilderness and in pursuit of Bigfoot than the* Finding Bigfoot *team would typically be.*

But for all the differences and commonalities, there's one thing we can unequivocally declare about both shows. They have not found Bigfoot or any proof more conclusive than what's been presented over the last several decades. Despite their high-tech drones and thermal imagery, the best they've provided is circumstantial evidence similar to what we've already seen.

Of course, these shows, sincere though they may be, are edited and produced to provide drama and suspense. Nobody expects the show to unveil proof that Bigfoot exists.

If researchers on such a show were to make a remarkable discovery, we would know about it long before the end of a several-week television season. Proof of Sasquatch would be one of the biggest scientific discoveries of our lifetimes. It wouldn't wait around for a series finale. The world would be watching, not just the Travel Channel's Wednesday night viewership.

And speaking of the world, why don't we take a quick spin around it before we meet back here to wrap this book up with some conclusions, opinions, and hot takes.

It's true that most Sasquatch sightings and the bulk of research occur in Canada and the United States. There could be several reasons for this that aren't related to the supposed Bigfoot population in these areas, including the number of people and the free time they have available to be out in the wilderness. We tend to be spoiled, with more expendable income and time on our hands than is probably good for us.

We've already noted that sightings tend to increase around population centers. And while we will mostly stick to these areas as we begin to summarize the theories and evidence and draw some opinions and conclusions, we would be remiss not to expand on sightings in other parts of the world that aren't North America or Nepal—home of the Yeti.

We can start *near* the home of the Yeti, across the Himalayas, in China. Specifically, the western, remote, mountainous regions of the country spawn many of the tales of this Asian Bigfoot. But it's the Shennongjia Forestry District of the Hubei Province that is the most famous for sightings of the region's hairy hominid, known as the Yeren.

Sightings of "hairy men" in this area have been constant at least as far back as 340 B.C.E., continuing through the Tang dynasty, and solidifying in a generally accepted version that has become the modern legend of the Yeren. The creatures are described as savage, strong, and fast. They live in mountain caves and descend to raid villages for food and women. Interest in the Yeren

True Tales from Across America

coincided with that of Bigfoot and the Yeti in the 1950s and 1960s but was suppressed by the Maoist government, which was eager to leave such legends and folk stories in the past.

Ancient writings tell of fast-moving, long-haired creatures that would eat people. The Feifei (this Chinese character is often translated as "baboon") had a number of supernatural and strange physical characteristics. Shaped like an ape, it was said to use human speech but sound like a bird. It was able to foretell life and death, and drinking its blood would make one able to see ghosts. The creature was immensely strong, with heels that faced backwards, and no knees.

Another description uses the character for "orangutan," which is not a native Chinese animal. More generally, the interpretation could simply be "ape." The Xingxing was said to have the face of a human but the body of a beast.

These "apemen" were said to lack females of their species and therefore had to abduct and rape women for breeding purposes. There are some vicious and graphic accounts of women having been ravaged by these creatures. I find this to be one of the stranger recurring themes in monster lore in general and Bigfoot lore in particular.

At the end of the Mao era, interest in the Yeren (the Hubei Province name which would come to serve as a catch-all moniker for the beings) renewed amid translations of Western works regarding the Yeti and Bigfoot reaching China. In 1977, the Chinese Academy of Sciences launched the first of several Yeren expeditions that gathered evidence such as footprints, hair samples, and witness accounts.

Most Chinese scientists investigating the phenomenon worked to prove that the "ape-men" were offshoots of humanity rather than some supernatural being, assuming it was a remaining descendant of an ancient, giant ape species. Another hypothesis was that the creatures were an unevolved, backward race of modern humans. This was often supported with racist comparisons to local ethnic minorities. It's suspected that this hypoth-

It's a Mad, Mad, Mad, Mad World

This inscription on a cliffside near Yeren Cave in the Shennongjia Forestry District in Hubei Province, China, reads "Ye Ren Dong" (Wild Man Cave).

esis was encouraged for political purposes to promote Marxist theories.

In the 1980s, interest was so high that funding from the Chinese Anthropological Society helped to found the Chinese Yeren Investigative Research Association. A lack of convincing evidence caused scientific interest to plummet, and after the 1989 protest and massacre at Tiananmen Square, government discouragement of private organizations and public research led to the Yeren Association being subsumed by the Chinese Association for Science and Technology. Further study of the creature's possible existence does not appear to be encouraged.

Remaining on the Asian continent, we slide over to the southeastern shore of the East Sea. Though tales come from Borneo and Laos, the bulk of accounts of the muscular, hair-covered "Jungle People" in this region come from Vietnam, and most often from the Vu Quang Nature Reserve. Tales of the Nguoi Rung, or the Batutut, were unknown to the outside world until the Vietnam

War, when encounters were reported by U.S. soldiers on missions in the dense jungle landscape.

While not as tall as its North American cousin, standing only five to six feet by most accounts, the Batutut were known to U.S. soldiers as "Rock Apes" due to their propensity for throwing rocks, with velocity and accuracy, at humans.

According to one American G.I., his platoon witnessed a Batutut during a pause in a firefight with the Viet Cong. The soldiers prepared for close-quarters fighting when they heard rustling from a nearby bamboo grove, but instead of a human wave attack from the enemy, a heavily muscled, six-foot-tall creature covered head to toe in reddish-brown hair emerged. Bounding on its hind legs, like a human but faster, the creature moved in the direction of the enemy soldiers.

Suddenly, the normally ghost-quiet Viet Cong could be heard screaming in terror. The Americans stayed put until the jungle was silent again and then, cautiously, made their way toward the Viet Cong position. As they advanced, they came across the body of a VC soldier that had been torn in half. They reported that the body looked like it had been attacked by a grizzly bear.

Gibbons, such as this Nomascus gibbon common to China and Vietnam, stand only about two feet tall, so it seems unlikely they would be confused with a large Rock Ape.

While there were many stories of run-ins with these creatures from American soldiers, many more came from the Viet Cong—so many that the North Vietnamese government sent scientists in to investigate. Dr. Võ Quý, a respected environmental researcher, discovered a large footprint in the Central Highlands of South Vietnam, of which he made a cast. The print was too large for a human or an ape. More prints were found during further investigations after the war.

Bigfoot Sightings

It's a Mad, Mad, Mad, Mad World

It's been suggested that what the soldiers saw were gibbons—common in the area—and that the mistaken identity could have been caused by the extreme psychological pressures of war. It seems unlikely that the gibbon, at around two feet tall, would be mistaken for something the size of a gorilla. Others say that it could have been an undiscovered species of orangutan, a species of which once lived there. However, those creatures went extinct thousands of years ago.

That theory and counterargument play out in a conversation among soldiers of the 11st Airborne Division during an encounter with a Rock Ape, as documented in Kregg P. J. Jorgenson's book *Strange but True Stories of the Vietnam War*:

> *The purported cryptid wasn't taller than 5 feet and it walked upright. It stopped, looked at them as though scrutinizing each and one of the soldiers.*
>
> *"What the hell is that?" one of the soldiers recalls muttering.*
>
> *"It's a rock ape," said another.*
>
> *"No, it ain't," a third man said.*
>
> *"I've seen rock apes, and that sure as hell isn't a rock ape!"*
>
> *The warriors didn't take their eyes off the creature.*
>
> *"It's an orangutan, isn't it?" asked the first soldier again.*
>
> *"Well, if it is, then he can't read a map. There are no orangutans in Vietnam."*

Like so many of the other Sasquatch-like beings around the world, a continued lack of substantial evidence leads people to believe its existence is less likely. Perhaps they shouldn't be so quick to judge.

True Tales from Across America

The local people of Vu Quang who tell of encounters with the Batutut, including times when the creatures have boldly entered village, accepted food, and spoken in an unknown dialect that sounded more human than animal, also told of a creature called the saola, or Asian unicorn. Scientists suspected this was another mythical creature, nothing more than a figment of their imagination, until one was captured and photographed in 1993.

The saola, which is native to Laos and Vietnam, is a very large animal, which makes the fact that it wasn't discovered as a species until 1992 quite surprising.

Continuing our trek southeast brings us to the island nation of Indonesia and the Orang Pendek. As elusive, furry, mysterious bipeds go, the Orang Pendek is a bit of an anomaly in that it's not really large and it doesn't seem to possess the podiatric prominence of similar creatures around the world.

The name *Orang Pendek* has nothing to do with the creature's color or diet. The name is Indonesian for "short person." It is said to inhabit the remote, mountainous forest on the island of Sumatra and has been seen and documented by forest tribes, local villagers, Dutch colonists, and Western travelers for at least 100 years. The consensus among witnesses is that it is a ground-dwelling primate, covered in short fur, standing anywhere from two and a half to five feet tall.

According to the Suku Anak Dalam—also known as Orang Kubu, Orang Batin Simbilan, or Orang Rimba people—the Orang Pendek has been a coinhabitant of their world for centuries. These nomadic people of the lowland forests of Jambi and South Sumatra also speak of a similar being known as Hantu Pendek that is more supernatural demon than animal. The Hantu Pendek is said to travel in small packs, eating yams and hunting animals with axes—a much more human trait than their larger "cousins" in other parts of the world.

Bigfoot Sightings

It's a Mad, Mad, Mad, Mad World

It would be tempting to dismiss tales from remote tribes as being superstition or another case of the mistaken identity of a monkey or lemur-type animal. When visiting Indonesia in 2024, I toured a monkey reserve and the macaque monkeys—which, coincidentally, stand around two to two and a half feet tall—were human-like, unintimidated by humans, and scary. They were reminiscent of the "bad monkeys" in the movie *Congo* (though considerably smaller). It would be easy to see how they could be mistaken, from a distance and if unknown by the observer, as a race of small, hairy people. However, there are a several reported encounters with the Orang Pendek from others, including Westerners.

An artist's concept of an Orang Pendek, with inset comparing its size to an average human.

One of the first such accounts was from Louis Constant Westenenk, a former Dutch governor of Sumatra. He recorded multiple sightings that allegedly occurred in the early 1900s. Two different accounts claimed to see the creature at close range: 15 and 30 feet, respectively. In both cases the witnesses, other Westerners, were certain they had seen something that was neither human nor ape.

Another report in the same era comes from Dutch surveyor J. Van Herwaarden in 1923. He writes:

> *I discovered a dark and hairy creature on a branch.... The sedapa was also hairy on the front of its body; the colour there was a little lighter than on the back. The very dark hair on its head fell to just below the shoulder-blades or even almost to the waist.... Had it been standing, its arms would have reached to a little above its knees; they were therefore long, but its legs seemed to me rather short. I did not see its feet, but I did see some toes*

> which were shaped in a very normal manner.... There was nothing repulsive or ugly about its face, nor was it at all apelike.

Based on witness testimony, British cryptozoologist Richard Freeman, who has traveled to Sumatra many times to find the Orang Pendek, describes them as having broad shoulders and long, muscular arms. They have dark hair and a mane that runs down their back. While shy and nonaggressive, they have been known—like other Bigfoot and Sasquatch—to grab sticks and throw stones to ward off threats. Freeman suspects the being is an unknown species closely related to the orangutan.

Cryptozoologist, journalist, and lecturer Richard Freeman is the director of the Centre for Fortean Zoology.

You might notice the similarity in the names "orangutan" and "Orang Pendek." *Orang* is the word for "person." Sometimes written "orang utan," the name means "forest person." And descriptions of the Orang Pendek are not dissimilar to the description of these endangered apes. But witnesses have, in some cases, stated very specifically that they were certain that what they saw was not an orangutan.

One such witness was Debbie Martyr, a British journalist who became interested in the creature during a camping trip near Mount Kerinci in western Sumatra in 1989. Her guide told her the Orang Pendek had been sighted in nearby forests, and when she scoffed, he vouched for the reports and claimed to have seen the creature twice himself.

Martyr began researching reported sightings. In 1990, she claimed to have seen the cryptid walking like a human, though she was certain it was not one. She described it as a small but strong-looking primate, similar to a gibbon, with an impressive upper body build. It moved quickly on two legs.

The journalist would claim multiple sightings after that first. She teamed up with photographer Jeremy Holden to film the creature but came up empty despite 15 years of effort. Holden claimed to have also caught a glimpse of the Orang Pendek, but he did not have his camera ready and was not quick enough to capture it on film.

Moving on to Australia, Yowie is the name of the ape-like creature common in Aboriginal legends. It is also the most popular name of this particular Bigfoot relative, which may actually take the prize for number of names. In various regions of the continent, the creature also goes by *quinkin, joogabinna, Ghindaring, doolaga, yahweh, pangkarlangu,* and *jimbra,* among other names.

With the Yowie, we return to the stereotypical large, brutish creature with abnormally large feet. Yowie are described as being between 7 and 12 feet tall, with wide, flat noses. Various alleged Yowie tracks have varied in shape and even number of toes.

The Yowie legend seems to trace its lineage back through Aboriginal folklore, such as that of the yahoo, a being described as resembling a man with long white hair and extraordinarily long arms. This creature was said to have talons and feet turned backward (a particularly interesting characteristic that it seemed to share with a version of the Chinese Yeren).

The first reported sighting of the Yowie in Australia is said to date back to as early as 1795. Reports of "indigenous Apes" appeared in an 1850s newspaper, and one in 1876 asked, "Who has not heard, from the earliest settlement of the colony, the blacks speaking of some unearthly animal or inhuman creature ... the Yahoo-Devil Devil, or hairy man of the wood?"

In an 1882 article, amateur naturalist Henry James McCooey claimed to have seen apes that stood around five feet tall, covered in long black hair.

While these don't seem to be descriptions of the 12-foot-tall creature we started with, it's important to note that Australia has no native primates. So seeing even relatively normal-size primates would border on a mythical experience. It wouldn't be much of a leap to move to an exceptionally large, more human-like creature, particularly if influenced by similar stories from around the world.

Australian historian Graham Joyner doesn't believe in the Yowie and claims it was unknown before reports began in 1975. He maintains that reports and descriptions of the subject of his interest, the Yahoo—a nineteenth-century phenomenon also called the hairy man or Australian Ape, which was believed to be an undiscovered marsupial that has gone extinct—has been muddled with the relatively new mythology of the Yowie. In any case, sightings continue.

Most recent sightings of Yowie come from the eastern side of the country—Queensland, the Northern Territory, and, especially, New South Wales, which includes Sydney and is the most populous state. Footage from 2000, known as the *Piper Film*, purports to catch the being on film. There are reportedly additional films, photos, and vocal recordings of the creature.

The hottest of the hotspots for Yowie reports is the Springbrook region in southeast Queensland. Former Queensland senator Bill O'Chee reported that he had seen a Yowie on a school trip to the area. He likened it to the Chewbacca character in *Star Wars*.

In 2014, a man from Gympie, Queensland, claimed to have not only seen a Yowie but also to have engaged in regular conversations with the creature in which he taught it some English. This is possible if, as the creature's whistling would suggest, it has a similar physicality for vocalizations as humans.

One of my favorite reports of a Yowie encounter comes from

This Yowie statue can be at Yowie Park, Kilcoy, Queensland, Australia.

Canberra. In 2010, a man described his run-in with a "juvenile" Yowie that he said was "covered in hair, with long arms." He claimed the creature was attempting to steal his car.

Australia has an active paranormal community, and interest in the Yowie remains high. There are a number of prominent investigators, such as Andrew McGinn and author and Yowie witness Tim the Yowie Man (his legal name). The late Rex Gilroy and his partner, Heather, spent 50 years collecting over 3,000 reports of Yowie encounters and believed it was a relative of North America's Bigfoot. Rex believed the creatures to be relict populations of the extinct ancestor of *Homo sapiens*.

Let's move back to the Northern Hemisphere and reports of the British Bigfoot. While many trace the British Bigfoot's roots back to England, Scotland, Wales, and Ireland, it's not an area well known for sightings of Sasquatch-type creatures. Like Australia, the UK doesn't have any native primates other than people. This is the case all across Europe.

The first modern humans appear to have reached England around 40,000 years ago, over 250,000 years after they first appeared in Africa. Earlier species of humans occupied Great Britain as long as 900,000 years ago, and Neanderthal fossils have been dated back to 400,000 years ago. There is a consensus, however, that Britain was unoccupied by humans from approximately 180,000 to 60,000 years ago. Even since then, it was only intermittently occupied as the climate swung between a tundra habitat with low temperatures and severe ice ages that made the region uninhabitable.

Of course, we know that the Yeti of the Himalayas is a cold-weather creature, so why couldn't it have a British cousin with the same low-temperature adaptations? In fact, an otherwise unoccupied island would make an excellent place in which such a creature could thrive and eventually adapt.

While there aren't many reports of Bigfoot in Britain's more distant past, there was a report of a Yeti-like creature in Staffordshire in the 1800s. However, there have been some recent sightings of the British Bigfoot. Some speculate this is because of the inevitable interactions that a potentially increasing Bigfoot population and an ever-encroaching human one would naturally cause.

Lee Brickley has been searching for a Bigfoot in England for more than a decade. He claims to have located tracks nearly twice the size of a man's size-eight foot in Cannock Chase, as well as claw marks on a tree near a mutilated deer.

> *Lee Brickley... claims to have located tracks nearly twice the size of a man's size-eight foot in Cannock Chase, as well as claw marks on a tree near a mutilated deer.*

Brickley has been fascinated by the hairy cryptid since he was a child and watched Bigfoot documentaries from America. He began researching any local sightings and has written *On the Hunt for the British Bigfoot* that discuss his findings.

Bricklet found a surprising number of reports of "man-monkey type creatures" in Staffordshire alone. He claims to have seen one of the elusive creatures but admits that it was dark outside and the figure was in shadow.

"It definitely moved more like an animal than a man, and it was easily seven feet tall," Lee said. "I tried to run after it, but it was too quick and disappeared into a dense section of trees."

In 2002, Bigfoot researcher Deborah Hatswell shared a map plotted with decades of Bigfoot sightings across the UK. It suggests the British Isles are overrun with Sasquatch.

Hatswell has collected reports from Scotland, Wales, Ireland, and England. She has also received accounts from other European countries including Sweden, France, and Germany. The witnesses cover a wide spectrum of humanity, from army personnel and police officers to game wardens, campers, and dog walkers.

Now in her fifties, Hatswell says she had her own encounter with an eight-foot tall, hairy, ape-like creature when she was a teenager. While enjoying a sunny day, Hatswell and a friend noticed some slight movement in the bushes.

The next thing that happened was a huge, hairy, gorilla type-face was thrust at us from the bushes. It was a huge thing, like a man and an ape had been pushed together. It had amber dark eyes, with dark brown hair, and yet it had a redness to it. Its jawline was thickly muscled, and its teeth were like a human's. His nose was flattish, like a boxer. It was the most terrified I've ever been in my life. I pushed my friend over and ran screaming for my life.

Due to that experience, Hatswell has been investigating Bigfoot and other weird phenomena since the early 1990s. For her, it's personal.

Understanding that not all the reports she receives will be genuine, Hatswell says that she has developed "tools" for weeding out the hoaxers, though that largely seems to be her opinion of the person's honesty. She also points out that even though there is the occasional "lone report" in areas, most of the sightings cluster in certain areas like Cannock Chase, Thetford Forest, and the Highlands.

It's not just glimpses of the hairy creature that we find in England. Tree structures and suspected Bigfoot nests have been found there as well. The British Bigfoot appears to be closely related to the North American version in both appearance and behavior.

As recently as March 2024, there have been claims of Bigfoot evidence in the southwest of England. A group of walkers taking a scenic path along the coastline of Devon came across footprints in the mud that they believe were left by the creature.

They said the prints came from the woods, followed the muddy path for about 20 meters, and then veered back into the trees. Although no accurate measurement was taken, one walker stated that the print was half again as big as his own size-eleven foot.

Moving across the Atlantic, we find ourselves in South America's largest country, Brazil, which encompasses 60 percent of the Amazon rainforest. In Brazilian folklore, the protector of that rainforest and its animals is the Mapinguari. Traditionally, it was described as a shaman (or holy man) that turned into a hairy humanoid. Said to be a cyclops, often with a gaping mouth on its abdomen, the creature is described as having backward feet, making it hard to track.

Beginning in the second half of the twentieth century, cryptozoologists began to speculate that the Mapinguari could be an unknown primate, a southern version of North America's Sasquatch. Others have theorized that these are sightings of a giant ground sloth, though that creature is estimated to have gone extinct almost 12,000 years ago.

A Mapinguari is a beast from Brazilian folklore that has one eye and a fanged mouth in its belly.

Recent sightings of this Brazilian Bigfoot claim it is over seven feet tall, with reddish fur and long claws. It is said to be carnivorous, attacking cattle and other large animals. The Maringuari is said to dislike water, tending to remain in the forest.

Like other versions of Bigfoot, Brazil's beast is said to have a putrid odor, which can serve as a warning of its presence. If you come across an area that the Maringuari has passed through, it reportedly leaves a path of destruction in its wake as it tears down brush and trees with its powerful claws.

According to a member of the Karitiana tribe, who insisted his son encountered one of the giants in the forest, the area of the sighting looked "as if a boulder had rolled through and knocked down all the trees and vines."

The Amazon is a strong candidate for housing an undiscovered primate. The habitat supports many diverse species. Thirty percent of the world's plant and animal life calls the Amazon home.

Bigfoot Sightings

Brazilian biologist Claudio Padua points out that scientists believe the Amazon is hiding thousands of undiscovered species. He says that this is prime primate property and that ten new species of monkey have been discovered in the last decade alone.

Amazon ornithologist David Oren was a subscriber to the ground sloth theory, or, at least, that the Maringuari was evolved from the ancient primate. From 1988 until his death in 2023, Oren promoted the idea. He wrote two scientific papers on the subject and led ten expeditions into the Amazon in search of evidence.

Oren collected hundreds of accounts from people claiming to have seen the Maringuari and interviewed seven hunters who had claimed to have shot specimens. He said he began his investigations as a skeptic but came to believe in the primate's existence after hearing several personal accounts from people in the Tapajós River basin.

Oren never discovered a Maringuari, and hair and stool samples he suspected to be from the beast turned out to be from an anteater and a tapir. He did own a photograph of "claw marks on a tree, eight of them about a foot long and an inch deep" that he suspected were made by the Maringuari, and he claimed to have heard its vocalizations four times on two separate occasions. He also discovered large, round paw prints with characteristics of a ground sloth.

Oren died without being able to provide definitive proof of the existence of his giant ground sloth, but stories of the Maringuari continue. Witnesses claim the creature is shy but can be fierce when confronted. People do their best to avoid places where sightings have occurred.

The Amazon is also home to the largest number of uncontacted peoples. Most of the more than 100 of these isolated populations live in the Amazonian rainforest. These "primitive" groups may be the inspiration for the "wild men" beings on the continent. Or they may just exist alongside another unidentified species.

The Maricoxi is a more general term for several large ape-like creatures that have allegedly been seen in the jungles of South America. British explorer Lieutenant-Colonel Percival H. Fawcett claimed to encounter a group in 1914.

According to Fawcett, the beings were extremely hairy and stood as tall as 12 feet. Despite their primitive look and language—said to be a collection of grunts—they were reportedly intelligent, used tools and bows and arrows, and lived in villages. Here is Fawcett's fascinating account from his 1914 expedition from Bolivia into southwestern Mato Grosso.

Geographer, cartographer, archaeologist, and explorer Percy Fawcett disappeared in the Amazon jungle in 1925.

As we stood looking from right to left, trying to decide which direction was the more promising, two savages appeared about a hundred yards to the south, moving at a trot and talking rapidly. On catching sight of us they stopped dead and hurriedly fixed arrows to their bows, while I shouted to them in the Maxubi tongue. We could not see them clearly for the shadows dappling their bodies, but it seemed to me they were large, hairy men, with exceptionally long arms, and with foreheads sloping back from pronounced eye ridges, men of a very primitive kind, in fact, and stark naked. Suddenly they turned and made off into the undergrowth, and we, knowing it was useless to follow, started up the north leg of the trail.

Bigfoot Sightings

It was not long before sundown, when, dim and muffled through the trees, came the unmistakable sound of a horn. We halted and listened intently. Again we heard the horn call, answered from other directions till several horns were braying at once. In the subdued light of evening, beneath the high vault of branches in this forest untrodden by civilized man, the sound was as eerie as the opening notes of some fantastic opera. We knew the savages made it, and that those savages were now on our trail. Soon we could hear shouts and jabbering to the accompaniment of the rough horn calls—a barbarous, merciless din, in marked contrast to the stealth of the ordinary savage. Darkness, still distant above the treetops, was settling rapidly down here in the depths of the wood, so we looked about us for a camping site which offered some measure of safety from attack, and finally took refuge in a tacuara thicket. Here the naked savages would not dare to follow because of the wicked, inch-long thorns. As we slung our hammocks inside the natural stockade we could hear the savages jabbering excitedly all around, but not daring to enter. Then, as the last light went, they left us, and we heard no more of them.

Next morning there were no savages in our vicinity, and we met with none when, after following another well-defined trail, we came to a clearing where there was a plantation of mandioca and papaws. Brilliantly colored toucans croaked in the palms as they picked at the fruit, and as no danger threatened we helped ourselves freely. We camped here, and at dusk held a concert in our hammocks, Costin with a harmonica, Manley with a comb, and myself with a flageolet. Perhaps it was foolish of us to advertise our presence in this way; but we were not molested, and no savage appeared.

In the morning we went on, and within a quarter of a mile came to a sort of palm-leaf sentry-box, then another. Then all of a sudden we reached open forest. The undergrowth fell away, disclosing between the tree boles a village of primitive shelters, where squatted some of the most villainous savages I have ever seen. Some were engaged in making arrows, others just idled—great apelike brutes who looked as if they had scarcely evolved beyond the level of beasts.

I whistled, and an enormous creature, hairy as a dog, leapt to his feet in the nearest shelter, fitted an arrow to his bow in a flash, and came up dancing from one leg to the other till he was only four yards away. Emitting grunts that sounded like "Eugh! Eugh! Eugh!" he remained there dancing, and suddenly the whole forest around us was alive with these hideous ape-men, all grunting "Eugh! Eugh! Eugh!" and dancing from leg to leg in the same way as they strung arrows to their bows. It looked like a very delicate situation for us, and I wondered if it was the end. I made friendly overtures in Maxubi, but they paid no attention. It was as though human speech were beyond their powers of comprehension.

The creature in front of me ceased his dance, stood for a moment perfectly still, and then drew his bowstring back till it was level with his ear, at the same time raising the barbed point of the six-foot arrow to the height of my chest. I looked straight into the pig-like eyes half hidden under the overhanging brows, and knew that he was not going to loose that arrow yet. As deliberately as he had raised it, he now lowered the bow, and commenced once more the slow dance, and the "Eugh! Eugh! Eugh!"

A second time he raised the arrow at me and drew the bow back, and again I knew he would not shoot. It was just as the Maxubis told me it would be. Again he lowered the bow and continued his dance. Then for the third time he halted and began to bring up the arrow's point. I knew he meant business this time, and drew out a Mauser pistol I had on my hip. It was a big, clumsy thing, of a caliber unsuitable to forest use, but I had brought it because by clipping the wooden holster to the pistol-butt it became a carbine, and was lighter to carry than a true rifle. It used .38 black powder shells, which made a din out of all proportion to their size. I never raised it; I just pulled the trigger and banged it off into the ground at the ape-man's feet.

The effect was instantaneous. A look of complete amazement came into the hideous face, and the little eyes opened wide. He dropped his bow and arrow and sprang away as quickly as a cat to vanish behind a tree. Then the arrows began to fly. We shot off a few rounds into the branches, hoping the noise would scare the savages into a more receptive frame of mind, but they seemed in no way disposed to accept us, and before anyone was hurt we gave it up as hopeless and retreated down the trail till the camp was out of sight. We were not followed, but the clamor in the village continued for a long time as we struck off northwards, and we fancied we still heard the "Eugh! Eugh! Eugh!" of the enraged braves.

In 1925, Fawcett and his men disappeared while on an expedition to find a lost city. Though there is no evidence to support it, many claim they were killed by the Maricoxi.

Some theorize that the discoveries in Mexico's Chiquihuite Cave, which suggest human occupation as many as 33,000 years ago, may have been the leavings of the Maricoxi.

So, where does this leave us?

It leaves us with thousands of reports, from all over the world, that support the existence of a species (or multiple species) of a giant, hairy, half human–half ape kind of creature that is either among the most elusive of large mammals or that has some supernatural ability to remain hidden and to affect the quality of film and video cameras.

Are these cases of mistaken identity? Hoaxes? A mass psychosis?

Well, what kind of Bigfoot book would this be if we didn't share some opinions of our own?

Is Bigfoot real or just a mythological construct? It's time we addressed it in detail. As I said in the preface, I am an "optimistic skeptic," so I come at things with more of a "prove it to me" perspective. My coauthor Jim Willis's notes are clear about his view:

> I must admit that when I started this project, I was a Sasquatch agnostic. I wanted to believe. I really did.

On the one hand, we have mountains of circumstantial evidence consisting of sightings, pictures, plaster cast, some DNA anomalies, and thousands of years' worth of oral history. It is a remarkable body of evidence, and we should try to address as much of it as we can.

Before we get too far, I want to address a couple of things that we first discussed, if only briefly, in the chapter "The Elephant in the Dark." Some people believe Bigfoot is an extraterrestrial capable of traveling between dimensions. Others believe Bigfoot is a supernatural entity or a shape-shifter with magical powers.

It's difficult enough to convince skeptics that an undiscovered, intelligent, hairy, apelike humanoid exists without adding in supernatural aspects. Most people dismiss these ideas. It's more likely that legends of supernatural beings have been inspired by an animal, another living creature, or even some natural occurrence like the rising of the sun or an eclipse that couldn't be explained by the known science of the time than it is that actual magical or supernatural beings exist.

The idea that Bigfoot is a being from another dimension or time, using portals to travel in and out of our world, is at least *slightly* more plausible than the "magical being" theory.

The idea of alternate or parallel universes has been around since the early 1960s. Like many scientific theories, the idea mostly began in the minds of science fiction writers. These days, multiverses, parallel dimensions, and alternate realities are often argued in the context of other major scientific concepts such as the Big Bang and quantum mechanics.

One theory about Bigfoot is that the creature originates from another universe or parallel dimension.

String theory and particle physics open the possibility of parallel dimensions, and the scientific community at large does not discount the possibility. Well-known and respected scientific minds like Stephen Hawking, Brian Cox, and Neil deGrasse Tyson have supported the multiverse hypothesis.

Some have even suggested that we are more likely to find intelligent life in these other universes than we are within our own—*ultra*terrrestrials instead of *extra*terrestrials. The late ufologist John Keel theorized that beings from other dimensions visited our own dimension and influenced human culture throughout history.

Keel believed that the unexplained creatures from folklore and religious texts—such as angels, demons, fairies, and monsters—were visitors from other universes. He thought these "aliens" could somehow travel between dimensions using portals and magnetic anomalies.

Is it possible that Sasquatch is an ultraterrestrial being from another universe? This would help explain the lack of bodies and the elusiveness of a population large enough to sustain itself.

Perhaps they are, according to principles of physics, entities who inhabit a dimension parallel to the perception realm that we arrogantly think of as the only reality that exists. Just because *we* have not learned how to travel back and forth between realities that some scientists assure us are there doesn't mean *other* species can't do it. They wouldn't even necessarily need to be smarter than us. It could be a matter of instinct that enables this movement between dimensions, or it could be entirely out of their control. In their world, portals could just open, and the occasional inhabitant gets caught up and transported by accident.

If we allow this idea to answer the question of where Bigfoot comes from and why it's such an elusive creature, a couple other significant questions would come up.

First, why would we assume that beings from another universe would look even remotely like us, whether an ape or a person or something in the middle?

From what we know of our own universe, it seems ludicrous to expect aliens to look, think, or act like us. The universe is vast and diverse, and any other intelligent lifeforms have likely evolved under different circumstances than our own. But it's hard to grasp those concepts, so we arrogantly convey aspects of our own likeness onto these beings. Our concepts of them make them out to be almost human when it's far more likely they would be like nothing we have imagined.

> *From what we know of our own universe, it seems ludicrous to expect aliens to look, think, or act like us. The universe is vast and diverse, and any other intelligent lifeforms have likely evolved under different circumstances than our own.*

If we accept that these creatures are advanced and have some ability, either in their physiology or in altering our perception, to appear to us in any form they choose, does it make sense that they would show up as an ape-like humanoid, drawing comparison to a "missing link" in our own evolution?

And even if this were the visage they chose to display, what would be their purpose? Why would this advanced being, choosing to visit our universe, decide upon arrival to play an epic game of hide-and-seek? Conversely, appearing as a giant, hairy hominid would be a silly choice if the idea were to quietly observe us and our world.

To get past this, we might return to the suggestion that Bigfoot does not deliberately visit our dimension but ends up here accidentally. This unintended overlapping of universes is sometimes what people think causes other supernatural/paranormal experiences, like ghost sightings or unexplained disappearances.

But I doubt it. I think these ideas stem more from a desire to explain away the lack of evidence rather than being driven by any actual experiences or discoveries. It's sort of a "God of the gaps" situation—we can't answer some nagging questions, so ... multiverse!

Once again quoting Carl Sagan: "Extraordinary claims require extraordinary evidence." When some of that is presented, I'd be willing to reconsider my opinion on Bigfoot being an extra- or ultraterrestrial. For now, it seems unlikely, and other than being a convenient reply to difficult questions, there is no reason to accept it.

If Bigfoot is a space alien or visitor from another dimension is what we would consider the most "out there" theory, the idea that the creature is a surviving species of early humans may be the next hardest for skeptics to accept.

The number of references to races of giants in ancient texts and folklore are hard to ignore. If these were isolated among a certain culture or region, they would be easier to dismiss as "bogeyman" stories or exaggerations that evolved over time. As these stories are found all over the globe and essentially cover the breadth of human history, it would seem foolish to write them off as simply primitive fear and superstition. We give a lot of weight to superstitions with much less to support them.

Today there are still many people whose ignorance or spiritual beliefs refuse to allow for the idea of evolu-

I'm Just Sayin'

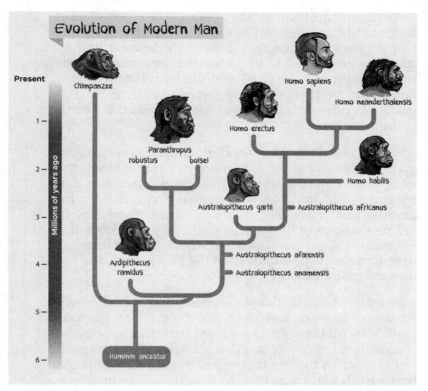

Evolution is not a linear progression that has one species evolve neatly into another. It resembles more a tree with many branches.

tion. Even early believers only had a basic grasp of the idea and viewed evolution as a linear concept in which you start with one creature that, over time, continues to change incrementally until becoming a different creature altogether. Many of those who argue against the idea of evolution still use this view to make their case.

"If we came from apes," they ask, "why are there still apes?"

Of course, that's not how it works. The simple answer to their question is that we didn't evolve from apes but, rather, we and apes both evolved from a common ancestor somewhere along the way. This occurred four to seven million years ago when the genus *Pan* (chimpanzees) and *Homo* (humans) both emerged from the tribe *Hominini*.

We haven't quite sorted the path from our most distant ancestor to ourselves and all the other existing primates. Nor do we know exactly which of the ancient human species were related to us and which were separate, or how many may have lived and died out that we don't know about. But we do know that as recently as 300,000 years ago, nine distinct human species walked the earth at the same time.

We've discussed the Neanderthals of Europe briefly and the Denisovans of Asia more in depth. During the same period that these ancestors existed—ancestors that we *know* we share DNA with—*Homo erectus* lived in Indonesia and *Homo rhodesiensis* in Africa. Short, small-brained species of humans existed alongside these others, such as *Homo naledi* in South Africa, *Homo floresiensis* in Indonesia, *Homo luzonensis* in the Philippines, and the mysterious Red Deer Cave People in China.

In many cases, it doesn't appear that these known "cousins" of ours met their fate through an obvious environmental catastrophe driven by volcanic activity, climate change effects such as Ice Ages, or an asteroid impact such as the one that wiped out the dinosaurs. As best we can tell, it was the proliferation of our own species, *Homo sapiens*, that led to the demise of these other humans.

Accompanying the theory of evolution is the mechanism of natural selection called "survival of the fittest." This often means that species that can adapt best to environmental change and resource availability are the ones that will manage to endure, evolve, and proliferate. On a more immediate level, it also means that the species that can eliminate its rivals to access those resources obviously stands a better chance of surviving.

We often think of ancient humans as relatively peaceful creatures without much more than the basic concerns of food and shelter to occupy their hunter-gatherer lifestyle. Of course, these early humans would also have developed social constructs among themselves and with any other human or animal species they would encounter. We can assume most of these encounters weren't particularly friendly.

Bigfoot Sightings

I'm Just Sayin'

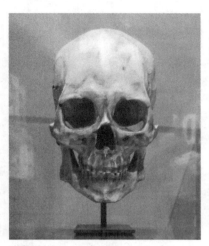

The skull of Kennewick Man is preserved at the Natural History Museum in Karlsruhe, Germany.

Our recent history is full of examples of war, conquest, and genocide. It's unreasonable to think early *Homo sapiens* would be less intrinsically violent. All evidence suggests that our increased intelligence and knowledge have allowed us to temper these instinctual tendencies toward killing each other.

And that's just among our own species. We need only to look around us to understand how much less we regard *other* species.

Archaeology and historical accounts demonstrate that primitive cultures engaged in intensive, pervasive, and lethal warfare. We have examples of neolithic weapons such as clubs, spears, axes, and bows. Our more distant relatives would have utilized rocks and sticks and whatever else was available. The 9,000-year-old Kennewick Man was found with a spear point embedded in his pelvis, and a brutal massacre is documented at the 10,000-year-old Nataruk site in Kenya.

This isn't to say that *Homo sapiens* were just running roughshod over the globe, wiping out every peaceful human species they encountered. There's reason to believe that the now-extinct hominids were every bit as bent toward violence and warfare. Neanderthal skeletons show trauma consistent with warfare. We can also see cooperative violence in modern chimpanzees, suggesting that "war" predates human evolution.

Homo sapiens, with their big brains, were just better at it.

That big brain helped us develop more complex tools and weapons and gave us the ability to develop complex plans, strategize, and be creative. We've been thinking "outside the box" for a long, long time.

True Tales from Across America

We were also able to communicate more effectively, which led to our ability to cooperate, eventually leaving the nomadic hunter-gatherer lifestyle and its small clans and forming permanent settlements, where farming and collective efforts resulted in a culture that encouraged larger tribes and strategic advantage in numbers.

We bred like rabbits.

As we lived and worked together for survival, we largely eliminated our risk of being prey. We became the apex predator and, unchecked, we reproduced exponentially. While expanding, we took over the resources of our rivals as our own needs increased, eliminating them through violence or driving them to extinction through habitat encroachment, as we continue to do today to various animal species.

The various species of humanity's ancestors were more apelike in many ways. If such a species somehow managed to survive to modern times, it's easy to see how they might be considered "monsters."

The DNA evidence tells us that *Homo sapiens* mated with some of these early humans. This could have been as simple as a matter of opportunity as the species overlapped, or a result of forced sexual intercourse as a "spoil of war." This information solidifies the fact that early human species interacted with each other.

Between natural events such as climate change that certain human species were unable to adapt to, and the genocide directly or indirectly caused by the expansion of *Homo sapiens*, it seems we modern humans were the only one of our species to survive. But ...

We continue to discover fossils of previously unknown human species, as well as those of other ancient primates, still today. As our understanding increases and our scientific methods improve, we will continue to shed light not only on our own evolution but on those of other branches of the hominid tree.

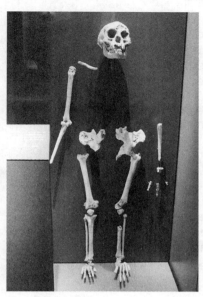

Remains of a Homo floresiensis *on display at the London Museum. The species was discovered only recently on a remote Indonesian island.*

Recent discoveries have not only enlightened us about the fact that *Homo sapiens* shared the planet with a number of other human species but also that many of those species appear to have existed more recently than first imagined. *Homo floresiensis*—small humans also known as Hobbits—survived until about 12,000 years ago. That's only about 7,000 years before the pyramids were built.

Could small populations still exist, or could those early species have evolved into something in between modern humans and our Great Ape relatives? Have these beings influenced the folklore and legends of monsters and giants?

While small tribal communities that have remained cut off, and even unknown, to the modern world have been discovered, none have appeared to be a distinct human species from ourselves. The tribes we have found are as genetically identical to us as we are to our next-door neighbors.

At best, we have been able to determine a small measure of shared DNA among ourselves and one or two other early human species. However, most species of early humans seem to have simply died out, ceasing to pass on their genes to another generation, even in a small quantity transferred to a more dominant species.

Ancient stories of giants and the lore of ape-like monsters among early, indigenous cultures can be explained in a few ways.

On the one hand, these stories could be exaggerations meant to serve as a parable, a warning that dangerous beasts lurk in the woods and prowl the night. They would serve to remind people to take precautions to protect themselves and to not stray needlessly from the safety of the village. Perhaps the protagonists of these stories developed from the "memories" of our ancestors' interactions with more primitive human species.

The stories could also have begun as the misidentification of a primate or other animal that we can now identify, such as a gorilla or an orangutan. Those first encountering such a beast could have easily assumed it was a very hairy species of human, much like themselves. Recent DNA evidence would support such a theory. For instance, the scientific conclusion after analysis of DNA gleaned from hair samples of nine purported Yeti specimens was that five of them were Tibetan brown bears, two were Himalayan brown bears, and one, a relic that looked like a fossilized hand, belonged to an Asian black bear.

We shouldn't underestimate our own tendency toward exaggeration and misunderstandings. A recent podcast mentioned the "freak shows" that used to travel circuits through the United States and Europe. I was struck by the realization that those "freaks" were simply genetic anomalies of our own species.

While popular at least as far back as the medieval period, the peak of "for-profit" exploitation of people with physical, mental, or behavioral rarities was more recent—from about the 1840s to the 1940s. Only a couple of decades before putting man on the moon, we were apt to believe that the "dog-faced boy," "wild men" from Borneo, or the "elephant man" were hybrid human-animal creatures or species entirely their own.

The descriptions of early explorers and colonizers may have been exaggerated descriptions of other *Homo sapiens* that simply appeared different; perhaps they were dirty, with unruly hair and long beards, speaking in unknown languages that sounded like grunts, hoots, and howls. Could Colonel Fawcett have simply encountered an "uncivilized" tribe of humans, never

> *Only a couple of decades before putting man on the moon, we were apt to believe that the "dog-faced boy," "wild men" from Borneo, or the "elephant man" were hybrid human-animal creatures or species entirely their own.*

before contacted by the outside world, like the many we know still exist today?

It is also possible that "giants" did exist. Maybe not a Jack and the Beanstalk giant but certainly taller than average humans. Nine-foot-tall Robert Wadlow is an example of the occasional genetic anomaly. A Guinness World Record lists 30 people eight feet or taller (including three women). It's common to see seven-foot basketball players. There's no reason to believe that this didn't occur in the past.

Goliath, the giant mentioned in the Bible, is said to have stood either 6'9" or 9'9", depending on the text. In our minds, hearing the story of a young David defiantly wielding his slingshot against the behemoth, we picture Goliath towering over the lad. A couple feet taller? Surely, we see him in the same way the artist renderings depict him—twice as tall, or more, than the future king.

That's no surprise. Think of how you might describe your own encounter with an NBA center. He would seem enormous to most of us. A foot taller surely wouldn't account for it, despite the realities of a tape measure. And so those ancient stories would be no different from your uncle's exaggerated fishing story about "the one that got away."

If Bigfoot were some version of human species, or some hybrid of ape-human, with a level of intelligence greater than a monkey but, perhaps, less than our own, it seems unlikely that we would be unaware of them. For starters, this would seem to necessitate bestowing the creature with human-like genetics that would again raise the issue of a population large enough to sustain itself.

Excluding those who bestow supernatural or magical properties to Sasquatch, most witness accounts suggest that the creature is more animal than human. While this could just be human arrogance, even the claims of those who purport to understand the habits of Sasquatch suggest a primitive evolution.

Fossil evidence and DNA analysis seem to show that while other human species were supplanted by *Homo sapiens*, the intermingling with those species—particu-

If you speak with sherpas, guides, or monks who have seen the Yeti in the Himalayas, they won't argue with you about the verity of what they saw. They know what they saw.

larly the Neanderthals and Denisovans—contributed to the survival of our early ancestors. While cultural exchange would aid innovation, interbreeding could have helped the invading population of *Homo sapiens* quickly acquire genes that helped them adapt to the new environment and previously unencountered diseases.

Unless we discover new evidence, the story of other human species seems to be clear. Like so many other species, they died out, lacking the ability to adapt to changing environments or to fight off the spread of a more dominant species. They survive only in the genetic traces they contributed to our own DNA, as we eradicated them through genocide or assimilation.

Of course, to those who have claimed to see a Sasquatch or a Yeti, all this science is just a bunch of smoke. For them, the truth is that science is yet to "discover" the true identity of Bigfoot. When confronted with the scientific findings of analysis on the hair samples and other physical evidence they claim has come from the Yeti, the local Sherpas and monks who have lived in the small Tibetan village monasteries simply shake their heads and refuse to talk any more about the subject. They have seen what they have seen, and no self-appointed expert from the outside is going to tell them anything different.

So, what of the argument that Bigfoot is an unknown species of ape, or a descendant of one that we believe to have gone extinct, like *G. blacki*? It's not a ludicrous idea. Frankly, this seems the most plausible, if still unlikely, scenario.

Even if we can't settle on what, exactly, Bigfoot may

I'm Just Sayin'

be, how do we address the evidence that there's *something* out there?

So far, things such as hair samples have not stood up to any serious level of scrutiny. Inevitably, they turn out to be hairs from deer, elk, bear, or other local animals.

This would suggest a case of mistaken identity in regard to encounters where such samples were obtained. If a witness has claimed to see a Bigfoot and has obtained a hair sample from that encounter, and we later discover that the hair sample belongs to an already known animal, the logical conclusion is that the witness saw this known animal, not Bigfoot.

It's ludicrous to believe, for instance, that early sightings of the Orang Pendek weren't actually some of the first human encounters of orangutans. And anyone who has seen a circus bear performing can understand how easily, especially in less-than-ideal viewing conditions, such a creature moving on its hind legs could be mistaken for something more human.

At the very best, some hair samples are inconclusive.

Does "inconclusive" mean that they come from an animal not yet identified, so a comparative sample doesn't exist in a database? Of course not. It could be that the sample is too deteriorated or otherwise contaminated.

Claiming that the hairs belong to Bigfoot because we can't otherwise identify them is a long reach.

What about nests and mysterious tree structures? The easy explanation is that these are man-made hoaxes.

Most of us have seen videos of island natives easily scurrying to the top of a palm tree, so the argument that the heights at which some nests have been seen could only be accessible to a climber more adept than a human doesn't hold water. In fact, some of the nest locations—high in the trees, where branches become thinner and less capable of bearing weight—would, as a matter of physics, be inaccessible to a creature the size of Bigfoot, often described as weighing at least twice that of the average man and being as tall as 12 feet.

True Tales from Across America

Tree structures could be the work of hoaxers. While we can't condemn all findings based on the known hoaxes such as the sites that show clear use of tool marks, they certainly taint the evidence pool. We also can't dismiss that this is the behavior of an animal, such as a bear.

The idea that these nests and tree structures require an advanced level of intelligence is quickly dismissed by pointing out the skills of beavers building lodges and dams, or birds weaving intricate nests. Instinct is often mistaken for creativity and intelligence. I don't think we'd be signing up any spiders for MENSA membership, despite the marvels of engineering that they spin in silk.

Likewise, vocalizations can only be given a certain amount of weight. Not knowing what kind of animal is making a particular sound doesn't prove that a certain creature is the one doing it. Also, it's generally possible to find a vocalization from a known species (loons, wolves, foxes, owls, etc.) that mimics the recorded sounds. This leads skeptics to suggest the recordings are either misidentifications or deliberate fakes.

Photos and casts of footprints are intriguing and among the most convincing pieces of evidence available to prove the existence of a large, bipedal creature. Regardless of whether that creature is covered in hair or as nude as a newborn baby, it left prints unlike anything we can identify. Unfortunately, this is also the most often faked evidence.

Finally, what of the film and video evidence? If there was any that could be proven as conclusive evidence, I wouldn't be writing this book. Perhaps the creatures are camera shy because their past encounters with our human ancestors have proven to their satisfaction that we are not to be trusted—and who could blame them?—but the lack of proof persists.

Footprints, remains, photos, films, and even DNA evidence have been faked and debunked in the past. As Mark Wilson, geology and natural science professor at the College of Wooster, explained during a presentation entitled "A Scientific Perspective on Bigfoot," "There are too many doubts, too many errors, too many possibilities of fraud."

I'm Just Sayin'

Evidence of Bigfoot such as footprints can obviously be faked, as can movies and photos. Thus far, convincing evidence has been rare, to say the least.

I'm not saying that these suggestions are my conclusions or opinions, but they are the holes that can be shot through the current body of evidence by those who demand more concrete proof. After analysis of all the physical and circumstantial evidence, we are left with scientific conclusions—admittedly on a relatively small sample size of evidence—against generations' worth of legend, folklore, and eyewitness accounts.

It's difficult to disprove an eyewitness account. After all, you are arguing about someone's personal experience and perception. Even if they *were* mistaken in what they thought they saw, they are often absolutely convinced they saw it. Obviously, we can't see what they saw, so how can we draw an absolute conclusion?

That's not to say that we can't examine the circumstances, evidence, and plausibility of their account and determine whether we believe their account. If their recollections are mistaken, this doesn't make them liars—though certainly some of those who have claimed to have encounters with Sasquatch certainly are.

Unfortunately, witness accounts are often not reliable and therefore not scientifically convincing. According

True Tales from Across America

to Mark Wilson, "The problem is that eyewitness accounts are shockingly poor in reporting what actually happened. They make good stories, but they don't make good science."

Even within the realms of our established and agreed-upon reality, eyewitness are notoriously unreliable. Seventy-five percent of false convictions are caused by inaccurate eyewitness statements, and 80 percent of overturned convictions include at least one mistaken eyewitness.

Often eyewitnesses recall false facts because they are led to do so through subtle, even unintended, clues from interrogators. In the same way, stories passed down through oral tradition and folklore, as well as information gleaned from other witness statements, can influence one's perception and ability to properly remember details and events.

For all these reasons, even an optimistic skeptic must lean toward the opinion that Bigfoot is not a real creature that still walks among us but, more likely, is an enduring myth that was probably based on a human or ape relative of the past.

Despite my investigations and research to this point—admittedly, not as exhaustive as others nor yet concluded—it comes down to the same four words that most skeptics eventually fall back on: *Show me a body*.

I understand that it's maddening to most Bigfoot enthusiasts that so much detailed, personal, and episodic evidence could be thwarted and brought low by a simple sentence, but there it is. The plain truth of the matter is that until a captured or dead Sasquatch is produced, most people will not believe such a creature exists.

The personal accounts are, by far, the most difficult evidence to dismiss, if only for the sheer number that exist.

Those who have experienced a Bigfoot encounter are almost universally changed. Seeing is believing. It's as simple as that.

It's like a religious conversion. Like Thomas the

Doubter, the disciple of Jesus who said he would not believe until he had seen a risen Christ with his own eyes, or people who don't believe in an afterlife until they undergo a near-death experience, a Bigfoot encounter changes everything. Doubters become believers.

But the lack of a physical body, after all these thousands of years, is a formidable obstacle and must be dealt with. According to the Bible, Doubting Thomas eventually believed not because his faith grew but because he was able to see the physical wounds still evident on the body of Jesus.

A few hypotheses exist to why a Bigfoot carcass has not been located. One is that we've done very little to actually look for one. Without a serious effort to look for Bigfoot remains in the areas they are believed to reside in, what are the chances of stumbling across one?

It's a solid argument. I've spent a good portion of 50 years in the woods of Michigan as a hunter and outdoorsman. The areas I've frequented boast substantial deer populations. Just driving around the few square miles where my family has property in the "the Thumb," my kids and I have counted as many as 200 deer out in the fields during the early twilight of a summer night.

In an area with a deer population this dense and an avid hunting community, I have stumbled across a deer carcass in the wild perhaps two or three times.

Another explanation, bordering on the supernatural, is that we're unable to see what we don't believe exists. A myth that is gaining popular exposure might help at this point.

> *A few hypotheses exist to why a Bigfoot carcass has not been located is that we've done very little to actually look for one. Without a serious effort to look for Bigfoot remains in the areas they are believed to reside in, what are the chances of stumbling across one?*

The story stems from the voyages of either Captain Cook, Columbus, or Magellan, depending on which version you hear. It's said that when one of these voyagers arrived at the coast of either Australia, Cuba, or South America, the native peo-

True Tales from Across America

ple completely ignored them, presumably because huge ships were so outside their perception realm that they couldn't see them. Apparently, the shaman of the tribe could see a disturbance, but it was not until they performed a ritual that the ships became visible to the entire tribe.

The story may have some backing in the historical record. On James Cook's 1770 voyage in the 106-foot-long *Endeavour*, botanist Joseph Banks observed that the natives paid virtually no attention to them as they sailed along the coast. Then, on April 28, sailing north along the east coast of Australia, he recorded in his diary that fishermen "seemd to be totaly engag'd in what they were about. The ship passd within a quarter of a mile of them and yet they scarce lifted their eyes from their employment. Not one was once observd to stop and look towards the ship; they pursued their way in all appearance intirely unmovd by the neighbourhood of so remarkable an object as aship must necessarily be to people who have never seen one."

Only when the explorers approached the shore in longboats were their attempts at landing resisted. "As soon as we aproachd the rocks two of the men came down upon them, each armd with a lance."

Of course, there are many explanations for this behavior, but somehow, when the story was passed down, it became almost a statement of faith that the ships were visible, but the people could not see them because such vessels were totally outside the perception realm of the natives. It was only when their eyes were opened to a previously unknown reality that they could see with unveiled sight.

Can we apply this myth to an understanding of what Bigfoot might be? Maybe this will help.

For thousands of years, and even to this day in some cultures and areas, our ancestors believed they could receive messages and guidance from forces and powers that inhabited and governed the natural world. Sometimes these messages were delivered by acts of nature or mysterious animals.

I'm Just Sayin'

This belief system was, and maybe still is, the most predominant faith system in the history of humanity. We drew pictures on cave walls in Spain, dragged megaton boulders across the landscape of England, buried our dead along with tools they would need in the next life, raised huge pyramids in the deserts of Egypt, and built medicine wheels on the tops of mountains in America's Northwest, all to contact or appease these messengers. We spread pollen, traced the stars, and studied animal entrails. We observed the paths of planets and suns, went on vision quests, feasted, fasted, and contemplated sunsets. We talked to the trees, listened for voices from the ocean's foam, and consulted hermits and oracles, all of whom went to the wilderness to be close to natural spirits.

For thousands of years, and even to this day in some cultures and areas, our ancestors believed they could receive messages and guidance from forces and powers that inhabited and governed the natural world.

Then came the Age of Enlightenment when, at least in academic European circles, we left our "primitive" superstitions behind and became fully "mature," rational, scientific adults who no longer believed that the great and wonderful natural world, awesome as it was, really possessed anything that could be construed as consciousness in physical from, let alone the ability to converse with us.

We still wondered how fish could find their way to the streams in which they hatched after spending years in the oceans, how birds and butterflies could keep such a precise schedule, and how a million and two minor miracles of coincidence and process could exist within the world of plants and animals, but we assumed it would be only a matter of time before we figured it all out.

I understand that kind of thinking. That describes me completely. I'm rational and of scientific bent, despite being an incurable romantic. I lived most of my waking hours in the left side of my brain, meaning I am normally self-contained to a fault. Often, for me, things like religion were matters to "know about" rather than to "experience."

True Tales from Across America

We have, indeed, been able to answer those questions that we assumed we would figure out through science rather than mysticism. I still find it an interesting mental exercise to consider this idea of some sort of commingling between belief and perception.

I remain open to the idea of Bigfoot, hopeful that such mystery and magic exists in the world and hungry to experience it. Over the last few years especially, I have immersed myself further into the realm of the unexplained, the spiritual, and the natural wonders of the universe that I had previously closed my eyes to.

If I *had* to make a conclusion, I'd say I remain a skeptic and that Bigfoot does not exist. I hope someday I can answer the question more confidently.

AFTERWORD

Despite Jim and I sharing the authorship of this book, the bulk of the writing and compiling was completed after his death. He was at least as instrumental in its completion as I was, but by necessity, most of the opinions put forth in the book are mine—particularly in the last chapter.

I felt it was important to let Jim's voice on the matter be heard, however, as much as it was possible to do so. The following words are from Jim's notes.

As the twentieth century drew to a close, I spent time one summer at a cabin I had built in central Massachusetts. The idea was to commune with nature and get in touch with some issues that were on my mind.

Five feet in front of the porch of the cabin was a rock, about four feet long, lying on its side. The best way to describe it is to recall the old "Weebles wobble but they don't fall down" craze. Remember Weebles? This rock looked just like that, right down to the flat face—but it had fallen over. Obviously, forces other than those found in nature had been employed to work the top smooth, and I had often wondered why it appeared to be almost face-like.

This was the setting where I spent afternoons for four days, meditating on whatever came to mind, trying to go deeper into myself than I normally do. By the second day, I was conscious of sounds I first thought were caused by cars on the highway about a mile away. It was not until the fourth afternoon that I realized I was

True Tales from Across America

hearing the sounds in my right ear, which is completely deaf.

After a moment, it came to me that what I was hearing was not highway noise but drums. Suddenly I was aware that I had snapped my eyes wide open and was experiencing a fully formed sentence ringing in my head. My heart was racing. I didn't hear a voice, and I saw no apparition. Up to this point in my life I had never experienced a conscious out-of-body experience. I hadn't been thinking about dancing at all, but the sentence that seemed to appear, almost floating before my eyes, was, "It's not that you can't dance, it's that you won't dance!"

As soon as I saw, heard, or somehow experienced that message, I felt, rather than figured out, that the reason I could not dance was because at one time dance was so sacred, either to me or the people who danced, perhaps even on this spot of ground, that I could not sully it by making it mere entertainment.

In short, I surrendered, if just for a moment, to a very real magic that seemed to have taken on almost physical form.

I am one of the most rational people you will ever meet. At that point in my life, I wasn't sure if I believed in reincarnation or not, and I only believed in spirits on the occasional second Tuesday. But in that instant, I looked down at the rock I had been contemplating for the last four days, and knew, just knew, that it was meant to be standing upright.

Fearing that any minute I would have a perfectly acceptable psychological explanation for what was happening to me, I immediately got a shovel and began excavating around the rock. It took about an hour to dig down to bedrock, only about a foot deep on this ledge, clearing a six-foot circle surrounding the stone. I knew long before I finished what I was going to find.

Hidden beneath the soil at the base of the rock was a tripod of stones, obviously placed by human hands, formed to exactly fit the bottom of the rock that had fallen over. And in a semicircle, spread fan-shaped to

Afterword

the east, were seven hammer stones that could only have been made by pre-European, stone-age New Englanders.

The next day, when I used a hydraulic jack and ropes to stand the stone on its pedestal, the smoothed face of the stone swung just a fraction around toward the southeast, facing exactly where my previous observations had marked the place I knew the sun peeked over a faraway ridge on the morning of the spring equinox.

In doing research about the indigenous people of thearea, I later discovered a possible explanation for the rock. It stands on a natural divide. All the water from the stream to its east eventually flowed into a huge, man-made reservoir to the south. The water draining from the swamp to the west flowed out to the Connecticut River, and then to the Atlantic Ocean at Long Island Sound. This would have made the area a natural place of power to the people who lived here.

The rock itself stood on a small plateau, a natural stage. On all four sides, a tribe could have gathered to watch a religious ritual "in the round," so to speak. And right on top of the stage stood a boulder I once nicknamed "Dru." (You can read more about Dru in my book *Journey Home: The Inner Life of a Long-Distance Bicycle Rider*.)

One explanation for this stone being knocked over might be found in unsubstantiated stories about religious disagreements between Indians and Europeans in early New England. When Indians watched Puritans burying their dead, they thought they must be worshipping a common deity. The Puritans used four-foot rocks as grave headstones. Some Indian tribes had similar rituals and would dance around the rock as they prayed for the departed. But Puritans believed that while their rocks were sacred, Indian rocks were heathen idols, so they knocked them down whenever they came across them.

Back then, however, this was just conjecture. I now wonder if they were honoring quite a different force of nature.

I had compiled a list with the names of every person who had owned that property since 1798, when the

True Tales from Across America

town was first settled. It is easy to believe the very first pioneer who farmed this land, which was awarded to his ancestral family as payment for participation in King Philip's War, came across this spot in his sheep pasture and, recognizing it for the pagan idol it was, knocked it down, to the glory of God.

There it lay until I, his future town minister, put it back up, also to the glory of God.

The story doesn't end there. I was so impressed by the whole affair that I told some folks about it. One thing led to another, and we wound up having a dedication service there on the night of the winter solstice. Not knowing what to do or what we were honoring, we drank some mead and burned some incense, hoping the spirit of the place would accept our good intentions.

And that was that until March. On a day of early thaw, I walked out to the place for the first time since December. The snow had melted back from around the base of the rock, just as it had around many other rocks in the area. But at the foot of this special rock lay the feathers—not the carcass, just the feathers—of a ruffed grouse.

My first thought was that a hawk had killed a grouse on this spot. Sometimes I still believe that. But I called my daughter that day to tell her the story. She knows a lot about all things Indian, and I mentioned the grouse. She called me back a few minutes later and I could hear the excitement in her voice.

"Dad, I looked up the meaning of having the ruffed grouse as your totem animal." She then read to me: "When the Creator sends you the grouse as your spirit guide, it is a message to attune yourself to the dance of life. Its keynote is sacred dancing and drumming, both powerful ways in their own right to invoke energies. Rhythmic movement is a part of life. All human activity is a kind of dance and ritual."

What do I make of all this? My rational self accepts the coincidence of a grouse being killed by a hawk at this particular time and place. But why a grouse, with its ancient meaning relating to my own dance phobia? And why this particular time? And why this rock, out of all

Afterword

the many others? And why does it tie in to my discovering the secret of the rock after my time of meditation, exactly when I was attempting to let the woods sort out my confused mindset? And why just feathers, with no carcass?

I don't really know. Do I believe a Bigfoot somehow arranged this offering for me in exchange for the "gift" I had given him by restoring an alter ancient people might have once built to honor him?

Of course not! Or at least I don't think so. But something did, and it was a very real something! The feelings I experienced that day, and still experience when I recall that story, are real and profound. The best I can say is that there was some kind of magic at play. There are strange forces that operate out there just beyond the periphery of our physical senses. They are found in the natural world quite often by those who venture forth alone to find them. Our indigenous, native ancestors knew this. It was part of their religion. As was Bigfoot, or Sasquatch, as many Native Americans remind us the mysterious creatures prefer to be called.

Is Sasquatch a part of a magical, mystical web to be found in a dimension that exists parallel to our own, so close as to peek over our perception fence occasionally? Does it exist in a world of entities that sometimes are described as UFOs, angels, spirits, ghosts, fairies, large hairy primates, partially revealed shadows, or beams of light?

By suggesting this, I'm not saying that Bigfoot is a figment of imagination but rather something real that is beyond our perception realm, just like the mythical remembrances of the ships of Columbus or Captain Cook. That would certainly explain the lack of a body that could be examined.

Such a statement will be welcomed by some, understood by a few, and scoffed at by many. When I am confronted on podcasts or radio shows by those who prefer the latter response, I am sometimes moved to reply with sympathetic understanding. It's a hard idea to embrace. At other times, I am tempted to shout, "Believe in magic, you muggle!"

True Tales from Across America

I have been privileged to have spent a lot of time by myself in both woods and desert. I have seen a lot of strange and wonderful things. I fully understand that those whose lives have been spent in loud, noisy cities, surrounded by activity, do not, and probably cannot, understand the solitude experienced by indigenous people and even by the European frontiersmen who moved into the wilds of early America. Even today, days go by when I don't see or even hear other people, but even what I normally experience is nothing to those who spend long periods of solitude in the Himalayan home of the Yeti, the northwest forests of Sasquatch, or the true desert wilderness of the Navaho Ye'iitsoh.

I thus understand the argument of the skeptic who has never experienced such a thing and, understandably, considers their individual experience as "normal."

But I have come to believe that there is another type of understanding that accepts the Reality (notice the "R") that exists beyond what we call reality (with a lower case "r"). It is more than a supernatural or metaphysical idea. It is a totally foreign realm that our ancestors explored through their intuition. It was the only way they could explore it. But today, physicists explore the same reality through math. They call it the Quantum, and it exists on the other side of the newly discovered Higgs field.

Are the two methods, which have until now sped down separate roads, finally beginning to merge onto one superhighway? Only time will tell, but it should be interesting to see.

Imagine the incongruity of it all! The search for Sasquatch could actually be the vanguard of an exploration into the mystery of physics and parallel dimensions! It almost takes my breath away.

We now come to the bottom line. Does Bigfoot really exist? In my own mind I have come to a resounding conclusion. Yes!

It might not be what we expect it to be. It might need to be defined in much broader terms than a simple undiscovered primate. It might be much more than that.

Afterword

But the thousands of eyewitnesses, going back in time as well as spreading out around the world, are seeing something very real that will be revealed when the proper time is upon us. Of that I have no doubt.

Until then, all we can do is wait, while keeping our eyes and minds open to greater realities yet to be discovered.

Photo Sources

Allthatsinteresting.com: p 125.
AscendedAperature (Wikicommons): p. 185.
Christen Ballew: p. 221.
Beloit.edu: p. 194.
Lee Roger Berger: p. 35.
Tim Bertelink: p. 241.
Caroline (Flickr): p. 51.
Centre for Fortean Zoology: p. 242.
Charles R. Knight: The Artist Who Saw Through Time: p. 207.
Charleston Gazette: p. 56.
Community Archives of Belleville and Hastings County: p. 198.
Concavenator (Wikicommons): p. 9.
John D. Croft: p. 14.
Emőke Dénes: p. 263.
Discovering Bigfoot (YouTube): pp. 161, 162, 178.
Melissa Eagan, WNYC New York Public Radio: p. 122.
Tim Evanson: p. 105.
Expedition Bigfoot (YouTube): p. 231.
Fernando (Wikicommons): p. 25.
Finding Bigfoot (Animal Planet): pp. 165, 227.
A Flash of Beauty: Bigfoot Revealed (YouTube): p. 151.
Ghedoghedo (Wikicommons): pp. 102, 261.
Miranda Gleilson: p. 18.
Dylan Kereluk: p. 192.
Aden Kowalski: p. 127.
Library and Archives Canada: p. 202.
Media.liveauctiongroup.net: p. 21.
MikesMegapixels (Wikicommons): p. 215.
Rolf Müller: p. 237.
National Portrait Gallery, London: p. 95.
Neanderthal-Museum, Mettmann, Germany: p. 39.
Nicholas School of the Environment, Duke University: p. 110.
Jamling Tenzing Norgay: p. 53.
OpenStreetMap: p. 129.
Ordercrazy (Wikicommons): p. 113.
Roger Patterson and Robert Gimlin: p. 60.
Popular Science: p. 52.
Haisam Rahal: p. 22.
Nick Redfern: p. 70.
The Sasquatch Files (YouTube): p. 167.
Scyrene (Wikicommons): p. 80.
Shutterstock: pp. 2, 5, 10, 13, 26, 28, 30, 33, 41, 43, 44, 48, 64, 67, 72, 75, 83, 84, 86, 88, 94, 96, 98, 114, 119, 137, 138, 145, 159, 160, 168, 170, 172, 175, 183, 186, 189, 195, 205, 206, 213, 216, 217, 219, 222,

238, 240, 248, 256, 259, 262, 266, 269.
SimplisticReps (Wikicommons): p. 37.
Smithsonian Institution Archives: p. 106.
Smithsonian Natural History Museum: p. 152.
Somersetpedia.paul (Wikicommons): p. 244.
Squatch Mafia (YouTube): pp. 146, 149.
Statistics Canada: p. 201.
TonyTheTiger (Wikicommons): p. 176.
Tracking the Sasquatch: With René Dahinden: p. 142.
U.S. Geological Survey: p. 17.
Willow Creek (YouTube): p. 230.
Alexander Frederick Richmond Wollaston: pp. 92, 93.
XxxJohnDoExxxx (Wikicommons): p. 126.
YouTube.com/watch?v=mQ2kU6e8Huo: p. 225.
Public domain: pp. 63, 250.

Further Reading

AJ. "The 'Sierra Sounds': Our Most Impressive Evidence for Bigfoot?" *Bigfoot Base*, January 25, 2017. https://bigfootbase.com/bigfoot-evidence/sounds/sierra-sounds

Alberta Sasquatch Organization. "David Thompson's Story." *Alberta Sasquatch*, January 16, 2018. https://sasquatchalberta.com/classic-encounters/david-thompsons-story/

Alley, J. Robert. *Raincoast Sasquatch*. Surrey, BC: Hancock House Publishers, 2003.

Ashton, John and Tom Whyte. *The Quest for Paradise: Visions of Heaven and Eternity in the World's Myths and Religions*. New York: Harper Collins, 2001.

Bartholomew, Paul, Bob Bartholomew, William Brann, and Bruce Hallenbeck. *Monsters of the Northwoods*. New York: privately printed, 1992.

Bayanov, Dmitri. *In the Footsteps of the Russian Snowman*. Surrey, BC: Hancock House Publishers, 2004.

Blackburn, Lyle. *Lizard Man: The True Story of the Bishopville Monster*. San Antonio, TX: Anomalist Books, 2013.

———. *The Beast of Boggy Creek: The True Story of the Fouke Monster*. San Antonio, TX: Anomalist Books, 2012.

Boirayon, Marius. *Solomon Island Mysteries*. Kempton, IL: Adventures Unlimited Press, 2010.

Bord, Janet and Colin. *Bigfoot Casebook*. Enumclaw, WA: Pine Winds Press, 2006.

Christensen, Christian. "The Giants of Norse Mythology: Meet the Jotnar." *Scandinavia Facts*, 2023. https://scandinaviafacts.com/the-giants-of-norse-mythology/

Clark, Jerome. *Unexplained! Strange Sightings, Incredible Occurrences, and Puzzling Physical Phenomena*, 3rd edition. Detroit: Visible Ink Press, 2013.

Coleman, Loren. *Bigfoot! The True Story of Apes in America*. New York: Paraview-Pocket Books, 2003.

———. "The Myakka Skunk Ape Photographs," *Fate*. May 2001.

——— and Jerome Clark. *Cryptozoology A to Z*. New York: Simon & Schuster, 1999.

——— and Patrick Huyghe. *The Field Guide to Bigfoot and Other Mystery Primates*. San Antonio, TX: Anomalist Books, 2006.

Collins, Andrew. *The Cygnus Key: The Denisovan Legacy, Göbekli Tepe, and the Birth of Egypt*. Rochester, VT: Bear & Co, 2018

Colvin, Andrew B., and Jeffrey Pritchett. *Praise for the Hairy Man: The Secret Life of Bigfoot*. Seattle, WA: Metadisc Books, 2013.

Dobie, Frank. *Tales of Old-Time Texas*. Austin, TX: University of Texas Press, 1984.

Douglas, Ed. *Tenzing: Hero of Everest*. New York: National Geographic, 2003.

Downes, Jonathan, and Richard Freeman. *Surviving Neanderthals? Expedition Report: Russia*. Woolsery, UK: CFZ Press, 2007.

Doyen, Claire. "The Oldest Known Burial Site in The World Wasn't Created by Our Species." *Science Alert*, June 20, 2024. https://www.sciencealert.com/the-oldest-known-burial-site-in-the-world-wasnt-created-by-our-species

FBI Bigfoot Files. https://vault.fbi.gov/bigfoot/bigfoot-part-01-of-01/view

Gordon, Stan. *Really Mysterious Pennsylvania: UFOs, Bigfoot & Other Weird Encounters Casebook One*. Greensburg, PA: Bulldog Design, 2010.

Green, John. *Sasquatch: The Apes Among Us*. Crypto Editions, 2019.

Grossinger, Red. *Nahganne: Tales of the Northern Sasquatch*. UpRoute Books and Media, 2022.

Guttilla, Peter. *The Bigfoot Files*. Santa Barbara, CA: Timeless Voyager Press, 2003.

Hall, Mark A., and Loren Coleman. *True Giants: Is Gigantopithecus Still Alive?* San Antonio, TX: Anomalist Books, 2010.

Hancock, Graham. *America Before: The Key to Earth's Lost Civilization*. New York: St. Martin's Press, 2019.

Heuvelmans, Bernard. *On the Track of Unknown Animals*. London: Routledge, 1995.

Hoyland, Graham, with Hector Boece, William Stewart, William Barclay Turnbull. *Yeti An Abominable History*. New York: William Collins, 2019.

Hunt, Brigadier Sir John. *The Ascent of Everest*. London: Hodder & Stoughton, 1953.

Hunter, Don, and Rene Dahinden. *Sasquatch: The Search for North America's Incredible Creature*. Toronto, ON: The Canadian Publishers, 1993.

———. *Sasquatch*. New York: New American Library, 1975.

Jones, Dr. Russell. *The Appalachian Bigfoot*. San Diego, CA: Beyond the Fray Publishing, 2021.

Joy, Julia. "What's the Big Deal about Bigfoot?" *Columbia Magazine*, Spring/Summer 2024. https://magazine.columbia.edu/article/secret-history-of-bigfoot-john-oconnor-review

Kadane, Lisa. "The True Origin of Sasquatch." BBC, July 21. 2022. https://www.bbc.com/travel/article/20220720-the-true-origin-of-sasquatch

Kent, Lauren. "The 10 Most Convincing Bigfoot Sightings," *Outside*, July 19, 2024. https://www.outsideonline.com/outdoor-adventure/exploration-survival/10-convincing-bigfoot-sightings/

Kowalski, Kyle. "The Blind Men and The Elephant: A Short Story about Perspective," *SLOWW*, October 2022. https://www.sloww.co/blind-men-elephant/

Krantz, Dr. Grover. *Bigfoot Sasquatch Evidence*. Boulder, CO: Johnson Books, 1992.

Lapseritis, Jack. *The Psychic Sasquatch: And Their UFO Connection*, Blue Water Publishing, 1998.

Little, Becky. "Bigfoot Was Investigated by the FBI. Here's What They Found," *History*, June 26, 2023. https://www.history.com/news/bigfoot-fbi-file-investigation-discovery

Long, Greg. *The Making of Bigfoot: The Inside Story*, Amherst, NY: Prometheus Books, 2004.

Further Reading

Margaritoff, Marco. "Astounding Bigfoot Facts That Delve into the Legend of the Notorious Ape-Man." *All That's Interesting,* May 22, 2024. https://allthatsinteresting.com/bigfoot-facts#24

Mayes, Michael. *Texas Cryptid Hunter,* July 10, 2023. https://texascryptidhunter.blogspot.com/

Mayor, Adrienne. *Fossil Legends of the First Americans.* Princeton, NJ: Princeton University Press, 2023.

Matthews, Rupert. *Bigfoot: True-Life Encounters with Legendary Ape Men.* London: Arcturus Publishing, 2008.

Mills, Emily. "Science Professor Explains Why Bigfoot's Likely Not Real," *Mansfield News Journal,* April 18, 2017. https://www.mansfieldnewsjournal.com/story/news/local/2017/04/17/science-professor-explains-why-bigfoots-likely-not-real/100543942/

Mooney, James, and George Ellison. *History, Myths, and Sacred Formulas of the Cherokees,* Fairview, NC: Bright Mountain Books: 1992.

Napier, John. Bigfoot: *The Yeti and Sasquatch in Myth and Reality.* New York: E. P. Dutton, 1973.

Narr, Karl J. "Prehistoric Religion." *Encyclopaedia Britannica,* April 14, 2021. https://www.britannica.com/topic/prehistoric-religion

Nelson, R. Scott. "Sasquatch Phonetic Alphabet and Transcription Standard." *Bigfoot Encounters,* June 2010. http://www.bigfootencounters.com/biology/scott-nelson-spa.htm

Patterson, Roger, and Chris Murphy. *The Bigfoot Film Controversy.* Blaine, WA: Hancock House Publishers, 2005.

Peters, Hammerson. "How the Sasquatch Got Its Name." *Mysteries of Canada,* July 12, 2018. https://mysteriesofcanada.com/bc/how-the-sasquatch-got-its-name/

Powell, Thom. *The Locals: A Contemporary Investigation of the Bigfoot/Sasquatch Phenomenon.* Blaine, WA: Hancock House Publishers, 2003.

Radford, Benjamin. "Yeti 'Nests' Found in Russia?" *Live Science,* November 18, 2011. https://www.livescience.com/17104-yeti-nest-russia-evidence.html

Redfern, Nick. *The Bigfoot Book: The Encyclopedia of Sasquatch, Yeti, and Cryptid Primates.* Detroit: Visible Ink Press, 2016.

———. *Man Monkey: In Search of the British Bigfoot.* Woolsery, UK: CFZ Press, 2007.

Sanderson, Ivan T. "The Strange Story of America's Abominable Snowman." *True Magazine,* 1959. http://www.bigfootencounters.com/articles/true1959.htm

Sebti, Samir. "New DNA Study Reveals Neanderthals Survived and Interbred with Modern Humans." *Daily Galaxy,* December 16, 2024. https://www.msn.com/en-us/news/technology/new-dna-study-reveals-neanderthals-survived-and-interbred-with-modern-humans/ar-AA1vX3Ip?ocid=msedgdhp&pc=LCTS&cvid=e05696c6b-43f449eafa61463979c5bbe&ei=9

Simpson, Victoria. "How Many Undiscovered Species Could There Be on Earth?" *World Atlas,* May 11, 2020. https://www.worldatlas.com/articles/how-many-undiscovered-species-could-there-be-on-earth.html

Steenburg, Thomas N. *Sasquatch: Bigfoot: The Continuing Mystery*. Blaine, WA: Hancock House Publishers, 2004.

———. *In Search of Giants: Bigfoot Sasquatch Encounters,* Blaine, WA: Crypto Editions, July, 2000.

Steiger, Brad. *Real Monsters, Gruesome Critters, and Beasts from the Darkside*. Detroit: Visible Ink Press, 2011.

Tench, C. V. (as told by J.W. Burns). "The Hairy Giants of British Columbia." *The Wide World*, January 1940. http://www.bigfootencounters.com/legends/jwburns.htm

Ward, Tom. "When Edmund Hillary Went in Search of the Yeti." *Atlas Obscura,* February 15, 2022. https://www.atlasobscura.com/articles/edmund-hillary-yeti-hunt-nepal

Waters, Frank. *Book of the Hopi*. New York: Penguin Books, 1977.

Waddell, L.A. *Among the Himalayas*. Philadelphia: J. B. Lippincott, 1899.

Waller, Dennis. *In Search of the Kushtaka: Alaska's Other Bigfoot*. Bedford, TX: Dennis Waller, 2014.

Wells, Jeffrey. *Bigfoot in Georgia*. Enumclaw, WA: Pine Winds Press: 2010.

Willis, Jim: *Lost Civilizations: The Secret Histories and Suppressed Technologies of the Ancients*. Detroit: Visible Ink Press, 2019.

Wong, Kate. "Why Is *Homo sapiens* the Sole Surviving Member of the Human Family?" *Scientific America,* September 1, 2018. https://www.scientificamerican.com/article/why-is-homo-sapiens-the-sole-surviving-member-of-the-human-family/

Zada, John. *In the Valleys of the Noble Beyond: In Search of the Sasquatch*. New York: Atlantic Monthly Press, 2019.

Index

A

Abominable Snowman (name), 1–2
Acord, Russell, 40, 230
Alberta Bigfoot sightings, 50–51, 170–74, 172 (ill.)
Alexander the Great, 2
Algonkian, 128
Allen, Betty, 4
Almas, 5
Altamaha-ha, 136
amateur "hunters," 30–31
Amazon jungle Bigfoot sightings, 249–54
Anakites, 24
Ape Canyon, 51 (ill.), 51–52, 58
archaeology, 261–71
Arizona Bigfoot sightings, 221–23, 222 (ill.)
Arkansas Bigfoot sightings, 216
Athapaskan Indians, 123
Australia Bigfoot sightings, 243–45
Aziz, Saba, 157

B

Banks, Joseph, 272
Barackman, Cliff, 227
Barberis, Stephano, 176
Baril, Michelle, 180
Batutut, 237–40
Bauman, 124–25
bears, 42
beavers and beaver eaters, 205–7, 207 (ill.)
Belanger, Jeff, 130
Bering Land Bridge, 16–17, 17 (ill.), 103, 104
Berry, Alan, 78–79, 80, 81
Bible, 22–26
Bigfoot
 Amazon jungle sightings, 249–54
 archaeology, 261–71
 Australia sightings, 243–45
 behavior of, 86–89
 Brazil sightings, 247–48
 Canada sightings, 50–51, 157–210, 170 (ill.), 172 (ill.), 201 (ill.), 202 (ill.)
 capture of, 121
 China sightings, 235–37, 237 (ill.)
 circumstantial evidence, 69–76, 70 (ill.), 72 (ill.), 75 (ill.)
 communication of, 83–84
 Denisovans, 13 (ill.), 13–18, 14 (ill.)
 emergence in North America, 101–15
 evolution, 258–60, 259 (ill.)
 extraterrestrial theory, 8, 34–35
 footprints, 47–58, 48 (ill.), 52 (ill.)
 as giants, 21–31
 Himalayas, 91–99
 and Indians, 118–20, 119 (ill.), 121–36, 125 (ill.), 126 (ill.), 127 (ill.)
 Indonesia sightings, 240–43
 lack of physical evidence, 33–46
 name, 4–6
 Pacific Northwest, 84–85
 photographs and videos, 59–67, 60 (ill.), 224–27, 225 (ill.), 268
 Russia, 84
 sounds of, 77–82
 supernatural theory, 8, 255–58
 throwing rocks, 81–82
 UK sightings, 245–47
 undiscovered ape theory, 8–12
 U.S. sightings, 51, 55–57, 59–67, 78–79, 81–82, 211–31
 Vietnam sightings, 237–40
Bigfoot Collector's Club (podcast), 229–30
Bigfoot Field Research Organization (BFRO), 195–98, 212–14
Bigfoot Okanagan, 163–64, 166
Bindernagel, John, 69–70, 138, 178, 178 (ill.)
Bishop, Barry, 98
Blanco, Ernesto, 206
Bluff Creek, California, 55–57
bonobos, 10, 10 (ill.), 12–13
Boone, Daniel, 124

True Tales from Across America

Brazil Bigfoot sightings, 247–48
Breedlove, Seth, 220
Brickley, Lee, 246
Bridgewater Triangle, 129 (ill.), 129–30
British Columbia Bigfoot sightings, 159–70
Brown, Joe, 53
Buffalo Bill (William F. Cody), 124
Bullock, Guy, 92 (ill.)
Burns, J. W., 159
Burns, John Walter, 3
burying the dead, 35–36
Byrne, Peter, 44, 45, 141, 151 (ill.), 152–55

C

California Bigfoot sightings, 55–57, 59–66, 78–79, 224–26, 225 (ill.)
Canaanites, 24
Canada Bigfoot sightings, 50–51, 157–210, 170 (ill.), 172 (ill.), 201 (ill.), 202 (ill.)
Catches, Pete, 122–23
Chehalis people, 3–4
Chenoo, 199
Cherokee, 131–36
China Bigfoot sightings, 235–37, 237 (ill.)
Chiquihuite Cave, 17
chu-the, 94
Clarke, Bobby, 179–80
Clovis people, 103, 104, 105 (ill.)
Cochran, Jay, Jr., 44–45
Cody, William F. (Buffalo Bill), 124
Coleman, Loren, 188
Comanche, 124
Connors, Sara, 203
Cook, James, 271–72
Cook, Steve, 218
cougars, 175 (ill.), 175–76
Cox, Brian, 256
Cree, 126, 188–89
Creek tribe, 136
"The Cremation of Sam McGee" (Service), 202
Crew, Jerry, 55–56
"Cripplefoot" plaster casts, 150–51

D

Dahinden, René, 141–44, 142 (ill.), 147–48
Dakota, 123
Darwin, Charles, 97
David, 26, 26 (ill.), 265
Denisovans, 13–18, 13 (ill.), 14 (ill.)
DNA analysis, 38–42, 76, 108–9
Dogman, 5, 217 (ill.), 217–18
Dostert, Casey, 218
Douglas, Ed, 96
Dufresne, Andy, 149
Dzoonakwa, 169
dzu-the, 94

E

East, Greg, 178
Egypt, 24–25
elephant parable, 7–8
Elliott, T. C., 170
England Bigfoot sightings, 245–47
environmental DNA (eDNA), 73, 76
evolution, 97, 258–60, 259 (ill.)
Expedition Bigfoot (TV series), 39–40, 75, 229–32, 230 (ill.)

F

Fariña, Richard, 206
Fawcett, Percival H., 250 (ill.), 250–54, 264
Fay, James "Bobo," 227
Feaser, Jerry, 226
Feifei, 236
Finding Bigfoot (TV show), 227 (ill.), 227–29
Florida Bigfoot sightings, 215 (ill.), 215–16, 216 (ill.)
Flying By, Joe, 122
Followill, Mark, 176
footprints, 47–58, 48 (ill.), 52 (ill.)
Ford, Bobby, 216
Ford, Don, 216
Ford, Elizabeth, 216
Fouke Monster, 5, 216
Four Horseman of Sasquatchery, 141–55
Freeman, Paul, 66
Freeman, Richard, 242, 242 (ill.)

Index

G

Galyon, Carl, 216
Genzoli, Andrew, 4, 9, 56
Georgekish, Melvin, 189
giant squid, 11
giants, 21–31, 265
gibbons, 238 (ill.), 239
Gigantopithecus blacki, 9 (ill.), 9–10
Gilroy, Heather, 245
Gilroy, Rex, 245
Gimlin, Bob, 59–64, 146, 229
Göbekli Tepe, 113–15, 114 (ill.)
Goldthwait, Bobcat, 229
Goliath, 25–26, 26 (ill.), 265
Goodall, Jane, 83 (ill.), 83–84, 111
Grassman, 219–20
Gray Wolf, Ralph, 123
Grayson, Donald, 106
Great Britain Bigfoot sightings, 245–47
Great Flood, 25
Green, John, 141, 144, 146 (ill.), 146–49
Grossinger, Red, 203–5

H

Haida, 163
hair as evidence, 41–43, 44–46
Hance, Jeremy, 107
Hantu Pendek, 240
Harrison Hot Springs, British Columbia, 159–60, 160 (ill.)
Hatswell, Deborah, 246–47
Hawking, Stephen, 256
Heironimus, Bob, 64, 64 (ill.)
Henry, John, 180
Heron, Alexander, 92 (ill.)
Herwaarden, J. Van, 241
Heyerdahl, Thor, 185
Highcliff, Josh, 66, 226–27
Hill, Sharon, 72
Hill, William Charles Osman, 153
Hillary, Edmund, 52–53, 53 (ill.), 94, 96, 98
Himalayas, 2, 91–99
Hocking Hills, Ohio, 220–21, 221 (ill.)
Hockomock Swamp, 129–30
Holden, Jeremy, 243
Holland, Ranae, 227, 229
hominin species, 37, 37 (ill.)
Homo floresiensis, 263, 263 (ill.)
Homo naledi, 35, 35 (ill.), 36
Homo sapiens, 260–66
Hopi, 121, 125
Howard-Bury, Charles, 92 (ill.), 93, 93 (ill.)
Hoyland, Graham, 96
Huffman, J. H., 51
Hunt, David, 151
Hunter, Don, 143
Hunter, Kim, 63 (ill.)

I

Independence Day Footage, 224–26, 225 (ill.)
Indians, 118–20, 119 (ill.), 121–36, 125 (ill.), 126 (ill.), 127 (ill.). *See also* Native Americans
Indonesia Bigfoot sightings, 240–43
International Cryptozoology Museum, 44, 44 (ill.), 45
Iroquois, 121, 128
Irving, Washington, 128
Israelites, 24
Ivanov, Dmitry, 84

J

Jacobs, Rick, 66, 226
Jesuits, 77–78
Johnson, Bryce, 39, 229–30, 230 (ill.)
Jones, Russell, 132
Joogabinna, 5
Jorgenson, Kregg P. J., 239
Joyner, Graham, 244

K

Keel, John, 256
Kennewick Man, 261, 261 (ill.)
Kent, Bonnie, 160
Kentucky Bigfoot sightings, 223–24
Ketchum, Melba S., 39, 108, 109
Kilpatrick, Anna, 134
Kilpatrick, Jack, 134

True Tales from Across America

King Philip's War, 129–30
KIondike Gold Rush, 201–2, 202 (ill.)
Kiowa, 128
Kirlin, R. Lynn, 79
Knox, Shawn, 178
Kootenay Region (British Columbia), 165–66
Krantz, Grover, 10, 141, 149 (ill.), 149–52, 152 (ill.), 182
Kwakwaka'wakw First Nations tribe, 169

L

Lagina, Marty, 198
Lagina, Rick, 198
Lakota, 122–23
Leakey, Louis, 106 (ill.), 106–7
LeBlanc, Ronny, 40, 230–31
Leif Erikson, 191
long-beaked echidna, 11
Lyles, Trey, 176, 176 (ill.)

M

Mallory, George, 92 (ill.), 93
Manitoba Bigfoot sightings, 179–82
Mapinguari, 248 (ill.), 248–49
Maricoxi, 249–54
Martyr, Debbie, 242–43
Matthiessen, Peter, 122 (ill.), 122–23
Mattson, Harold, 59
Maushop, 130–31
Mayes, Michael, 133
Mayor, Mireya, 39, 230, 231 (ill.), 231–32
McCooey, Henry James, 243
McCune, Robert, 220
McGinn, Andrew, 245
McMillian, Michael, 229
meh-the, 94
Meldrum, Jeffrey, 62–63, 72, 75
Methoh-Kangmi, 1–2
Meyer, Richard, 218
Michigan Bigfoot sightings, 217 (ill.), 217–19
Midnight Whistler, 223
Mi'kmaq, 199
Mills, Jim, 65–66, 224
Minerva Monster, 220

Mississippi Bigfoot sightings, 66, 226–27
Missouri Bigfoot sightings, 217
mitochondrial DNA (mtDNA), 108–9
Mogollon Monster, 221–23, 222 (ill.)
Momo the Monster, 217
Moneymaker, Matt, 80, 165 (ill.), 165–66, 227
Mooney, James, 132
Morehead, Ron, 78, 80, 81
Morris, Philip, 63
Morshead, Henry, 92 (ill.)
Mount Everest, 52 (ill.), 52–54, 92 (ill.), 93, 97
Mowat, Farley, 198, 198 (ill.)
Mulgrew, Peter, 98
Mulka, Angela, 218

N

Nàhgą, 208
Naish, Darren, 80, 80 (ill.)
Natchez tribe, 77
National Center for Biotechnology Information, 42–43
Native American Graves Protection and Repatriation Act (NAGPRA), 15, 38
Native Americans, 27–28. *See also* Indians
Navajo, 125, 125 (ill.)
Nearchos, 27
Nelson, R. Scott, 79
Nepal, 2
Nephilim, 23–26, 25 (ill.)
Nevison, Tom, 98
New Brunswick Bigfoot sightings, 195–97
Newfoundland and Labrador Bigfoot sightings, 191–95, 194 (ill.)
Newman, Henry, 1–2, 93
Norgay, Tenzing, 53 (ill.)
North American Wood Ape Conservancy (NAWAC), 138, 215
Northern Athabascans, 121
Northwest Territories Bigfoot sightings, 207–9
Nova Scotia, 198
nuclear DNA (nuDNA), 108

Index

Nunavik Bigfoot sightings, 184–88
Nunavut Bigfoot sightings, 209–10

O

O'Chee, Bill, 244
O'Connor, John, 211
Ohio Bigfoot sightings, 219–21, 221 (ill.)
Ojibwa, 14–15
Ojibway, 126
Olympic Project, 72–73
Ontario Bigfoot sightings, 182–84
Orang Pendek, 240–43, 241 (ill.), 267
Oren, David, 249
Owen, Ray, 123

P

Padua, Claudio, 249
Paiutes, 27–28
pandas, 145 (ill.), 145–46
Patterson, Roger, 57–58, 59–64, 146
Patterson-Gimlin film, 59–65, 150
Pauls, Grant, 203–4
Pawnee Indians, 124
Pennsylvania Bigfoot sightings, 66, 226
Perkins, Marlin, 98
Persians, 27
photographs and videos, 59–67, 60 (ill.), 224–27, 225 (ill.), 268
Pimm, Stuart, 110, 110 (ill.)
Planet of the Apes, 63, 63 (ill.)
Pliny the Elder, 2
Plummer, Rachel, 124
Preston, William, 200
Prince Edward Island Bigfoot sightings, 198–200
Puglia, David J., 192
Pukwudgies, 129–31
Puritans, 277
Putin, Vladimir, 84, 84 (ill.)
Puttkamer, Peter von, 141

Q-R

Qingalik, Maggie Cruikshank, 187–88
Québec Bigfoot sightings, 184–91
Queskekapow, Linda, 180
Quý, Võ, 238
Rabesca, Michel Louis, 208–9
Radford, Benjamin, 69
Raeburn, Harold, 92 (ill.)
Rahal, Haisam, 21, 22 (ill.)
Ramos, Miroslava Munguia, 40–41, 75
Ransburg, David, 154
Raymond, Charlie, 223
Redfern, Nick, 34–35
Rephaites, 24
Reyerse, Robert, 159, 160
Roberts, Tom, 177
Robertson, Joey, 180
Romanes, Wally, 98
Roosevelt, Theodore, 124
Rudolph the Red-Nosed Reindeer, 1, 5, 201
Rugaru, 126, 126 (ill.)
Rutkowski, Chris, 177

S

Sagan, Carl, 258
Sanderson, Ivan T., 56 (ill.), 56–57, 85
Sarmiento, Esteban, 42
Saskatchewan Bigfoot sightings, 174–79
Sasq'ets, 117
Sasquatch. *See* Bigfoot
Sasquatch (name), 4, 5–6
Sasquatch Museum (Harrison Hot Springs, BC), 160
Schmidt, Klaus, 113, 113 (ill.)
Seaview, Peggy, 169
Sergeant Preston of the Yukon (TV series), 200–201
Service, Robert W., 202
Sewid, Thomas, 169
Shipton, Eric Earle, 52 (ill.), 98, 98 (ill.)
Sierra Sounds, 78–81
Si-Te-Cah, 27–28
Six Nations Confederacy, 128
Skin-walkers, 125, 125 (ill.)
Skunk Ape, 5, 215 (ill.), 215–16, 216 (ill.)
Slick, Tom, 147, 153–54
sloths, 205–6, 206 (ill.)

True Tales from Across America

sounds of Bigfoot, 77–82
Spink-D'Souza, Erica, 164–66
Stack, Liam, 43
Standing, Todd, 161, 161–63, 162 (ill.)
Steenburg, Thomas, 167 (ill.), 167–69, 170
Stewart, Jimmy, 153
Stollznow, Karen, 79
Striker, Fran, 200
Sts'ailes Nation, 163
Suchet, David, 143
Sumatra Bigfoot sightings, 240–43
Swan, Larry, 98
Sykes, Bryan, 42, 185–87

T

Taft, Michael, 192–93
Thompson, David, 50–51, 170–72
Thompson, Leon, 163, 166–67
Tim the Yowie Man, 245
Tlicho, 207–8
tree structures, 267–68
Trendle, George W., 200
Trent University Sasquatch Society (TUSS), 182–84, 183 (ill.)
Tschemezky, Wladimir, 9
Tsul 'Kalu, 131–36
Turtle Mountain Ojibway, 126
Tyson, Neil deGrasse, 256

U-V

UK Bigfoot sightings, 245–47
undiscovered species, 11–12, 18–20
United States Bigfoot sightings, 51, 55–57, 59–67, 78–79, 81–82, 211–31
Upper Peninsula Bigfoot/Sasquatch Research Organization (UPBSRO), 218
Ursus minimus, 102 (ill.), 102–3
Utah Bigfoot sightings, 66, 81–82
videos and photographs, 59–67, 60 (ill.), 224–27, 225 (ill.), 268

Vietnam Bigfoot sightings, 237–40
Vikings, 191, 192 (ill.)

W

Waddell, Laurence, 95 (ill.), 95–96
Wade, Jeff, 176–77
Wadlow, Robert, 21, 21 (ill.), 22 (ill.), 265
Wall, Brad, 176–77
Wallace, Ray, 56, 59, 64, 146
Wallace, Wilbur, 56
Wampanoag, 129
Washington Bigfoot sightings, 51, 66
Welch, William, 51
Wells, Jeffery, 136
Wendigo, 126–27, 127 (ill.)
Wheeler, Oliver, 92 (ill.)
Whillians, Don, 53–54, 99
White Thang, 136
Wilde, A. G. de, 150
Williah, Tony, 208
Willis, Jim, 255, 275–81
Willis, Ryan, 182–84
Willow Creek (film), 229
Wilson, Mark, 268, 270
Windigo, 117
Witiko, 117
Wollaston, Sandy, 92 (ill.)
wood ape, 138–39
Wood Booger, 5
Worm, Boris, 11

X-Z

Xingxing, 236
Yahoo, 244
Yeren, 5, 235–37, 237 (ill.)
Yeti. *See* Bigfoot
Yeti (name), 2–3, 6
Yowie, 243–45, 244 (ill.)
Yukon Bigfoot sightings, 200–207
Zada, John, 168–69
Zimmer, Carl, 13
Zoe, John B., 207